OBSERVATIONS FROM THE TREADMILL

Poems

Observations from the Treadmill

by my

Foreword by Nat Hentoff

THE VIKING PRESS : NEW YORK

First published in 1973 in a hardbound and paperbound edition by
The Viking Press, Inc., 625 Madison Avenue, New York, N.Y. 10022
Published simultaneously in Canada by
The Macmillan Company of Canada Limited
SBN 670-52016-0 (hardbound)
670-00388-3 (paperbound)
Library of Congress catalog card number: 72-10343
Printed in U.S.A.

ACKNOWLEDGMENTS

Harcourt Brace Jovanovich, Inc.: From *The Complete Poems of Carl Sandburg*
Harcourt Brace Jovanovich, Inc., and MacGibbon & Kee Ltd.,
from *Complete Poems 1913–1962* by E. E. Cummings.

I am until I am not.

Foreword

One of the reasons I am delighted that these *Observations from the Treadmill* are now in one place is that this book will make my sometime teaching a lot easier. I'm part of the Media Ecology program at New York University's Graduate School of Education; and what we do—teachers and students—is examine what my colleague, Neil Postman, calls "language pollution."

There is no government funding to deal with this ecological problem, nor can there be. The First Amendment, of course, is paramount. Newspapers, newsmagazines, television—all the ways in which we are presumably connected with each other—have every right to be simplistic, confusing, deceptively bland, unwittingly—or wittingly—distorting. The citizen, yearning to make some kind of sense, and even maybe to find a fragment of believable hope, in all that's going on out there, has basically three choices.

He can believe everything he reads and sees, thereby being in a perpetual state of vertigo. He can fit what he reads and sees to what he wants to believe, discarding all else, thereby creating a most comforting cocoon—until he gets mugged by an actuality he chose to overlook. Or he can sift and weigh and try to piece together some coherence from a multitude of informational sources. The third way is difficult, unsettling, always partly unsatisfying. It requires both skepticism and openness and also, as students rightly keep insisting, some kind of measure, some kind of criterion.

You can't try to control language pollution for yourself, they point out, unless you have some relatively clear source of information to judge the rest by. So, for a start in the assaying business, I send them, of course, to Orwell. And for a contemporary measure, I used to send them, so long as it was being published, to I. F. Stone's four-page newsletter. It's not a matter of your agreeing or disagreeing with Stone's politics, I would point out. See what one man is able to do—without tiers of editors above him and an institutional consensus to smother him. He does it all himself—the leg work, the digging, the interpreting—and then shows it to you. Without any tricks of language, without any tricks of personality to beguile or otherwise cozen you into accepting him as the one true light. He tells you how he found out what he did, how he came to his conclusions, and then you can argue with him. He's not pretending to ubiquitous omniscience or irrefutable "objectivity" or the shaman-superiority of the more egregious "personal journalism." ("My antennae are the most sensitive of all; trust me because *I* was there.")

I. F. Stone was—and is—a measure because he is as vulnerable as you or I. The difference is that he does a lot more empirical work to find things out, to make connections. And he doesn't play games with you—shell games, ego games, meaning games.

Some two years ago I found another one-man measure. Those are the best kind, but exceedingly rare. For me it is never a particular newspaper or magazine or network cadre I depend on for purposes of comparison in media ecology. It's always a *particular* writer or reporter hooked into one of those institutions; but even when I find one I can reasonably trust not to mislead me, I'm never quite sure how much of his story as he originally conceived it finally got through the layers of editors and other "supervisors." On the other hand, a one-man information shop is like a family bakery. There's no packager in the middle.

Anyway, an issue of *Observations from the Treadmill* (author-editor: *my*) arrived in the mail. I read it, and wrote for back issues, and asked to be sure to be put on the list for all future issues. (Here I must confess that to this day I am a free-loader. Because of *my*'s Pay-What-It's-Worth Subscription Plan, I have procrastinated and rationalized and forgotten, and I am ashamed. I confess this, Reader, in the hope of sparing you that shame.)

I became indebted (figuratively and literally) to the *Treadmill* because it is one of those very few information sites where the air is clear. *my* becomes curious about a subject, an undertaking he's heard about, a person he's met. He then goes out to find out as much as he can. He does not make himself the center of the story (sometimes, like the mouse in *Goodnight Moon*, you have to look very hard to find him at all). If he does have preconceptions, he does not shape the story or the person to fit them. And I should add that whatever his politics are, I don't know them. *my* is not a polemicist or an ideologue or a savior or a muckraker. He tries to be, as he puts it, a bridge connecting people. And because his curiosity is so extensive you never know what the next issue of *Treadmill* will be about.

I open the mail, and I get "A Handbook on Death"—something I did not want that dour morning. But when, as sometimes happens, I next thought on death, I read it all. And then later, again.

Another day, I open the mail, and there is "Big John" measuring me from the cover. When I read about him, I know why. Have I got what it takes to more than survive what he's experienced? I hope I'll never have to find out; but I have seldom gotten so full a sense of a man (a *mensch*, my father would have said) from print as I did from the "Big John" issue of the *Treadmill*. And where else could I have read about Big John or Russell or Doctor Jim? Oh, conceivably, in a few magazines structured by editors and space salesmen, but not at the length that only the author decides is the right length, and not entirely in the way only the author decides is the right way.

So, one of the values of the *Treadmill* is that you never do know what's coming, and consequently you can't set your defenses against it. By taking you off guard each time, *my* can surprise you into learning something you didn't expect you wanted to know about. And since it's coming directly from his sensibility to yours, without any flattening intermediaries, you have a one-to-one connection that is very hard to come by in these days of conglomeratized "communications." You want to take issue with him, so to speak, his address is right there, and he's likely to answer.

There's another satisfying element in the *Treadmill*, in addition to its high rating in terms of media ecology. *my* is specific, concrete. You get some idea, particularly in the bridges constructed for this book, of what he thinks and would like to believe; but there's no lengthy attitudinizing or *ex cathedra* exegesis in his work. The people in these pieces—and they are only about people, not abstract "systems"— speak for themselves. And when you're all done, if it's that kind of piece, there are specific references to where you can get more information—bibliographies and addresses. And if it's another kind of piece, and you want to connect directly—without *my* in between—with what's going on, he tells you how. What I mean is, it's all real—it's all happening. It's not about how marvelous it would be *if* we could connect. A lot of the time he actually gives you a way to. That's very annoying, I expect, to some of his readers. To me sometimes. I should have sent some bread to the Washington Free Clinic. Well, *my* doesn't make you pay for a subscription; but he makes you pay some kind of dues.

Another reason the *Treadmill* is more than somewhat singular has to do with *my*'s stubborn emphasis on possibility. He can be as angry as the next person—in this case, me—about all manner of thoroughly unnecessary injustices and neglect; but he keeps finding people who are *doing* something to fill some of those helping gaps—the Washington Free Clinic, Doctor Jim, the teachers involved in Philadelphia's Parkway Program (full of doubts as some of the latter are). His is not a *Reader's Digest* sentimentality. He sees what isn't being done too, but he won't surrender the possibility of more possibility. His credo, tucked into "The Alternative to Public School Is Public School," is:
"We have given up too easily."

Not him, which is another reason I welcome the *Treadmill* when it comes (even, at a later time, when it's about death). There's an indomitability there. Not a posture, but a habit of the man's spirit.

Now, about that man. What's this *my* business? Why just the initials? Well, as he puts it in one of the bridges: "I have the feeling that if you know too much about a writer, it can be a distraction. Yet the reader should have some protection against anonymity, some identity on which to heap praise or scorn. *my* is the compromise."

I understand the point. I don't practice it—too much ego—but I understand it. What you read in this book will provide more than enough of the essence of *my*'s identity. He doesn't loom over the pieces, but he's there, in every one. As for the rest, I've met him and I know what he does for a living (in addition to and while living), but that's not germane here. Besides, he's not all that mysterious. He's been on television to plug his book, and he hasn't worn a mask. It's just that he feels that the focus of these pieces ought to be on what they're about, not on *my*. It's not non-personal journalism. It's anti-*personal* journalism. Mailer at his best is one thing, but most of the rest of the front-and-center journalists are like the guy who sits next to you on an airplane and talks far too long past Toledo.

I do think, however, that you ought to know—or might want to know—how this *Treadmill* got started. Or, as the cops say, what *my*'s m.o. is. For this Foreword I asked him for some notes about the beginning. He sent in a backgrounder, in Washington terms, but I think it's worth quoting because it gets to the core of why I'm asking all my students henceforth to read this book. You're worried about the state of media ecology? Then do something. This guy did. It's not all that hard. Well, yes, it is hard, but far from impossible.

A note from *my:*

"In the spring of 1969, I got interested in SDS, so I spent my vacation—a day or two a week—visiting with student radicals at various universities. After six or seven, I decided I was getting a different picture than the one which the Media had offered, and thought I might write about it. *Look* was interested, but when the piece was done, the Editorial Board decided not to run it. I mimeographed it and sent it out to friends."

(Note from *nh*: Observe that term, "Editorial Board." My most useful advice to students: If you write for a publication that's edited by committee, you are going to be unhappy, no matter what the size of the check, or of your name in type.)

my continues: "That summer I got curious about the stockade riot at Ft. Dix. Peace groups in New York, New Jersey, and Pennsylvania planned a demonstration for the 'Ft. Dix 38.' Only I found out there was no Ft. Dix 38. Again, *Look* said we're interested, but when I wrote it—complete with a paranoid meeting with the Commanding General and his staff; phone tapping (mine—they didn't believe I was a concerned citizen); New York Weathermen (nobody yet knew about them) who tried to take over and lead an attack on Ft. Dix, etc.—*Look* said thanks anyway, we did the Army coffee-house scene already but who are the Weathermen? I sent that one out to my friends too.

"Then I figured: hell, who needs *Look*, I may as well do it myself. So I took off on the local school system that had just about ruined my oldest daughter and called it *Observations from the Treadmill*. That was in the Fall of '69. Then I wrote to every state and most major city school systems for innovative programs and ran a survey of them early in '70.

"In the spring of '70 I went to Washington to see what the Washington Free Clinic was all about, and I mimeographed another *Treadmill*. By now my list of friends grew to include a few hundred of theirs as well, so I switched to offset and did the 'Report on the Use of Behavior Modification Drugs on Elementary School Children' (which you picked up) and so on.

"What with write-ups in your *Voice* column, *Behavior Today*, *Commentary*, *Psychology Today*, *Big Rock Candy Mountain*, *Last Whole Earth Catalog*, etc., the list is about 6000 and growing. Wish they all paid."

What one man can do is what the *Treadmill* is about. One curious man who figures that "surviving is such a full-time job that most people don't have the time to understand why they don't have the time to understand. So I do the leg work. I talk to strangers and I find out what they know. About drugs. Or free clinics. Or education. Or prison. Or death. And occasionally I meet someone special—like Russell or Big John or Doctor Jim—and I write about them."

That's all there is to it. So how come there aren't a lot of other connections like the *Treadmill*? Surely there are a few curious writers in the country who'd like to be wholly independent. The problem, however, is faith. Not faith in the sense the clerics use the term. (To *my*, as to this writer, "There is no Reason Why. . . . It is not important to know *why* you are. What matters is *who* you are.") No, I mean the kind of faith in the possibility that if one curious man writes about something that interests him—without lacing the work with word-drugs (ups or downs)—there'll be curious readers somewhere who'll want to see the next issue. And the next. Without the publication's having a suite of offices, a staff, promotion campaigns, and all those essentials of modern com-mu-ni-cations. I mean, in this day and age, who'd believe that?

I wonder what Henry Luce would have made of *my*. An eccentric, he'd probably have figured. And so, alas, he is. But he *is*, and that's what counts.

Nat Hentoff

August 1972

Contents

*Plus poems, pictures, and other comments
concerning life on the treadmill.*

OBSERVATIONS FROM THE TREADMILL

An Introduction, Preface and Prologue on why this book has Unity, Continuity, and One Central Thrust. To be followed later by Bridges.

I have two hemorrhoids. And a fissure.

They're pretty common, you know. Napoleon had hemorrhoids at Waterloo, poor bastard. If you think there aren't a lot of them around, just count up all the Preparation H shrink hemorrhoids and obtain instant relief ads. They don't advertise if there's no market.

I once asked a doctor why do we have so many hemorrhoids, is it our diet or our pace or what, and he said we are too sedentary. Sedentary, do you believe it? We sit too much! I don't know why it is considered indelicate to discuss hemorrhoids. Country folks do it all the time. Sex may be a four-letter word but they sure do talk about hemorrhoids, piles, and bowel movements. We urban sophisticates seem to find fronts less indelicate than rears. Worse comes from more mouths than rears, why not malign the mouth?

Well, there I was with my two hemorrhoids and my fissure, sitting in an overheated conference room on Madison Avenue (honest!) surrounded by editors, editor-in-chief, and chief. There I was, squirming for a comfortable position from which to explain to the editors, editor-in-chief, and chief why there is no beginning and no end to the Treadmill.

"But do they have Unity? . . . Is there Continuity? . . . One Central Thrust? . . . If we put these pieces together and put a cover on them, what is there to tell a buyer that it's a book? We must think of the reader. Why should he buy this book? And we have to have

[3]

*something to tell our salesmen. Could you write an Introduction? And
perhaps Bridges between these individual pieces? That would tie it
all together. Then it would be a book." they said.*

*I did what I could to explain, but it wasn't too comfortable I can
tell you. I was thinking about Napoleon at Waterloo, poor bastard. I
told them how I never talked to people I didn't know, but how
Elaine could wait for a traffic light to change and know the life history
of a stranger standing next to her. You're a snob, she said, why don't
you try talking to strangers, you might learn more than you think.
It wasn't easy, but I've got the hang of it now and I do it all the time.
She was right. Books are only substitutes for people. You can learn
more from the real thing.*

*I told them that surviving is such a full-time job that most people
don't have the time to understand why they don't have the time to
understand. So I do the leg work. I talk to strangers and I find
out what they know. About drugs. Or free clinics. Or education. Or
prison. Or death. And occasionally I meet someone special—
like Russell or Big John or Doctor Jim—and I write about them.*

*That's what I do. It started with a mimeograph, a list of friends, and
a gloriously impractical Pay-What-It's-Worth Subscription Plan
that may wipe me out but what the hell. Now it's printed, the list has
grown and I've added an understanding printer who probably wishes
he didn't understand quite so well with the circulation growing so
large. And now we've put some of the issues together and I'm supposed
to tell you why they have Unity, Continuity, and One Central Thrust.
To be followed later by Bridges.*

*Well let's see. The Unity is people, the Continuity is the treadmill
we are on, the One Central Thrust is forward. So? Why are we so
compelled to find limits? Spend a lifetime trying to comprehend a
Universe without end, now the astrophysicists say there may well be
many Universes. More than one Infinity! There you have it, friend.
Wrestle with infinities and the indignity of hemorrhoids. There's your
continuity, there's your thrust. No difference between Lassie,
Vietnam, and The Men On The Moon. They are all on the same
picture tube.*

Who then will set the priorities? Time *and* Newsweek *with the same
cover and no collusion you say? Listen Cindy, see that moon up
there? Well our boys are walking up there right now, this very minute,*

planting the stars and stripes isn't that marvelous? and we can see them on the teevee in Pop Pop's den! do you understand what that means, Cindy? Christ, that's really something!

To be perfectly honest, I don't know why you should buy this book. I really don't. But I do know why you should talk to strangers. Because they aren't what they look like they are and neither are you. But how can you know till you're inside looking out?

my

Big John

Agnew goes to Greece. Rogers goes to Israel. Kissinger goes to China. Chiao Kuan-Hua goes to New York. Tito goes to Washington. Castro goes to Chile. Hirohito goes to Europe. Mindszenty goes to Rome. Lady Fleming goes to England. Sir Alec goes to Rhodesia. Rehnquist and Powell go to the Senate. Colonel Herbert goes to Cavett. India goes to Bangla Desh. Atmospheric inversion goes to Birmingham. Mariner 9 goes to Mars. Phase I goes to Phase II. my goes to the hospital.

The last time I went to the hospital it was tonsils at six. They didn't tell me much then either. They never tell you much. It's part of the you-wouldn't-understand-only-we-do myth. Nothing to worry about, just a few tests. You're in good hands with the AMA. Have you ever noticed their hands? Plastic.

Sunday. Admissions is crowded and everyone has that I'm-really-scared-but-I-won't-show-it-look. Fear tastes funny. The people here are very efficient. They need your cash deposit, your age, your address, your Social Security number, your Blue Cross number, your Blue Shield number, your Medicare number, your Major Medical number, your Medical Assistance number, and your name . . . which they misspell. Also pee in that bottle and bleed in this tube. Please. Thank you. Routine. My number is 328730. My room is 1269. My phone is 215-829-7298. I wonder what's wrong with me?

Next door is John ———. Big John. A fifty-five-year-old, 225-pound bulldog with a George C. Scott rasp. Five-eight, thick combed-back gray hair, pencil-thin mustache, and a big square scowling face. Big Bad John. Only he's not so big and he's not so bad as he'd like you to believe. And there's a whole lot more to Big John than he wants you to see but what the hell, John, you said it was all right to tell them about you so now you get to see what it's like to take your clothes off in public. Shall we show 'em the boat tattooed on your chest, the one you were afraid to show your dad?

Big John's Problem

"February 2nd, 1968, at 12:05 p.m. That's a day I'd like to forget. I saw the truck in the rear mirror. I was stopped at a light. I said Jesus Christ—I remember that—just Jesus Christ. One of those god-damn things hits you, you know you been hit. You know, this business of havin' a dream about havin' an accident and makin' a lot of money is for the birds. Look at me now.

"We haven't had a preliminary hearing yet, so I have to pay it all out of my own pocket, whatever the insurance don't pay. I'm on a government pension. Two-eighty a month. I don't have any bread. My wife works now too. But it's been rough. I've had two operations on my back—I got five screws in there—they removed cartilage from my knee, I got an artificial hip—ball and socket—in this hip and now I'm in for the same operation on the other hip. Altogether it's been thirty, forty thousand at least, so far, and there's no tellin' how much more. I lost thirteen thousand a year at my job and I may have to get my neck operated on yet too. I go to sleep at night and my hands go to sleep—get numb, you know? But I can take that. It's the pain that's rough.

"This operation they did on my hip is still experimental. The FDA won't let them do it unless you're over sixty. It was invented by Doctor Charney in England. His brother-in-law was a dentist and it was his idea to use cement to hold the Teflon socket in place. It's the same stuff they use to hold caps on in dentistry. Then they put in a steel ball. The cement may cause cancer, but I figured nobody else got cancer so why should I? I'd rather take that chance than end up with a fused hip.

"I went all the way to Switzerland for the operation. What a trip that was! First the plane to Zurich from New York was canceled. So we had to fly to Paris, then to Zurich. But we got fogged in at Zurich, so we had to take a train to Berne, where the hospital is. Then that bastard doctor wouldn't do the operation unless I paid seven thousand in advance. In advance! The government said they would pay for the operation anywhere in the world, but that would be afterward. And I

[7]

didn't have that kind of bread. I told him, I said look you Pordorikan so and so—he was dark so I called him a Pordorikan—I don't have that kind of bread, I can't pay seven thousand dollars in advance.

"The guy's a multimillionaire—owns the hospital for Chrissake—and he needs the seven thousand in advance? If I'da had a gun, I'da shot him! On top of that he wouldn't talk English to me. Used his secretary to interpret. I talked to him on the phone in English before I flew over! I said you sonofabitch, you talked English to me on the phone, speak English to me now! So I had to leave without the operation. I couldn't even make connections right to come back. Had to take a Varga plane—from South America—to Rome, stayed overnight at the Rome airport and came back from there. Then they decided to make an exception and do the operation here even though I was under the sixty-year age limit, because I couldn't get the operation in Switzerland.

"It's a long operation. They cut you in half practically. And you're open a long time so you're susceptible to infection. I been here a couple days already and they won't do me till Wednesday. They shoot you full of antibiotics for a week. They did a culture on a pimple I have. Just a little pimple on my chest, but if they grow anything from it, they won't do the operation. Afterwards, I'll be strapped down in bed for forty-eight hours so I don't move. It'll be six months out of my life. That's what it was before, six months. There'll be two weeks with a helluva lot of pain. After that I'll hobble around on one of these four-legged walkers, then crutches, then a cane. And they don't know how long it'll last. If the Teflon wears out, they'll have to go in and replace it. I know one thing. I'll walk to the bathroom and I'll walk to the car, but that's all. I ain't gonna wear these hips out if I can help it."

Big John's Bed Partners

"I have this NPU government insurance. I was a tool and die maker at the Navy Yard. It's a hundred-thousand-dollar medical plan. Up to a hundred thousand dollars during your lifetime. Cost me thirty-three bucks a month. I have to pay the difference between semiprivate and private. Did you see the semiprivate? A room like this with two beds and no closet, just two metal lockers like in gym in school. And I've had five bed partners die on me. No thanks!

[8]

"I had one bed partner, he had lung cancer. Used to cough up big lungers with blood, wouldn't tell his doctor about them. He was kiddin' himself. Couldn't eat, used to cough his false teeth out. I used to try to feed him. I called his family and said, you better get up here, this guy's not gonna die of cancer, he's gonna die of starvation. He died that night. Five years later I was in for another operation. They put his twin brother in with me. He had lung cancer too. He looked at me and said, I know you from somewhere. I didn't want to tell him his brother died in my room. For a week he kept askin' me questions, tryin' to find out where he knew me from. I never let on. Then he died too one night. Christ, it's no fun havin' people die in the room with you! I mean your parents die and you gotta live through that, but then to have five guys die on you . . .

"They put a guy in with me once, a cement worker. He inhaled too much dust and his lungs collapsed. He had a big tube in his chest and they pumped air in that way. He was snortin' and wheezin', and he apologized for keepin' me up at night. Jesus Christ, let the guy die in peace, and he's worried about disturbin' me! I hadda move out. I told the nurse, put a bed up in the hall, I'm not sleepin' in there. I told his wife to take my bed if she wanted to. I was movin'. I slept in the hall, too!"

Nurse Shevani checks me in. Fifties or so. Frowzy hair and the seams in her uniform are splitting. She takes my temperature and blood pressure. I take her picture. Click. Oh I see we've got a comedian on the floor. Weighs me. Complains. No aides, no nothin', we got to do it all. Later young Doctor Mannes. Mustache, red goatee, stethoscope, and magic finger. Routine. Click. Cystoscopy tomorrow. Marvelous. General anesthesia. Far out. A urologist will be the first ever to see inside of me, whaddayaknow. In the meantime I visit John, he visits me. He sits awkwardly in a chair to spare himself pain, walks with a cane. Short bulging neck, huge muscular shoulders. He was a weight-lifter and a lifeguard. Now if he would stand in the ocean, his feet would give way in the sand. The television drones in the background. He sneaks it into the hospital because he can't afford to pay for theirs. Click. The anesthesiologist is from the Philippines. Dr. E. Cepeda in red on her white coat. Click. Tonight, cream of celery and dry hamburger. Tomorrow, sodium pentothal. Routine.

Big John and Demon Rum

"I drink pretty heavy. Let's face it, I ain't no social drinker. Once I start a bottle, I got to finish it. Some guys can drink a couple martinis and feel good, or drink a couple beers and roll on the floor laughin'. Not me. I knock off the whole bottle. I don't get potted, ya understand. But I get mean, I guess. I'm just liable to hit a guy if he gives me that much reason. But I'm no alcoholic. I can take it or leave it. It's just sometimes I get tired of takin' the pills, so I drink vodka. When I'm half tanked, I don't feel the pain. But I do get mean. I work off my frustrations that way, I guess.

"I don't miss the booze when I'm not drinkin'. I like a fifth when I'm fishin', but now I haven't had a drop since I'm here and I don't miss it. The Old Lady, she says I'm an alcoholic, I can't live without the stuff. She just don't like me to drink is all. One time I was in the Naval Hospital in Maryland, back in '55. It wasn't much, just a minor thing. I'm in this room with two other guys. It's like the army there. They don't let you keep a thing, not even your clothes. So this one guy, he leans over and says would you like a drink? I says sure and he says so would I, I been here three years and ain't had a drop! So I called my wife and told her to sneak in a pint when she came to visit. When she gets there I pour him a good three fingers and he downs it with one gulp. Then he drops back with his eyes open and he's out like a light! My wife says, my God you killed him! I was scared too. I was careful after that who I gave liquor to and how much."

The night nurse is Nini Cuaresma from the Philippines, here for two years' training after five there. She doesn't like the cold, the work is harder, she's an only child and this is her first time away from home. American food is good with gravy on everything. Small, brown, pretty, twenty-three. Click. I go to sleep with the noise of the city and wake up with it in the morning. Buses, horns, jackhammers and jets. We sure are stupid. At eight-thirty—I can't eat so nobody wakes me— Nurse Carolina Cano, like our North Caroleena, takes pulse, temperature, and blood pressure. Routine. Click. Shorter and browner than Nini, with a throaty voice. What ever happened to Liz Scott? Here comes lab tech Joann Kavchak to draw another three tubes of my crimson sap. Routine. Click.

Big John Knows His Way around a Hospital

"I order everything on the menu. Then I send back what I don't want. I got a can of juice in my closet I took out of the kitchen. At the other hospital they let you drink, so I always bring a couple of bottles in. Then I steal all the orange juice I can get for chasers. I even went down to Pediatrics and took all the kids' orange juice. They replace it anyway."

At the Naval Hospital in '55: "The other guy in the room was Pordorikan and he didn't speak much English. He was always playin' cards with his friends and speakin' Spanish. They'd talk about you and you wouldn't know what they was sayin'. So one day my wife and her girlfriend were comin' to visit me and I says look, my—wife —and—her—girlfriend—come—visit—me—you—play—cards—outside. He says that your bed, this my bed. I do what I want on my bed. I says okay, you do what you want, but if you're playin' cards when my wife gets here, I'm gonna throw—you—the—fuck—out— the—window! He didn't play cards, you can be sure of that. I didn't want them talkin' Spanish around her. I knew she would be embarrassed."

"Another story. I was at another hospital for the back operation. Well I had this nurse, she put me on the bedpan. That's pretty painful by itself, after a back operation, because you're arched the wrong way, ya know? So she goes outta the room. I wait and wait. I flash the light. Nothin'. So I pick up the phone and I call the Administrator. I says this is John ——— in Room 317. And he says yes sir, what can I do for you? And I says you can get one of those whores down there in the bullpen to get me off this potty because I been on it for twenty minutes and my back is killin' me! About two seconds later she comes back all flustered. Who told you to call the Administrator? Hell, that's the only way you get anything done!"

"I been in and out of these hospitals. Some of 'em are good and some are bad. But you either gotta take no shit or you gotta take all they give ya."

"I don't see any sense to suffering pain. What for? As long as I can get something to relieve the pain—I'm not drivin' or runnin' a machine or anything—why not? I bring my own Darvon. Even brought my own Talwin and a syringe one time. Shoot myself if I have to. They give me Darvon, two hours later they shoot me with Demerol. That way as one wears off, I get the other and there's no hour or so of pain in between.

"One time I was layin' in bed waitin' for a pill and the pain was pretty bad. I flash the light at three and nobody comes in till twenty of four. I says how 'bout my Darvon? She says there's nobody out there, everybody's downstairs on a big emergency. As soon as they're back, I'll get somebody to get it for you. See, only certain people can dispense from the medicine room. So I get my cane and I walk out to the goddamn bullpen and there they all are, sittin' around on their fat asses. I says when this big fuckin' emergency is over, you think somebody could get my goddamned Darvon? They got all flustered.

"See, it's the change of the shift. The old shift don't wanna do it 'cause they're goin' off and the new one don't wanna bother 'cause they think the old shift should do it. Meanwhile, you're in pain. They couldn't care less."

When Big John comes up from Recovery on Wednesday afternoon, he can hardly talk. They've rigged his bed with traction bars and it looks like a jungle gym. His wife swabs his lips and tongue to moisten them. He sees me and rasps: "It was rough this time, my. I feel like I been run over by a truck. Well I knew what I was gettin' into." He drifts in and out, snoring loudly on the outs. One time he opens his eyes and looks at the I.V. bottle above him. Deciding that it's not feeding properly, he scowls at the nurse. "Is it backing up?" he growls. Sure enough, it is. "Fix it!"

Big John on Women's Lib

"This Women's Lib don't bother me a fuckin' bit. Maybe they got a point. If they wanna go out and pay the bills, that's okay with me. If they wanna be the breadwinner, I think they made the wrong choice, that's my opinion. They got a better deal stayin' home. Then maybe some of those guys would have jobs again. I think a lot of guys are out of work 'cause the women are workin'. My opinion anyway."

Big John on Religion

"I'm not real religious. I was raised strict Catholic, but I don't go to Mass regularly. I say my prayers at night and I believe in God and Christ. But I get very religious right before I go to the O.R. When I'm down there, I'm in limbo. I guess if you never wake up you don't know it, eh? That's a pretty good way to go. My father died when he was eighty-five. He was perfect until a week before he died. Then he just went."

Big John on Vietnam

"Vietnam? I don't know much about that. And I never talk about things I don't know nothin' about. If I knew why we were there in the first place . . . But every day you read in the papers that some guy stole some secret papers that tell you somethin' else you didn't know. I always said we're like sheep. They only tell us what they want us to know. We don't know half of what goes on. I don't think it's right, but no other country tells its people everything either. I think this war is costing more money than it's worth, though."

Big John on Long Hair

"I don't like it much myself. I think a guy should be well groomed. His hair in back shouldn't be lower than his chin. Now, I always had a thin mustache, but these long mustaches that droop way down below the mouth, they're dirty lookin'. But I don't mind if somebody wants long hair. I'm not afraid to be seen with somebody with long hair. These days anything is in. Long skirts, mini skirts, all kinds. People do pretty much what they want. That's okay with me, that's the way it should be."

Big John on Politics

"I'm a Democrat. I was for Humphrey. I don't know about Nixon. I didn't like him then and I guess I don't like him now. Three or four per cent decrease in cost of living don't do shit for me. I think this time I'd go for Wallace. They'd hafta tame him down some. Not shut him off, just tame him down some. Who else they got? Who've the Democrats got to go against Nixon? If the two Kennedys hadn't of been assassinated, we'd of had Kennedys for twenty years. One would step down and another would take his place."

Big John on Morality

"You ever have to go on a bedpan and have a woman wipe your butt? Boy, that's embarrassing. I mean it's different if you got a woman in your room and you're gonna knock off a piece. Then she washes you in the shower and it's nice, but this is different. I was always raised to be modest. It's different now with the young people. They walk around in front of their kids with no clothes on. They say it's more natural. I know if I'm in the bathroom and my grandchildren are around . . . wham! I close the door. That's the way I was raised. I don't think it's right for little kids to pull on your dingaling and say what's that? That should come later. A person should have modesty. If you don't have no modesty, a guy would be walkin' down the street with no clothes on. You'd see it on TV. It wouldn't leave anything to the imagination. I think it could even hurt a kid's sex life later on."

Big John on Ethics

"Ain't nobody never give me nothin'. I figure if they're not some-body I know, fuck 'em. That's the way everybody else feels, that's the way I feel too. More so since the accident. Look, I had a hip x-ray here. So because I'm Gartland's patient and I'm in a private room, they give me a bill for forty-five dollars. So I wrote 'em a note. I said I haven't worked in five years and I'm on a limited disability pension of two-eighty a month. I'm only in a private room because there was no semiprivate available when I came in. My insurance only covers me for semiprivate. I'd appreciate it if there was anything you could do to reduce the bill. You know what they did? They sent me a goddamn note. Dear Mister ———, you're delinquint. Delinquint! Not a word about my note. Whadda they care? If I was a semiprivate patient, it'd be twenty dollars. If I was a nigger in the clinic, it'd be ten. But be-cause I'm Gartland's patient in a private room, it's forty-five. They got different charges for different people. It's the upper class that makes the rules, not the John ———s. The John ———s are just peons."

Big John on Blacks

"Blacks? You mean do I like them or don't I? I'll tell ya, I didn't work directly with colored at the Navy Yard but I knew some. They were all right. See, if they're middle class and they work like me and they buy a house and a car like me, I like 'em fine. It's these that are on Welfare. They don't wanna work, they're just milkin' it. Sure there's more whites on Welfare than colored. There's a hundred eighty million or so whites, so there oughta be more. But I think whites would rather work. I think now with more civil rights, they're ridin' the gravy train 'cause they think they was stepped on for so long. Do I think they was stepped on? Yeah, I think so."

Big John's Gums

"I figured as long as I was in the hospital I'd have 'em out. No good anyway. They hadda fix my jaw a little. Measured me for dentures, but I put it off and put it off. For three years. Now my gums are so tough I can eat nuts. I never caved in so you can hardly notice 'cept when I eat. My cheeks go up and down. It looks funny. I watched myself in the mirror."

Big John Mitty

"In 'Frisco when I was fishin', I told the boat captains I was a TWA captain. I used to go to the bar on Fisherman's Wharf where they let you taste the different kinds of wines? Well I'd start at one end and go right through 'em all. Drink every one. I told the guy there, I said I'm a TWA pilot, you got any cards? I'll give 'em to our girls to pass out to our passengers. He give me a whole stack and a bottle of wine for my room. I was there drinkin' with these boat captains and some guy taps me on the shoulder. Hey, he says, are you an airline pilot? Yes, I says, and I turn around quick 'cause I don't wanna get into a conversation. So he starts in, I invented the special hydraulic so and so.

"So I turn and I say listen, am I bothering you? And he says no. So I say, then stop bothering me or so help me I'll lay you out. I hadda say somethin' or it coulda got technical and I'd be cooked. I packed my bags and got outta there that night. I woulda got caught in a lie for sure."

"I was in Vegas once with the wife. I was out by the pool and I met this Major Wong. He was in charge of an airfield in Hawaii. I told him I was a pilot with TWA and we got pretty close. We started drinkin' pretty good at the pool. I was scared he was gonna ask me something technical. Every time it looked like that was gonna happen I'd jump in the pool. I had my wife have the hotel page me. It would come over the loudspeaker: Paging TWA Captain John ———. Then I'd pick up the phone, talk to her and hang up.

"Well, came four or five I was really drunk. Every time I'd try to get up, the whole Tropicana would start swimmin' around. I didn't want to make a fool of myself, so I just stayed there. My wife came and said come on, it's gettin' late. I said listen, I'm stayin' here, I'm drunk and I'm not gonna make an ass of myself. Leave me alone, I'll stay here till ten o'clock at night if I have to till I sober up. I got in the pool and floated on my back spurtin' water out of both my hands. I guess they figured I was a new fountain for the hotel. The life guard swam out to tell me to get out and I said listen, you stay the hell away from me or I'll make you eat your whistle, I'm too drunk to walk. Well I stayed there till about ten that night till I could walk to my room. I was sick as a dog."

Big John's a Soft Touch

The phone rings. It's his wife. She puts Big John's granddaughter on. Big John lights up, his rasping voice suddenly softer. "Hello, how ya doin'? I'm fine. Yes, my boo-boo's better. No, I'll be here a couple weeks yet. Why ya cryin'? What? Oh. Yes, my back's fine." He turns to me. "She's smart as a whip. Just learnin' to talk. Goin' on two. Repeats everything you say, only she says it funny. Cute little devil." Big Bad John.

Big John Has a Way with Words

"I feel as helpless as a one-legged man at an ass-kicking contest."

It's almost three. They said I'd go down at one. It's getting to me. I lose a game of chess to Elaine and I can't remember one move. Spoke too soon, here they come. Onto the table and Nini shoots me twice in the rear. 75mg Demerol. Good-by, I'm on my way. Hollywood cliché traveling shot of the corridor ceilings, squeaking wheels of the table, hollow footsteps of the little black girl in the yellow Patient's Escort jumper who complains she had to leave in the middle of her lunch to get me, then brags I'm not too big to wheel around. She once moved a five-hundred-pound pregnant woman. Routine.

Into the elevator. Passengers watch the ceiling, feeling strangely embarrassed by me on the table. They sneak furtive glances down at me when I'm not looking. They don't want to look, but they can't help themselves. Wish they'd let me take the camera. Fourth floor. Up one corridor, down another. Left, right, two lefts. Through a passageway into a new section. Now everyone's in green pajamas. They banter with each other. Must be the happiest floor in the hospital. Clock on the wall. Three-fifteen. She leaves me in the hall alone. Relaxed but alert. Prop my head up to see around. Not nervous. Two green pajamas stop at my feet, glance over at me. Our eyes meet. He has a big walrus mustache. Is it Elliot Gould? She has long red hair bunched in back. Candice Bergen. They kid back and forth with each other. Then he describes the operation he just left. It was his first amputation. In detail. Don't mind me, pal. I'm just part of the woodwork, right?

Here comes my doctor. He's walking alongside another patient being wheeled out. He smiles and tells me he'll be right back. I figured. Somebody wheels me into the room and slides me off the rolling table onto a metal one. Several people in green pajamas and masks. Doing things. One behind me says hello, I'm Doctor Mumble Mumble the anesthesiologist. We're going to start the intravenous now, okay? Do I have a choice? He sticks me in the back of the left hand, tapes it down. The bottle above me starts to drip. Everybody's busy. Doing things. Something's the matter. Feel strange. Light. Sonofagun, you slipped it in on me and I never saw it coming. Yeah, sneaky huh?

Somebody is snoring like hell. Can't focus. Turn my head. Something black is near me, snoring like hell. Thirsty. I hear an old woman, weakly: Nurse. Can't . . . focus. Blurred. Squeeze shut, open wide. Better. I.V. bottle over me. Drip, drip. Almost empty. Where am I? A woman's voice: Ann! Ann! Wake up, Ann! She's in white. A nurse. Head clearing. Must be in Recovery. Clock on the wall. Five. The black shape next to me is a woman. Christ, can she snore! The old lady keeps crying weakly for the nurse to give her chewing gum. The nurse tells her impatiently that we don't have any chewing gum here and you can't drink any water yet. She's been telling every patient the same thing since she came on this service, because every patient asks the same questions. Routine. Except it's not routine for the patients. It's always the first time for them. Don't look for compas-

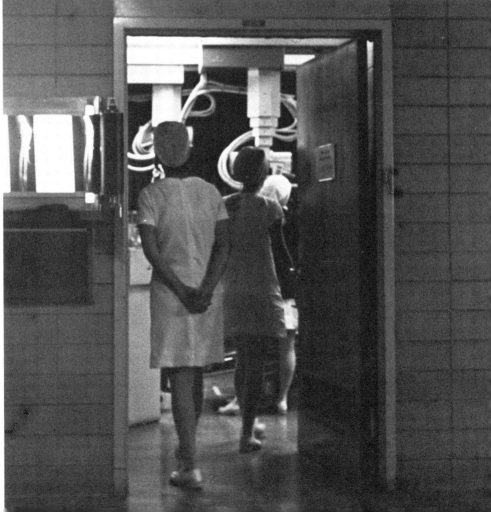

sion in a hospital. *Everybody's too busy doing their job. Of course, without patients there'd be no job. Oh well, there'll always be patients. Easy come, easy go.*

Still fuzzy. Slurring words. Here's my doctor: "How do you feel? Everything looked fine. We'll keep you here tomorrow to do the kidney function tests, then let you go home Wednesday morning, all right?" He smiles again and is gone before I can think up any questions. You've got to be fast, but they always have the advantage because you're either flat on your back or bent over or tripping on some magic juice. It's almost six, when can I go back up? The anesthesiologist has to sign you out. Where's he? Having dinner. I haven't eaten since yesterday. Drip, drip. Here come the boys in green. Mine signs me out. Fast trip. I'm back in my room already. This stuff is wild. Drip, drip. When can I eat? Sorry, the kitchen's closed. A hundred fifteen a day and the kitchen's closed? I'll eat my Blue Cross card. Bottle's empty. Disconnect.

Big John's Youth

"I was born in South Philly. I jacked up school after seventh grade. Didn't like it much. I worked in tailor shops—my father was a tailor. My Old Man fixed me up with a job as an armhole presser. They got paid the most. I got so good I was doin' more than the regular guys, so they complained to the union and I got fired. Next place there was an old Italian who was a mean bastard. He'd mark up the suit so you'd hafta do it over. One day he musta marked up twenty suits so I'd hafta stay late. When they pulled me off him, I had the sleeve half down his throat. I was gonna make him eat the whole damn suit, I was so mad. That was the end of my tailorin' career. Then I went to Vocational School to learn a trade. I ended up at the Navy Yard as a machinist. Civil Service. Seventeen years."

"When I was little, I was an Italian kid in an Irish neighborhood when we moved to West Philly. I got beat up morning, noon, and night, goin' and comin' from school. Finally I decided I wasn't gonna do that any more. I started liftin' weights and joggin'. Pretty soon I was the biggest kid on the block and I beat the shit out of every one of them little bastards. If they so much as looked at me funny, I beat their heads in."

"I have no regrets. I'd live my life over, day by day, hour by hour. I'd even marry the same woman. I dropped out of school because I didn't like it. I never regretted it. I worked on trucks—worked on an ice truck once—any kind of job, what the hell. I played a little football. A very little. Swimmin' was my sport. I could swim as easy as you could walk. And as far. I was a long-distance swimmer. I did running too, to keep in shape. And I lifted weights. I was a lifeguard in New Jersey in the summers and Florida in the winters. I worked at Wildwood. I won the nationals two years in a row with those big surf boats. I was a good rower. Really good. Then Beach Haven bought me—paid me more—for my rowin', ya know. But I did lousy that year, only pulled third place. They didn't get what they paid for."

Big John modeled "in between seasons" at the Academy of Fine Arts for a dollar and a quarter an hour, "but you couldn't do it too much. Five or ten minutes, then rest for five and pose some more. But they wanted your muscles tense and you'd start to shake after while." He shows me a picture of himself posing at twenty-three. That's when he got married. At twenty-three. The picture is pretty cracked, but it's Big John all right . . . skin oiled up and dressed in a jockstrap, tennis shoes, and sagging socks. There's the thin mustache and the thick straight hair, the front sticking out like a pair of wings.

"I started workin' the beaches when I was about nineteen. They used to hang around the tower. You could always spot the ones just arrived. There'd be six or seven together and no tan. If a girl had a dark tan, you knew she'd been around awhile and chances are she'd be as broke as you. But the white ones, they had some money. So you'd gather 'em in. Pretty soon you'd say who's a good cook here? There'd always be one good cook. So you'd dangle the keys and say how 'bout goin' up and fixin' us some dinner?

"It was usually only meat loaf or hot dogs, but it was a hot meal at least. And they'd wash the dishes and clean up, whiten the shoes and press your clothes. And you'd knock off a piece of ass. Maybe not all seven of 'em but five at least. Me and my three buddies did pretty good. Then the week would end and they'd leave and there'd be a new batch of girls arrivin' without tans. We did pretty good."

"My father used to take me all the way to Wildwood for crabbin' when I was a little kid. We'd get up in the middle of the night and travel for hours on trolleys and trains, then do the same thing comin' back. He didn't like fishin' but he knew how much I liked it so he took me. He was a pretty good man. He worked hard and he was good to us. My mom was a big woman. She started cookin' when she woke up and she'd cook until she went to sleep. Eggs and rice and cut-up peppers and soups, all kinds of stuff. She really cooked a lot of different things. We never had to figure what to eat."

"During the war I was on a Defense Deferment, workin' at the Navy Yard. But I got the word I was on my last deferment and I would have to go in the service. You work with a guy and train him for three years, you get a three-year deferment. Then you go in and he takes your place and trains somebody else. So I volunteered to go to California and train the Seabees. They had just formed the Seabees. I trained 'em basic machine shop stuff. How to work the lathe, the saw, the planer, stuff like that. So when they got to where they was goin', they'd at least be half-assed mechanics. I had my wife and the first kid with me—we only had the first one then. It was lousy there. Cold and wet and foggy. But it was better'n the service so I figured fuck it."

Big Charlie

"I like to fish. One weekend I went fishin' on Long Island with three other guys. There was a weekend! You could write a book about that weekend. There was Big Charlie who runs a bait and tackle place in Jersey, and Ed and Jay and me. Somehow we missed each other but we caught up with them at the Holiday Inn. Big Charlie was loaded to the gills already. He's a big sonofabitch. Must weigh three-sixty. A mountain of a man! We broke every rule in that place.

"They had a restaurant you had to wear a jacket and tie in. We didn't have no ties, we were goin' fishin'! But Big Charlie starts yellin' who's your boss, I'll buy this goddamn place! And he pulls out a wad big enough to choke a horse. I said you better give me that before you get stuck up—it was a pretty rough area. There musta been five thousand there! I gave it to the hotel to put in the safe. Ya know how they bring you a small loaf of bread? Well Big Charlie lets out a holler. Whadda ya call this? A loaf of bread and only two little pats of butter? You oughta be ashamed! Bring me a pound of butter! Put it on my bill! He says to the hostess, stir my Manhattan with your little finger, make it sweeter. And he hands her a twenty-dollar bill! The waiter brings the butter and he slips him a ten! It goes to show you, you can buy anything with money. From then on we owned the place. Every time I'd shove a ten out, they'd shove it back. They knew what kind of shape I was in and they wanted to show me a good time. We sure had a good time."

"I really like to fish. Big Charlie, he doesn't take many vacations, just a couple days like the weekend we went to Long Island, but we get away now and then. He's a hell of a guy."

Big Charlie's big, all right. Six one and a half, three-fifty-five. Hair thinning on top, a huge face speckled with red, and a near white mustache and goatee that would make him a good double for Burl Ives if it weren't for the black horn-rimmed glasses. Huge arms, scaly at the elbows from a nervous skin condition, and small fat hands. Forty-nine but looking older, Big Charlie was born and raised near Port Elizabeth, New Jersey. When I go to see him after getting out of the hospital, he tells me of the good old days when the fishing fleet sailed out of the mouth of the river and into the bay. We have a beer —Big Charlie drinks a case a day plus a fifth of scotch or so—and he shows me a picture of the near record catch of albacore that he and Big John pulled in once. They had to quit finally, both on their knees. It was either a hundred and seven or a hundred and eleven, he forgets which. He talks about his friend Big John.

"That John, he's a great fella. We've had some great times. We have a lot in common. Fishin', ya know. John's a hell of a fisherman, good as I ever met. And I've known a few. Doc Charlie Butcher and Old Man Hardstock and a whole lot of others. But John is really good. He knows his way around the waters. He has a hundred-ton captain's license, ya know. We had a high old time that weekend in New York. Tried to buy the place. I had eight hundred dollars on me. John took it off me, said I wasn't in no shape to have that much on me. 'Course, he wasn't in no better shape hisself. When John drinks, he don't wanna listen to nobody. He's crazy as a bedbug. He's a wild bird. But he grew up in a pretty tough area, so he hadda take care of hisself, I guess. Still, John'll do anything for anybody. But he won't take no shit neither. John'n I's been real close."

Tuesday. Technician Frannie Rosenberg draws a tubeful. Click. Breakfast: cold oatmeal, soggy toast, and the hardest driest scrambled eggs since Ranger School. The nurse gives me an intake-output chart to keep on liquids. Lunch: cold pea soup, watery, and a ham sandwich, dry, on phony rye bread that would never sell at Hymie's Deli. At two Joan Fedena takes an EKG and at four I'm wheeled down for a chest x-ray. Routine. Everybody's tagged. The yellows push us, the whites do us. They're color-coded. We're furniture. At five a kindly and overworked little old lady with her nurse's cap tilted crazily on her head, who can't read the little numbers on the chart any more and is all alone and tired and the phone's ringing at her station and she hopes someone will pick it up, brings me a big plastic bottle and tells me to pee into it for twenty-four hours.

Twenty-four hours? I'm supposed to be out of here in the morning! They said? Who's they? Somebody made a mistake. This was supposed to be started this morning. Nobody's worried. You've got Blue Cross, haven't you? They'll pay for the extra day. Routine.

Big John's getting edgy. He's seen the anesthesiologist and been shaved from chest to knees. He takes sleeping pills but they don't help. He's in and out of my room, watches his TV, paces the halls with his cane. He knows what's coming and it's no picnic. By morning, he's a little happier because his wife and daughter are with him. As the Patient's Escort wheels him away, his wife says so long. He turns his head and says, "Don't say so long. Say see you later."

Big John and the Fish

"Yeah, I'm pretty good. I got a seven-hundred-fifty-pound black marlin once. Fought him for seven hours. He'd of been a record, but I finally shot the bastard. I just couldn't keep goin' all night. It was him and me, me and him, him and me, me and him. For seven hours. Christ, what a battle!

"I was never cheap with bait. I used plenty of bunker and squid. I'd sometimes get a whole bushel of mussels. Scrape 'em off the pier.

Nobody else'd go to the bother. You get these Sunday fishers, they come back sayin' nothin's biting. Well I know where to find 'em and how. I guess that's why I like fishin'. I like the challenge. I like to come in after eight or nine boats have come in with nothin'. Then I like to come in and start throwin' the fish out on the floor. They say where'd you get those? And I say oh, out there. And I point to five different places.

"I'm out one time for winter flounder and I got this area pretty well chummed. I got it laid out so no matter if the boat swings around, it's still there. Then I wrap some in newspaper and tie it up and hang it down under my boat. After a few minutes the newspaper gets soaked. I jiggle it and it falls away. That way the bait goes to the bottom under my boat, instead of floating away on top. So it's pretty crowded. Sometimes, the boats get pretty crowded together. And they're gettin' nothin'. I keep pullin' 'em in. Each time I yell Jesus Christ, another flounder! Loud enough for them to hear. Pretty soon they yell hey what're you using for bait? I tell 'em blood worms. So they switch to blood worms, but they don't get a bite. They figure I'm usin' some secret bait. It drives 'em nuts. Sunday fishermen!"

"First time I met Big Charlie, I asked him what was what. When you get to a new area, you got to ask questions. No point in wanderin' around for two years when you can learn by askin'. Well he tells me there's loads of stripers in the creek. I ask him what bait and he says blood worms. So I buy some and try for awhile. Nothin'. So he says well the water's a little brackish, maybe they ain't runnin' there right now. That's legitimate. So then I see some people up by the dam and it looks like they're usin' grass shrimp. So I get some and try for a couple of days. I'm gettin' catfish and perch but no stripers. Each time, Charlie gives me some story. Finally I figure I took enough bullshit, it's time I showed 'em a few tricks.

"So I stop at the docks down here and I buy two big stripers. Maybe ten, twelve pounds. Then I buy some blood worms. I throw some away and a few on the floor of the car. I gaff the stripers so there's some blood on the gaffer and I wet the gear so it looks like they been used. Then I go to Big Charlie's. Well, he says, did you catch anything? Yup, I says, a couple of stripers. His jaw drops. Did you? How big? Oh, about ten or twelve pounds, I says, wanna see 'em? And I open the trunk. Wow, Big Charlie says, where'd you catch 'em? Right where you told me, I says. For the next couple of weeks they were out tryin' for stripers. Even used lanterns at night. I fixed 'em good. Nobody fucks around with me! Later Big Charlie and me became good friends, but I never told him that story. Let him go on believin' it. Serves him right."

"I don't like fresh-water fishin' much. It takes two. One to take the boat while the other fishes. You got to bucktail into the bank and reel it into the boat all the time. I like salt-water fishin'. I've fished Washington State, San Francisco, Hawaii, Canada, Jersey, and Florida. You gotta read the charts, look for the deep holes with forty or fifty feet of water, watch for nice sandy shores or washes. Things like that.

"It's a getaway for me. I don't have to think about anything out there. Just drink a fifth or two and catch fish. Don't think about troubles. Kind of a shelf to climb onto, I guess. Everybody's got to have a shelf to climb onto. After the accident, if I didn't have fishin', I'd of gone bugs. I've crawled onta the boat on my hands and knees already. It's the only hobby I have left."

"I have more friends than my Old Lady'd like me to have, I guess. Somebody's always askin' me to go fishin' somewhere every weekend. I try to even it out, but it never does. Even on vacations, I go where there's water. The kids did some fishin' when they was too young to know the difference. You know, too young to know they was girls instead of boys. But as they grew older, we grew apart. That's the way things go."

Wednesday. Big John is up from the O.R. Another total hip, another seven thousand dollars, another six months. As for me, I'm still peeing into the plastic bottle. When the twenty-four hours are up, I leave. My doctor—that's another part of the myth, this reference to my doctor—comes to see me. Fast, just friendly enough, efficient. No evidence of any obstructionary problem. There is evidence of a possible renal problem . . . glomeruli . . . creatinine elevation of three . . . manageable . . . medical problem . . . see your internist. Goodby and good luck. Five minutes. Can't even think up questions in five minutes! Like Sugar Ray. Jab, jab, and three steps back. Fast. Four days to find out what I haven't got. Two more weeks for the test results to reach my internist. When they do, there is a letter explaining that there was a clerical error in the lab. It wasn't three, it was one-point-three. Normal. A clerical error. A clerical error. A clerrriccalll eerrrooorrr.

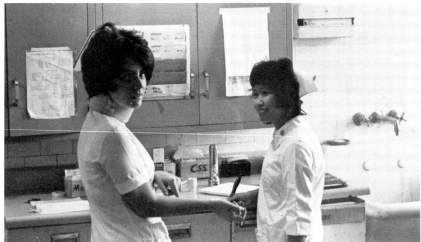

Big Bad John

"I hate it when I cry. Sometimes I get so depressed, I cry like a baby. My wife'll come in and say why ya cryin', John? I say get the hell outta here, I don't want ya to see me cryin'. I hobbled out on crutches once to give the mailman two bucks for Christmas. Merry Christmas, he says, and I start cryin'. If it hurts that much, he says, here take it back."

[28]

"I get depressed a lot. I say I don't think about the accident a lot, but I do. It really messed up my life. I had this total hip done last March and the knee in July. I know how bad that hip was but everybody kept sayin' it wasn't so bad John, so I started to believe them. You forget the pain. This one's been worse. A lot more painful. Sometimes I say what the hell, I oughta jump out the window. But then I figure I'd only end up back here, worse off."

"They keep sayin' one day you'll be a rich man, John. I sure hope so. Then maybe I could get to do some of the things I always wanted to but didn't have the money for. Sometimes, I take the whole pension check—two hundred and eighty dollars—and blow it on one weekend. Get drunk and fish and forget everything. Then I suffer for three weeks till the next check."

"They give me these happy pills here. Anti-depressants. But I think they make me more sleepy than happy. Maybe I'll be happy when this is all over and I don't need any more operations. Each one, I think this is the last one. Then I start gettin' the pain and I figure what the hell, I better get it over with. I hope to hell this is the last one."

"Someday, they tell me, you'll be a rich man. They say that to cheer me up. But I don't know, is it really worth it? I'm a cripple."
Big John.

Postscript

For sure somebody is going to ask why Big John? They will have missed the point. We have left the Age of Reason. Reason will no longer justify the unreasonable. We need new ways to survive this alien environment. Roth and Updike, Malamud and Bellow . . . they travel in circles with a generation left behind. A time of acid rock and Jesus freaks has clouded over Mailer's vision. He says his writing has become confusing because his head has become confusing because the times have become confusing. He can't separate his words from his cowboy boots. (Champ of what?) Let them entertain us, these intellectual prestidigitators, these electronically overdigested literati. But they will soften our teeth.

Big John, now, he's something else. Chew on him awhile and he may show you the way out. There never was a Joe, you see. He was just a caricature in the best Hollywood tradition. We have been suckered into a caricature reality. Big John is Joe and that's the way out. (See Schopenhauer's Stratagems.) If we don't, Skinner will. And who will know? Freedom is a state of mind and Control is benevolent manipulation. All our idols are fallen. They had clay feet, didn't you know?

Anarchy isn't something you do, it's something you let each other do. C'mon, Big John, let's you and me play frisbee in the park. You're a helluva guy.

[*January 1972*]

The Perils of Parity: Part I

Announcing: The Pay-What-It's-Worth Subscription, a Gloriously Impractical Plan

This constitutes a shift from our former Pay-Nothing Subscription Plan. Therefore, a few words of explanation. Circulation has grown considerably. First Class Mail is faster and more reliable than Third. The mimeograph was a Damn Drag. All of which taxed our philanthropic limits. Hence, the Pay-What-It's-Worth Subscription Plan which begins with this issue.

The *Treadmill* will continue to be published irregularly and sent to you at no charge. Read it, decide what the issue is worth to you and forward the cash, check or money order to *Observations from the Treadmill*. If an issue is worth nothing to you, send nothing. Should two consecutive issues prove so barren of interest, we will accept our inadequacy and no further issues will be sent to you. No advance payments will be accepted . . . the *Treadmill* will rise to its own occasions. Or fall, on the inertia of its readers.

The First Bridge

You have to admit this is a hell of a strange way to put a book together. I mean it's already done and now I'm supposed to go back and put in Bridges. I think the whole book is a bridge. Well it's their book so I'll put in the Bridges, but you go ahead and read what you want to read in the order you want to read it. I don't think it makes too much difference, it's not a mystery or anything like that.

What's a bridge anyway, but a structure that spans a river, a road, a chasm? Chasm. That's a good word for what separates people. No man is an island, John Donne said. Hell, every man is an island! That's the damn trouble. Ask Krishnamurti.

The Treadmill is a kind of a bridge. Between somebody like Big John and you, say. Or between you and the long hair barefoot bearded acid dropping street people who go to free clinics for help because there's nowhere else to go when you're on a bad trip or have the clap. Or you're knocked up, crashing down, or freaked out. That's what took me to the Washington Free Clinic. Your kids. The ones who ran away from your homes, from your values. They didn't want you on your terms. Nobody wants them on theirs. Except the people who volunteer to work at the Free Clinic. They don't take money. And they don't give morality.

Maybe it would help if we stopped moralizing. Those who criticize young sex have the oldest inhibitions. The strongest opponents of marijuana are often the biggest drinkers. Twenty million drinking problems in this country. Ten million alcoholics. And the maximum sentence for possession of marijuana in Texas is life. Just a social drinker, they say? Tell them you're just a social pot smoker. Watch their face.

The Treadmill is a kind of a bridge, I was saying, that connects people. You. And them. Come on, it'll hold you. It'll always hold one more.

A Bible Story from the Book of Grief

And God
   looked down
thru the smog
   and saw
Paranoia.

So God
   sent for Solomon
and said:
   "My children
are uptight.
   Go and
deal with it,
   wisely."

Then Solomon
      went to Harlem
and listened to Black Militants
   who said:
"No more shit
   from racist honkie motherfucker pigs. Power to the People."
And they raised their fists.

Then
Solomon
      went to Middle America
and listened to Concerned Citizens
   who said:
"Line the longhair dope fiends
   up against the wall support the President. God bless America."
And they raised their flags.

Then
Solomon
      went to Berkeley
and listened to Radical Students
   who said:

"Fuck the System. Fuck the Draft. Fuck the War.
    Fuck ABM. Fuck Pollution. Fuck Racism. Fuck Repression.
        Fuck it."
And they raised their middle fingers.

Then
Solomon
        went to Washington
and listened to New Left Doves
and Enlightened Conservative Hawks
    who said:
"It's their fault."
And they raised two fingers in the Bi-Partisan Peace Sign.

And Senate Committees held hearings.
And the President appointed Commissions.
And the Vice President made speeches.
And there was fear in the Land.

But Solomon remembered
    and smiled
and dealt with it,
    wisely.

            Then
            Solomon
                returned and said:
            "Lord,
                I dealt with it,
            wisely.
                I gave them
            my sword
                and told them
            to divide the child
                in two."
            (And God remembered and smiled.)

So they cut the child in two.

Washington Free Clinic

The sign on the door of the Georgetown Lutheran Church read: "Washington Free Clinic—Good Vibes." The arrow pointed to the basement. It was early on a warm Friday evening and people were strolling casually along Wisconsin Avenue, window-shopping the many small boutiques and shops that line the avenue. Inside, the hall was jammed with people standing in small groups or sitting on the floor. Past the hall at one end of a large room were tables set up with file baskets marked "VD," "GYN," "ABORTION," "DRUGS," "PSYCH." The walls were plastered with messages, photographs of missing children, astrological drawings, and drug posters ("Black is beautiful. Black and on stuff isn't!"). Donovan sang softly from an old phonograph in the corner.

I asked for Denise Horton, one of the administrators whom I had met at an educational conference in Chicago. She wasn't there yet, so I waited, watching the action. When she came in, she explained that she was on her way to Canada for a vacation, but we could rap a while before she left. After she showed me the Clinic, we went outside and sat on the steps.

Denni

A tall pretty girl with long straight blond hair and very dark eyes. Denni had been a pre-medical student in college majoring in psychology and working part-time as a lab technician in hospitals. Working at the Clinic will get her an advanced degree from Goddard. At twenty-four, she is the oldest of the three administrators. She told me about the Clinic.

"It started in May of '68, mostly because Steve Brown [Dr. Stephen Brown] couldn't hack doing it all himself in his apartment and everyone using it as a crash pad. He had help from the community, and the church donated its basement." Georgetown is a predominantly white middle-class area of Washington, D.C., that resembles New York's Greenwich Village with its mixed bag of students, artists, university professors, and communes of transient street people. It has two newspapers, a food co-operative and the Clinic. Residents refer to the area as "The Washington Free Community." "I helped set up the lab last year and they asked me to help administrate because Alex was fucking up trying to run it alone [Alex Fox, another administrator]. We have about forty doctors, a dozen psychiatrists, twenty lab techs, nurses, social workers, and six paraprofessionals trained for drug and psychiatric counseling by an excellent program at AU [American University]. They're all volunteers. We're the only ones who get paid." She smiled to let me know it wasn't much.

"Usually there are three doctors, a psychiatrist, a nurse, two administrators, one social worker, and some VD and abortion counselors on duty each night or afternoon. During the week we have regular sessions on birth control, child care, and draft deferment. We treat about seventy-five patients a night. We turn away twice that 'cause we don't have enough room to handle them." The Clinic consists of a hall and a large waiting-processing room, two examining rooms, a small lab, a smaller pharmacy, a few cubicles for screening and counseling, and two large rooms used for group therapy. It was obvious that equipment and space were both woefully inadequate.

What kind of work does the Clinic actually do?

Sex education and birth control: "Well, we have classes, but they really come for the pills. Some of our doctors are opposed to the Pill. We have them work on other cases. We don't give the Pill until they've menstruated about nine months—it has to do with the bones. We explain the pros and cons of using the Pill and of course rule out those who shouldn't use it. We measure and dispense diaphragms. We don't do IUD's [Intra-Uterine Devices] because we don't have the facilities. A lot of parents call and complain. They think we're teaching their daughters to fuck. One called the other day mad as hell. She found stilbestrol [the "morning-after pill"] with the WFC prescription label in her daughter's room. She was really uptight. We told her to talk to our lawyers. We treat these kids as adults. With the right information they can make their own decisions."

Abortion counseling: "In D.C. an abortion is legal and generally costs about six hundred dollars. We help chicks who don't have that kind of bread. There are psychiatrists who will certify for no fee, gynecologists who charge less, hospitals which accept patients as service cases. We try to counsel them. Do they really want the abortion or are they seeking another solution? Sometimes, they say that's all I can do, but they mean what else can I do. In the end, it's their decision. If they want it, we help them get it."

Venereal disease: "We have a lot of VD here, at least half of those that come in. Usually it's the guys. The chicks don't always know they've got it. They think it's just vaginal discharge. Sometimes the guys drag their chicks along to be safe. Mostly it's GC, sometimes syphilis. We diagnose and treat." The D.C. Department of Health provides the Clinic with penicillin and tetracycline at no cost. "We ask who they've been sleeping with and send polite little notes—'It is important to your personal health that you contact the Washington Free Clinic immediately!' If they come in, we treat them too. It's an uphill battle."

Drugs: "We get almost no skag [heroin] or coke [cocaine]. Most of the kids that come here are on bad acid trips, speed, mescaline, etc. If we get a real addict, we usually refer them to the Black Man's Methadone Center or one of the two Synanon Houses. Everybody's on grass, of course. I do counseling on drugs, but only the lighter stuff. We get a lot of bike chicks in here. They groove on bikin' [motorcycles], gang fucks, and dope. Occasionally one will come in freaked out—can't come down from an STP high or hallucinating. I don't relate with them. They like me but look at me like a straight, so after while I turn them off. I've used acid, mescaline, stuff like that, but I never shot up anything. They need to talk to someone who's done that, done the reformatories, done all that. Alex is terrific with them because he's been into heavy drugs. I've seen him sit up for twenty-four hours with someone doin' a bummer [bad trip]. He's really good.

"We're trying to get up a mobile unit which we can take all over the city. We got money from the Junior League, would you believe. It's drug year, I guess. They want us to do drug education, but our ideas are pretty different from what they expected. We try to help the kids get the most out of what they're using. It cuts down on OD's, keeps them from escalating to harder stuff. We do assays for them so they know what they're buying. It drives out bad pushers. We haven't

[3 6]

seen Mes for nine months, but they all thought they were on mescaline. It was bad acid cut with strychnine . . . gives all kinds of bad side effects, headaches, flashbacks, all kinds of things. We try to show them that there are other trips besides drugs. Most kids use drugs because there's nothing else for them, but when they see that there can be, some try. But we don't moralize."

Psychiatric therapy: "A lot of them have real emotional problems. Some are runaways. Others live with their parents in the suburbs. They're confused and hung-up and need somebody to talk to that knows. At first some of our psychiatrists were uptight about nonprofessionals doing therapy, but I picked most of them and they're damn good. They get good training here and at AU, and they're all in therapy themselves as well, so they get to know where their head's at. I've gone through analysis too . . . about three hours several times a week here and at AU."

How do people hear about you?

"Oh, word gets around. Strangers in town always ask where's the good vibes—where can they eat, shower, crash. There are seventy-five to a hundred free clinics now across the country. The underground papers do a good job of publicizing who, what, and where. We treat about seventy-five a night. Feed them a meal, too. Dan is into yoga and really knows about food." Dan Murphy, the third administrator, is a Conscientious Objector from Iowa working at the Clinic as alternative service to the Army. "But we don't have enough room. We have no dental facilities, no way to treat emergencies, do suturing, etc. That all takes room and room takes bread."

What about the police?

"For the first week or so we were busted about three times. Now they don't bother us. They don't bother people on the street much either. Most of them are paid off. The Mafia runs this town like all the rest, and the big pushers don't want their action broken up."

Do you have trouble with parents?

"We have never had to go to court, but we get plenty of parents who call up mad or come down here and try to hassle us. What are we doing to their kid . . . we should turn the kid over . . . you know. We try to protect the kid as much as we can, but we don't want to come between the kid and the parents. If they get tough, we ask them to call our lawyers, who may be able to answer their questions.

"People come to us and say we want to set up a clinic like yours in our town, tell us how. We tell them we'll help if they can answer yes to two questions. If they can't we tell them to go home and work on something else. The first is: 'Are you prepared not to moralize?' That's tough and it gets rid of lots of do-gooders. The second is: 'Are you and your doctors prepared to go to court and maybe to jail?' That takes care of the rest. Most of our patients are under-age. Our doctors risk law suits and possibly malpractice suits as well for treating minors without parental consent.

"We have lots of volunteers. They come and work. They bring food and stuff. Even the doctors come from the hospitals with their pockets loaded with things we need. But mostly we need bread. There's so much more we could do if we had it. Can you help us get bread?"

After Denni split for Canada, I went back in. Alex was in a group session and Dan was waxing a floor, so I had time to just look around. One pretty girl, well dressed in fur moccasins, corduroy bells, and a white lace blouse, kept asking to see a psychiatrist. There was none available, but finally a crew-cut psychologist who looked more like a fullback from Notre Dame quietly explained to her that if she could come back Monday or Tuesday there would be someone who could see her. I've been waiting for hours, she said, is there a free clinic like this with psychiatrists in Maryland? One of the counselors walking by said he wished to hell there was so there would be less turned away at this clinic.

A barefoot and long-haired boy of about seventeen with a drooping mustache was talking to a smooth-cheeked kid who couldn't have been older than thirteen.

"Once the pigs stopped me, searched me and made me strip. I had a joint on my ear the whole time and they never even saw it."

"They bust you there for grass? Man, that's a drag! They can't pick you up for one thing and bust you for another, you know. That's the law!"

A short-haired man in a green T-shirt and tattoos on both arms came in looking out of place.

"Where can I get a bath?"

"I just got cleaned up at a place where you can shave and stuff."

"Naw, I don't want a shave. I'm lettin' it grow. But I sure would like a bath."

Somebody told him where to go. An older man came in dressed in slacks and shirt, carrying a jacket and suitcase.

"Anybody know where I can crash tonight?"

"Call the Switchboard. Number's on the wall."

"I called them last night. Every pad was booked."

"Call them anyway. Maybe you'll get lucky."

He was and left. Somebody came in and announced no pregnancy tests tonight, come back Monday. Four girls left. About 11:30, Alex emerged from his long group session. We started to talk, but were interrupted by one of the doctors, who gave him hell because the lab tech and pharmacist had gone home early. He was apparently the only doctor around for the last couple of hours.

"No more, Alex. I can't examine patients, run out here and get medicine, run back and treat patients. I can't do it all myself. If you can't run it right, close it down. It's no damn good, Alex!"

Alex nodded and smiled quietly. The doctor seemed reassured and left. Everyone was gone. Dan was cleaning up. Alex and I went out and started walking down Wisconsin. The change was shattering. The casually strolling window shoppers were gone and, with the dark, Wisconsin Avenue had been transformed into Sunset Strip. Rock music blared. Bike gangs roared down the street. The sidewalks were jammed. Kids were walking, standing, sitting, and lying down everywhere. The air was thick with the smell of hamburgers, onions, incense, and the sweet smell of hash. As I walked with Alex, his long hair flying behind him, our conversation was constantly interrupted as someone said hello or he stopped briefly to talk to someone.

"Hi, how's Ted? Is he any better? Tell him to stop by the Clinic. Tell him I said so. Hey, what you trippin' on? Is it any good? Bring it in and I'll look at it. How do you feel? What are you on? Acid? Is it good? Come by the Clinic."

I kept worrying about his bare feet stepping on broken glass or burning cigarettes. If it bothered him, he gave no indication.

Alex

Small, frail, with long curly black hair and a beard to match. Barefoot, tattered pants, and open shirt. But his eyes are alert and direct, his smile gentle, and his voice quiet and reassuring. Alex is twenty-one. After high school in Maryland he went to New York to study acting.

"I tried the starving-actor bit. I was kicked out of YMCA's. I even lived at the Greenwich Hotel in the Village. After while I got to wearing this big old overcoat and carrying all my belongings in the pockets. They finally told me they could live without me and my starving-actor bit. I moved around a lot. Went to Israel on my mother's money. Stayed for eight months. It was cool. I dug the geography, but not the people. After twenty years they have a war mentality. I lived all over without any money in my pocket. Even stayed on a kibbutz. The only place where I found people I liked was Eilat. That's where all the dregs—the dreck dregs—go. The hippies. They're my people.

"I got into the Clinic in a funny way. When I came to Washington, I got to hangin' around the Clinic. Then they asked me to run it. I didn't want the responsibility, but the more they gave me to do, the more I seemed to take on responsibility. I came here to see my brother. He's pretty fucked up. I tried to put him in a hospital. My mother's pretty fucked up, too. It's really weird. I've become her counselor. She keeps calling me and asking where's my brother? These kids are all pretty fucked up. Mostly there's no one they can talk to. They're afraid of the hospitals, afraid they'll get busted. If they're runaways, they're afraid they'll get turned over. If they live at home, they're afraid to talk to their parents. They're afraid of everybody. They really have problems. Drug problems. VD problems. Hepatitis problems. Emotional problems. Man, they got problems.

"I like working at the Clinic. It gives me purpose. Making me a good counselor, too. I have this middle-class black family that I see. Man, they're fucked up. The kid's about fourteen and she started calling the Clinic and asking questions like can I take dope? Can I shoot up? Finally she called one night and talked about suicide and I said she better come in. She brought her parents. They start each session grudgingly like we don't belong here and what are we doin' here with this white hippie and we don't have any problems anyway. But I talk to them and after while it starts opening up and the shit starts to fly. The kid resents her parents' blackness because she grooves on a hippie life style and she thinks of herself as other than black. It's slow, but it's workin' out. It really makes me feel good. It's the first time I've had a family like this in regular session.

"I've messed around with a lot of drugs, but as an experimenter. I don't do that ex-junkie routine. . . . I don't know how long I'll keep this up, you know, stay at the Clinic. Nothing's permanent."

We stood on the corner, hitching a ride to Dupont Circle. Alex told me that a month ago he had decided not to be paranoid one night and took a ride with some rednecks. They beat him up and dumped him on a country road in Virginia. Dan joined us and after a short time we got a ride for the fifteen or twenty blocks. It was about 1:30 in the morning, and they walked me to Denni's apartment. She had sublet to two girls for a month, but had arranged with them for me to crash on the couch.

On the way, we saw a young girl sitting on the curb with her dog and a knapsack. Alex stopped and chatted with her.

"Have you got a place to crash?"

"No, my old man's lookin' for one now."

"Well, if he strikes out, you can crash with us."

"Far out."

He gave her the address and we left.

I have always distrusted the Twenty-Four Hour Expert and the Overnight Authority. Still, I learned something at the Free Clinic on a subject on which I had thought myself well informed. I had a brief glimpse at the other side of the Cool Scene . . . the one where you travel free, eat free, crash free, and love free . . . where no one need be uptight and paranoid . . . where you let it all hang out and trip when you feel like it. Instead I saw VD, bad trips, and abortions. I saw tired, hungry, confused, and uncomfortable kids who were beginning to realize that what they had found was just as bad as what they had left. When that happens, somebody has to be around to pick up the pieces. Somebody who doesn't moralize. Somebody who's been there. Somebody like Denni or Alex or Dan. Somebody like the doctors and psychiatrists and nurses and lab techs and counselors at the Clinic. It's a tough job, without end, it seems. They need your help.

The kid you help may be your own.

[*May 1970*]

"There is always a military officer somewhere who wants to win a battle by taking one more hill or dropping one more bomb. That is his responsibility."

—From a statement by General James M. Gavin (Ret.) in appearance before the Senate Foreign Relations Committee

Our Red Brothers Are in the Pink

Approximately 470,000 Indians live on or adjacent to more than 420 reservations and other sanctuaries set aside for them by the federal government. About 200,000 live in the larger cities of the nation. The American Indian was granted United States citizenship in 1924 and, according to the Bureau of Indian Affairs (BIA), life for the red man is getting better all the time. Says the BIA, his health is better, his living conditions are better, his education is better, his economy is stronger.

The average Indian now has 8.4 years of schooling. The average for the rest of the country is 10.6 years. The Indian school drop-out rate is almost 50 per cent. The school drop-out rate for all American pupils is 27 per cent.

The Indian income previously has been so small as to be virtually unmeasurable. It is now up to $1500 yearly for a family of four.

The Indian's health level is the lowest in the nation, as is his life expectancy. His suicide rate is the highest in the nation and among the highest in the world.

Indian unemployment runs to about 50 per cent, more than ten times the national average. Of the 10,000 new jobs created on or near reservations since 1962, less than half have gone to Indians.

If life is getting so good for the American Indian, wonder why they wanted Alcatraz?

The Perils of Parity: Part II

An Interview with the Editor Concerning the Glorious Impracticality of the Pay-What-It's-Worth Subscription Plan

In the last issue, a new subscription plan was introduced under which the reader would receive a copy free of charge, read it, decide what it is worth, and forward the sum to the Treadmill. *Should it be worth nothing, nothing would be sent, but should consecutive issues prove so devoid of interest, then no further copies would be sent. Advance payments would not be accepted. "The* Treadmill *will rise to its own occasions. Or fall on the inertia of its readers."*

OFT: Is the new plan working?

my: No, of course not. Well under ten per cent have responded. The least has been a quarter, the most has been ten dollars, the most unusual has been a half-gallon of genuine Vermont maple syrup. We don't expect to change to a barter-what-it's-worth plan, though, because our mailman threatens to quit. He's getting too old.

OFT: Then why not a regular subscription plan like other publications?

my: Because the *Treadmill* is not "like other publications." We can't say how many issues there will be or even what they will be about. Besides, why shouldn't you have the opportunity to decide for yourself what something is worth *after* you use it?

OFT: But your readers don't seem to care for the idea.

my: You're right there. Many have said they would gladly pay if we told them how much, but if not they won't. Strange. They can't decide how much an issue is worth after they read it, but they insist that we decide before we write it. Well, we want them to think for themselves.

OFT: You'll never get rich that way.

my: That's what my mother says.

OFT: It won't work.

my: That's what my wife says.

OFT: It's impractical.

my: I know.

Don't Cry, Lady

Where do you feel?
Do you feel here
(points to heart)
or here
(points to head)
        ?

If you feel here
(points to heart)
and I feel here
(points to head)
. . . do you feel more
than I
        ?

Why?

I Had a Dream

I've
    been to your
mountain, Martin,
    but I
didn't see
    what you
saw.
    (Did you
need
    glasses?)

Time

I think
  we should spend time
    like money.
  Each morning
we should put the day
  in our pocket
    and buy what we need.

Work. Love.
Ballgame. Snooze.
  Fellini or Myrna Loy or
    a confrontation
      with Mephistopheles.

Budget if you're cautious
  Squander if you're bold. Don't
    go broke too early.
  Nor recriminate when you're old.

I have spent enough time on this poem.

It's Relative

Tomorrow got here much too fast,
I blame it on Today.
If Yesterday'd been in less of a rush,
I'd have no more to say.

The Purpose of Punishment: a Requiem for the Bill of Rights

Cast of Characters

Dr. Edward Guy—Director of Psychiatric Services, Philadelphia Prisons. Tall, athletic, mid-forties, stylishly long hair and sideburns but thinning on top and bald spot in back, high forehead, deeply set blue-gray eyes, Southern accent, slightly out-of-sync humor, relaxed manner but tense vibes.

Jim Sheffer—Administrator of Psychiatric Services, Philadelphia Prisons. Short, stocky, mid-thirties, round face, glasses, thin tight lips, cold, mechanical, efficient.

Theodore—inmate-patient. Small, young, black, shy, quiet, double murderer awaiting result of Competency Hearing.

Speed Freak—inmate-patient. Tall, thin, nervous, twenties.

Hyper—inmate-patient. Big man, black, wide eyes, thirties, raspy voice, very talkative, not too coherent.

Plus various inmate-patients, mostly black and under thirty; several social workers, white hippie types; and a few guards, both black and white.

AT BUCKS COUNTY PRISON:

The Major—John D. Case, Warden. Retired twenty-one-year Marine Corps veteran, former Brig Commander at Camp Le Jeune, South Carolina, fifty, six-four, two hundred fifty pounds, stomach too big, neck grown paunchy, direct blue eyes, thinning gray hair combed neatly back, confident manner of an accustomed order-giver.

Larry—inmate. Slightly built, boyish eighteen, pimples, blackheads, long thin dark hair, a hint of mustache on the upper lip.

Plus assorted inmates, mostly young and white and often with long hair, beards, mustaches. Few guards, generally older and mostly white.

AT BUCKS COUNTY REHABILITATION CENTER:

Harold—trainee. Short and very heavy, forty-seven, graying hair combed straight back, round boyish face that belies his age, the easy manner of one that's been around, articulate, his shirt does not quite reach his pants revealing a good three inches of bulging flesh.

Plus assorted trainees, again mostly young and white, and guards not in uniform.

AT GRATERFORD PRISON:

Robert L. Johnson—Superintendent of the State Correctional Institution at Graterford, Pennsylvania. Forty-six, black, handsome, young-looking, fashionably dressed, former social worker and parole official, newly appointed, warm, friendly, hip, a cautious reformer.

Sgt. John Zaneski—guard. Forties, medium height and build, military-type hash marks denoting nineteen years' service, accent of upstate coal-mining region, manner correct but careful with opinions.

Lieutenant in the Hole—guard. In charge of day shift in Maximum Security, short and squat, beer belly, huge tattooed arms, biceps-size wrists, crew cut, cold as ice.

Runner—inmate. Black, allowed out of his cell in the Hole to carry food trays, clean floors, etc., jailhouse-lawyer type.

Junior—inmate in the Hole. Tall, about thirty, horn-rimmed glasses, very articulate, long-termer for armed robbery, reputed escape artist.

Biker—inmate in the Hole. Stocky build, long red hair and matching droopy mustache, speaks slowly with New York accent, member of upstate bike gang, convicted double murderer awaiting sentence.

Plus assorted inmates, mostly black, and guards, mostly white.

SCENE 5 COMPOSITE:

David Rothenberg—Executive Secretary, the Fortune Society. Early thirties, former publicity director for Off-Broadway play about prisons (*Fortune and Men's Eyes*), small and slightly built, sunken eyes, curly hair, the cold reserve of a man repeating the same lines too many times.

Ken "Red" Jackson—ex-convict. Thirty-one, tall, rangy, a thin mouth that never smiles and barely moves as he speaks in a New York accent; scowling eyes, thin hair with a deep widow's peak, tough and opinionated.

John Altman—detective, New York City Police. Late twenties, stocky but slightly overweight, sandy hair, long sideburns, and bushy turned-down mustache.

Honorable Edmund Spaeth—Judge, Philadelphia Court of Common Pleas. Tall, lanky, perhaps sixty, egg-shaped head, thinning hair, high forehead, large nose, silver-framed glasses, narrow chin held tucked in to his chest, nearly expressionless face except for raised eyebrows creating deep rolling furrows in his forehead, low measured tones that are friendly but reserved.

Ephraim Gomberg—Executive Director, Philadelphia Crime Commission. Early sixties, small, nearly white hair combed forward on top with long slanted sideburns, horn-rimmed glasses, confident eliteness of a savant on criminal justice, makes speeches rather than conversation, very intense, sincere but somewhat condescending.

Turner De Vaughn—Director, BarbWire Society. Twenty-four, black, high forehead, closely cropped hair, small mustache and goatee, soft-spoken.

Harry Bransom—Assistant head of Defenders Association, Juvenile Division, Philadelphia. Tall, medium build, longish hair, trimmed but straggly beard, horn-rimmed glasses, mid-thirties, bitter, cynical, concerned, speaks rapidly but confidently, no small talk and no time for anyone else's.

my—Narrator, quoter, reporter, compulsive prodder of the lazy conscience, advocate of radical reform, self-appointed Amicus Populae.

The action takes place in various prison settings, as well as offices, restaurants, and a railroad car. Each scene is briefly described. All prison settings contain high stone walls topped with barbed wire and search lights, many locked solid or barred steel doors, and an antiseptic smell. The prevailing colors are cream and light green, the prevailing mood is depressing gray. Throughout the action at Holmesburg and Graterford, groups of inmates stand around doing nothing, while guards continuously lock and unlock doors with huge keys and much clanging. All actors are dressed in prison-gray work clothes, but non-inmates each have some article to denote their function (e.g., Judge has a gavel, guards have keys, Dr. Guy has a large bottle of tranquilizers, wardens have a small box with a red button to push, etc.). It should grow progressively difficult to determine who are the prisoners and who are not. Throughout the action, my is under various types of artificial restraint. His discomfort should instill a vague uneasiness in the audience although it should not be a conscious distraction.

Prologue

my

[*Sits on the edge of the stage, legs dangling. He is handcuffed, a fact which he ignores, though his gestures are quite awkward.*] Dig it. If you came to be entertained, you better leave. Go home and watch the boob tube or read *The New York Times.* We're here to show you something you don't want to see. There's no plot, no heroes. You're here to think. About the purpose of punishment. About the injustice of justice. About a hundred-and-ninety-five-year-old piece of paper written by hypocrites and worshiped by hypocrites. The Sixth Amendment guarantees a speedy and public trial by an impartial jury. The Eighth Amendment guarantees no excessive bail, no excessive fines, no cruel and unusual punishment. Crap! Justice is a bummer, a nightmare of degradation for the poor and for the black and for the young and for Chicanos and Puerto Ricans and Indians and prostitutes and rum bums and junkies and ex-convicts of every description. And you know it. And you do nothing about it. "All animals are equal. But some animals are more equal than others."—Orwell. Law and Order, right? Lock 'em up, right? Well take a look, friends. Take a little look at a system that says you're innocent until proven guilty and then treats you as if you're guilty anyway, a system that treats humans like animals and takes away their pride and self-respect, a system that tells a released prisoner he has paid his "debt to society" and then refuses him a driver's license or a job, a system that still believes in a death sentence in all but nine states that is rejected by over seventy other countries. Take a look at the most expensive criminal justice and correction system in the world. It . . . doesn't . . . work. And because we have failed to hold it accountable, we are equally to blame for its incompetence. What is the purpose of punishment, anyway? Do you know? The people you will meet here are real, these are their actual words.

Scene 1. Holmesburg Prison, Philadelphia

The scene is the main building, shaped like an octopus with a central control desk at the middle of a high domed rotunda. Branching out from the circumference of the rotunda are a series of long corridors (cell blocks). Each has a barred entrance, locked. The action takes place in F Block. The sign over the entrance reads: Diagnostic Hospital. *On an easel nearby is a sign:* Thought for the day: He that lives only upon hopes will die fasting. *F Block is separated into three sections, each with a locked floor-to-ceiling barred gate. The first section is administrative, the second and largest holds most of the inmate-patients, the third is for maximum security. Cells line both sides, brightly lit and painted in the administrative section, dark and gray in the rest. Each cell is roughly nine by twenty-five feet with a high arched ceiling and a thin slit at the top for daylight. Most cell doors are open, revealing bare cots, an open toilet, and a wash basin. Doors are cross-hatched two-inch strips of thick steel, with a foot-square opening in the middle. my in straight-jacket stands with Dr. Guy outside the entrance to F Block.*

Dr. Guy

About ninety per cent of the inmates here at Holmesburg are black. That's what caused the riot here last July. This hall was covered with blood, guys were lying everywhere. One white inmate had his hand almost severed by a meat cleaver. It was hanging on by a thread. It was some show. [*A guard unlocks the gate, and they walk in to sit down in a cell-office in the first section.*] I've been in court all morning with a competency hearing. This kid had the shortest tour in Vietnam in history. Three hours. He got off the plane in Saigon and bumped into an Army psychiatrist who apparently thought the kid was acting strangely, so he had him shipped back on the next plane. He got out on a medical discharge. One day he came home and his wife said she was leaving because he didn't do anything for her in bed. She took the kids and went to live with her folks, he moved in with his best friend. But he was pretty tense and brooding. He told nine different people that he was liable to kill somebody if he couldn't get back with his wife. Nobody paid any attention. So he made a list of the nine people and decided to kill them all. The first on the list was his friend's wife. He went to her one day and stabbed her quite a few times. She didn't die too easily, so he dragged her to the bathroom and stuffed her in the tub. Her little kid came to see what was happening. She wasn't on his list, but he killed her too. Then he went to his wife and told her what he did. She didn't believe him, so he started to strangle her, but she was smart enough to tell him how much she loved him and how good he really was in bed and how she wanted him back. They went to several hospitals for help. Nobody believed the story. Finally somebody did and he was arrested. By then it dawned on him that he had killed his best friend's wife and his own godchild. He went into a catatonic stupor, expecting to lie there until he died. That's when they sent him to me. I put him on massive tranquilizers to bring him around. Now we'll get him to Byberry for treatment.

my

"Aggression is a drive as innate, as natural and as powerful as sex . . . the theory that aggression is nothing but a response to frustration is no longer tenable."—Anthony Starr.

Dr. Guy

They usually come here from low socio-economic groups. I almost never meet a high-school graduate. The incredible thing is their ability to adapt to a prison situation. Prison is like a confirmation of the life they've led. They always thought they had no freedom, now they know it. And there's a bitterness—why are they in prison for stealing a lousy few bucks when there are men stealing millions with a pen? This really is a "school for crime." They brag about their exploits. The more they talk, the more they learn from each other. By the time they get out, they know much more than when they went in.

my

[*Turns to audience.*] There are four prisons in Philadelphia. Three are at Holmesburg. The Detention Center, which is overflowing with adult males awaiting trial that can't make bail or are in on a non-bailable offense. The House of Correction, which was supposed to hold adult males sentenced to short thirty- or sixty-day terms, but instead is packed with men, women, and sixty-five juveniles-to-be-tried-as-adults—all in different wings and most awaiting trial or sentence. They spill over from both places into Holmesburg, where they mix detainees with convicted criminals and sentenced inmates. You can wait for six months or a year for trial, sometimes longer. And you can wait almost as long here to be sentenced. The most anyone can be sentenced to at Holmesburg is two years. The daily population is about thirty-five hundred. Twenty-five thousand are processed through here in a year. [*Turns to Dr. Guy.*] Homosexuality?

Dr. Guy

There is tremendous tension. What you hear is true. If it isn't forced on a new prisoner, he lives in constant fear that it will be. Often he will submit to someone who promises to protect him from the others. When he does this, his prestige in the prison community goes down, and his protector's goes up. He becomes the Pussy, his protector the Gorilla. The Gorilla never considers himself a homosexual.

my

Drugs?

Dr. Guy

So many have a drug problem. Heroin addicts aren't so bad to handle. It's nothing like I studied in school or like the movies. It's pretty easy to kick it. We help some with tranquilizers. If he's on a methadone program, we try to cooperate with the methadone centers by continuing treatment, but sometimes if he's done something particularly bad, they say "Fuck him, don't give him any. If he wants the program bad enough, he'll sign up again when he gets out." Anyway, we never had someone kicking die on us. Barbiturates can be a problem, though, they can go into convulsions just like that. There aren't many drugs available in prison, contrary to what you hear. They like to brag that they can get anything, but when it comes right down to it, I don't see that much.

my

Alcohol?

Dr. Guy

Many of these people simply can't hold liquor. They always seem to get in trouble in some bar. When they're sober, they're nice guys, even gentle, but give them more than a couple of drinks . . . and they can't seem to stay away from it. I think I'd have a bar in here and let them drink until they realize their problem.

my

"Violent crimes such as homicide, assault, and rape tend to be acts of passion among intimates and acquaintances. . . . The victim, the offender, or both are likely to have been drinking prior [to the crime]."—Report of the National Commission on the Causes and Prevention of Violence.

They get up and "make rounds." They are joined by Jim Sheffer, two social workers, and a guard. They stop as Dr. Guy talks to Theodore, the double murderer awaiting the result of a Competency Hearing. Theodore sits on a bench in the middle of the corridor, his head slightly bowed.

Dr. Guy

[*To my.*] This is Theodore. I told you about Theodore. How are you, Theodore?

Theodore

[*Smiles shyly.*] Fine.

Dr. Guy

I think we made out good with the Judge today, Theodore. I think you'll be going to Byberry. How do you feel about that, Theodore?

Theodore

[*Smiles again.*] Yes.
They move on as Dr. Guy asks each man how he feels, how he slept last night. They are stopped by Speed Freak, who does a nervous little dance as he talks.

[5 4]

Speed Freak

I didn't sleep last night, Doc. My feet and shins was burnin' awful. I've shot up these veins so often, I can hardly touch them. But it really burns from when they was frozen. I need somethin' for the pain, Doc.

Sheffer

Sure, he wants something with morphine in it.

Speed Freak

Naw, Doc, even aspirin would help better than these tranquilizers I'm getting. I think I may be a little psychotic, Doc, I been psychotic before. I think I was when I held up that bank, a voice told me to do it, I had a gun that didn't even work, no bullets. I think I'm innocent, Doc, I hear voices.

my

[*Turns to audience.*] In 1968 there were ninety million firearms in civilian hands in the United States, the highest gun-to-population ratio in the world. In opposition to gun-control legislation, the National Rifle Association says that guns don't kill people, people do.

They continue into the maximum security area where the guard tells Dr. Guy there is a "live one." He approaches the locked cell door and speaks to Hyper.

Dr. Guy

How do you feel? I'm Dr. Guy.

Hyper

I'm fine, Dr. Guy. There's no problem. I'm in control of my emotions. I know . . .

Dr. Guy

[*Interrupts.*] Have you been on any kind of drug or medication?

Hyper

No sir I don't need no medication I didn't do nothin' I just went into that Adams store to borrow some money from Mister Adams I

didn't have no gun I was just gonna borrow some money cause I
needed some money 'cause you ain't no man if you ain't got no money
. . . [*takes a big breath*] . . . you a man Doc so you know I got to
be a man if I had a gun I'd a got that money I'd a shot somebody
that's what I'd a done I just needed some money so's I could be a man
you know Doc and so I could go up to Boston where I got a cousin
. . . [*takes another big breath*] . . . so I don't need no medication
I'm in control of my emotions just let me go back to my cell block
'cause I'm just fine. . . . [*Guard and Sheffer, backs to the cell, are
smiling broadly.*]

Dr. Guy

[*Interrupts, but not easily.*] Well, I think you're pretty hyper. I
think you better take some tranquilizers for a few days.

*They walk slowly back towards the entrance to the Block, the
"staff" dropping off until finally my and Dr. Guy are standing at the
entrance gate to F Block.*

my

What is the purpose of punishment?

Dr. Guy

We call it the three Rs—removal, rehabilitation, and revenge. Deterrence? That would be a fourth purpose, but it's not practical, it
doesn't deter anyone, certainly not those who have committed the
crimes. Even capital punishment is no deterrent. These people have
nothing, so they are risking nothing. In seven years I've talked to
plenty of prisoners. None of them thought about punishment before
they decided whether or not to carry a gun.

my

[*Turns to audience.*] Why do we kill people to show people that
killing people is wrong?

Dr. Guy

As for removal, with the present set-up prison makes them worse
criminals. Unless you put them away forever with no chance for
parole, it does society more harm to remove them than to leave them

alone. Unless you are prepared to rehabilitate, and that doesn't exist here or in most places I've seen. Prisons are overcrowded and under-staffed. Society doesn't care much, anyway. The purpose of punishment is revenge.

A guard comes from the center of the rotunda and unlocks the gate. my exits, leaving Dr. Guy standing at the gate with his bottle of tran-quilizers.

Scene 2. *Bucks County Prison—Doylestown, Pennsylvania*

*The outside looks like a movie set with a colorfully painted main gate entrance decorated with red and yellow. To the left of the entrance are instructions to press the big button and announce your business into the speaker. my in handcuffs presses the button and a voice booms over the speaker: "Yes?" my answers: "my to see Warden Case." There is a buzz and the thick door opens. Inside, my is greeted by an inmate, who leads the way to the Major's office. Paneled, built-in shelves on one wall with stacks of mimeographed papers, cluttered desk with console push-button phone. A sign on the desk reads: "Be reasonable—*DO IT MY WAY." To the right of the desk is a small blackboard mounted on the wall. Scrawled backwards on the blackboard are the words: "Help! I'm a prisoner behind this blackboard." Around the room are numerous framed pictures of family and of military groups including the Major sans stomach, also several citations and civic resolutions. On one shelf is a glass display with military medals and ribbons. The Major is emptying the contents of several brightly colored metal boxes onto his desk.*

The Major

These are my suggestion boxes. If the men have a gripe, they put it in here. Pretty good ideas, some of 'em. You want to see my jail, eh? Okay. I'll have someone show you around, then we'll talk. [*Presses button and barks into speaker-phone.*] Larry. Come in here. [*Enter Larry.*]

Larry

Yes, Major?

The Major

Larry, this is my. Show him through the jail, answer any questions he may have, then bring him back here.

Larry

Yes sir, Major.

They exit. Larry shows my through the jail. The main entrance leads into a large very high-ceilinged hall. Just inside the entrance is a glass-enclosed control booth manned by one guard watching TV monitors. He sits at a control panel which operates most of the main gates by remote control. There are three branches off the hall—a Juvenile Block, a Maximum Security Block (the "Long Line") and a Medium Security Block (the "Short Line"). Cells line both sides of the blocks. They resemble those of Holmesburg but are not as deep. Inmates in the Long Line stand in clusters doing nothing. The Short Line is empty except for some inmates moving through it. The Juvenile Block appears to be empty. There is much coming and going of inmates in ones and twos moving through the Short Line to the Kitchen and the Laundry, and in and out of the main entrance to this building. There is a stairway to the basement, also heavily trafficked. In one corner are two barred lockups with several inmates sitting on long benches in each. They are waiting for interviews. In the basement, there are shops, offices, and a "research lab" that pays inmates to take experimental pills, give blood, test soaps and ointments, etc. my stands with Larry near the control room.

my

[*Turns to audience.*] This jail was built in 1884 for $85,000 and opened the following year as a maximum-security prison. Until the Major came here in 1963, inmates were locked in their cells for twenty-two hours a day. Now, they are locked in only at night.

Larry

On nice days, visitors can come with kids, bring box lunches, and spend all day outside with inmates. If it's bad out, they can meet in the dining room, but not with the kids. I'm from Levittown. I was a juvenile when I was brought here the first time. I was seventeen. I was just a petty crook, passing bad checks for twenty or so. Not like the real professionals. They write checks for five hundred or a thousand, but they know what they're doin', 'cept they get caught so I guess maybe they don't know after all. I was in on about nineteen or twenty charges. I was lucky. They sent me to the Rehab Center and then I got out on parole. Now they got me back on armed robbery which I didn't do. Somebody said I did it, but I didn't. I don't like to think about my trial. I could go to the Pen this time. I'm scared.

my

[*Turns to audience.*] Nearly everyone who goes to prison is eventually released. Half to two-thirds are sooner or later arrested and convicted again, most on greater charges than their last.

Larry

When I was on parole, I had trouble getting a job. When you fill out applications, you have to say whether you were ever convicted of a crime. Twice I said yes and didn't get the job. Once I said no and got the job. Mechanic at Two Guys. But they found out I lied and said they didn't need me any more. I felt pretty bad. I called my parole officer, but he wasn't there. I left word, but he never called back.

my

[*Turns to audience.*] The average case load of a city parole officer is 100-150 parolees at one time.

Larry

I was never a leader. I was always a follower. Whatever the guys talked about doin', I did, but somehow I was the only one ever got caught. When I get out I want to go back to Community College. I think I've learned a lot here. How to deal with myself. I always used to pull a job when I was depressed, but when I did it, it made me feel lonely. When I got in trouble, my folks' attitude was like they didn't care, like they didn't expect any more from me. But here it's different. My mom even comes here for classes. This place is far out. I don't know how to describe it. The inmates practically run it. I could probably walk out with you and nobody would even stop me. You can do plenty here if you want to. There's courses in English and Math and Imaginal Education. And you can get to go out and work. And the people from the town come here and meet with us. It makes you realize somebody cares. New guys don't mess around, 'cause they'd have to stand up to all the guys. But there's no fightin', 'cause nobody wants to get the Major in trouble. It's a great place. But they should tear down the wall. I don't believe in that wall. You put a wall around me, you put a wall around my brain.

What is the purpose of punishment?

Larry

I believe in laws, but I don't think you should punish people by putting them away someplace. Most people who commit crimes just don't ever think about gettin' caught. I never thought about what would happen. I don't think I'll get into any more trouble. I'm a leader here, not a follower.

They have strolled back to the Major's office. Larry exits as my re-enters the office and sits down. The Major works at his desk.

my

[*Turns to audience.*] When John Case came here, there was a nucleus of concerned citizens in the area, mostly Quakers, and he built on that base until today he has a very active community involvement in his reforms. There are weekly meetings of Alcoholics Anonymous. He was instrumental in the building of a minimum-security Rehabilitation Center in 1964. There is a free community bail program. There are drug and social counseling programs, a Work Release Program that accepts inmates with less than a year remaining to be served and permits them to reside at the Rehab Center and hold regular jobs on the outside. There are teachers who come in and conduct classes on a variety of subjects. The Major has even developed a form letter to be signed by inmates who are reluctant to take educational courses. It states that the inmate knows he has scored low on his tests, refuses to take any educational courses to improve himself, and knows that this letter will be forwarded to his trial judge. The Major calls it his "velvet fist" and has only ever had one inmate sign the letter. There is also a Sentencing Letter, opened by the trial judge only in event of conviction, evaluating the prisoner and signed by the Major. It carries a lot of weight and the prisoner knows it. Visitations are frequent and informal. The Major was strongly influenced by a course he took under Howard B. Gill, then Director of the Institute of Correctional Administration at American University in Washington. It changed his whole outlook on the penal system.

The Major

[*Looks up with a smile.*] I was Gill-ianized. Howard's slogan was: We operate a salvage business—not a junkyard. He also said that inmates are confined *as* punishment, not *for* punishment. I believe in Howard's theory of Challenging Uncomfortableness. I don't like the word rehabilitation. It presumes these people were once habilitated and went wrong. That's not the case. We have to try to change them into productive and acceptable members of the community. People say what can you do in so short a time? Plenty! I can accomplish something with just a fifteen-minute meeting. I can expose him to new ideas, to what's possible. That's something.

my

[*Turns to audience.*] In 1870, a Statement of Twenty-Two Principles of penal reform included: Reformation, not vindictive suffering, should be the purpose of penal treatment of prisoners. . . . The prisoner should be made to realize that his destiny is in his own hands. . . . Prison discipline should be such as to gain the will of the prisoner and conserve his self-respect. . . . The aim of the prison should be to make industrious free men rather than orderly and obedient prisoners. 1870! We've come a long way in a hundred years!

The Major

There are plenty of people in here that shouldn't be. They broke small laws and got caught. Oh sure, I have a triple murderer in here and a rape murderer, but I also have burglars, drug possessors, forgers, vagrants who can't pay their fines. Half are on drugs, the rest on booze. I suppose you noticed that we have a lot of long hair here. I decided two years ago that there are more important things to worry about than long hair. My daughter and her friends picked up on that hippie life style. She got picked up on a drug bust in New Hope. The papers had a field day, but I didn't judge her. I told her honey, I just came here to tell you that I love you and we'll work this thing out. It was the best thing I could have done. She's okay now, she had a good shrink, but it was really tough. These kids on drugs are sick, and they need treatment.

[62]

[*To audience.*] In 1968 Major Case was named U.S. Jailor of the Year by the American Correctional Association. His salary is $18,000, the highest in the state. His current inmate population consists of 167 in the jail including 4 women, 54 in the Rehab Center and 21 in the Juvenile Home. There have been rumors that he will be the next Commissioner of Correction. He'll find it hard to leave this place.

The Major

I'd like to increase the salaries and the training of the people in this work, improve the physical plant, get rid of a lot of bad laws. I'd legalize prostitution. Arrange furloughs so a man could visit his wife or girlfriend, get his ashes hauled. I'd change the bail system, change the whole judicial system. A lot of people running city jails have huge problems, like McGrath in New York. I can't comment directly, 'cause I'm not involved, but some of them hide behind their problems and use them for excuses.

my

What is the purpose of punishment?

The Major

I don't believe punishment is much of a deterrent for most crimes. If you charge a $25 fine for illegal parking, that's a deterrent, but when a man wants to rob somebody, that's different. Most murders are committed emotionally and someone emotional doesn't think about punishment until after it's done. I don't believe in revenge, but I do believe in restitution.

Scene 3. The Bucks County Rehabilitation Center

A small one-story gray brick building. It sits alone in the middle of county farmland. Twelve "trainee" rooms, four to a room in double-deck bunks, two or three non-uniformed guards, a mess hall and kitchen, a day room with TV and a beat-up pool table, two classrooms, a shower room, and a small canteen. No bars, no locked doors. In the basement, a dormitory for "guests" (former trainees, now re-

leased, who have nowhere to go). Trainees move freely throughout. There is a time clock with punch cards which trainees use on departing for or returning from work. The atmosphere is pleasant. my, still in handcuffs, chats with Harold as they walk around the Center, stopping finally in one of the rooms.

my

[*To audience.*] There are fifty-three trainees staying here. They are charged $17.50 per week for room and board. Deductions are also made for travel expenses, support and arrearage payments, court costs and fines, restitution. They promise no drugs or alcohol on or off the premises. Occasionally, they slip. Now and then, one doesn't come back. Not often. Work Release earnings through 1970 amounted to over half a million dollars, enough to pay for the building and the upkeep of its residents.

Harold

I'm just up from Atlanta. That was a hotel. I've been in a lot worse. San Quentin, where I was clerk for Warden Duffy. When he left, twenty-two years of hard work went down the drain, and it just went back to where it was. I was in Cook County jail three times on contempt charges. That's a filthy hole. But Atlanta was fine. I was there four years. The programs are excellent. A man can get a high-school diploma there and it doesn't say anything about where he got it. About sixteen colleges have courses there. I took a law course and did about ninety per cent of my last appeal myself.

my

[*To audience.*] Harold has been in several prisons as a result of what he calls a basic difference of opinion with General Motors, false securities, and so forth. He is a former army buddy of Huntington Hartford and has shown me some of his correspondence. He is also a writer and has shown me some press clippings. His job, which he has had for many years off and on, is publicity manager for the annual fund-raising sponsorship of the circus by the Shriners. He says that he is very good at his job and has sixteen phones in his office.

[6 4]

Harold

Prison's not so bad. It's like the army. Three square meals a day, a bed, and a roof over your head. Lots of guys save more money from their prison jobs than they could on the streets. And there's plenty of money around inside. I was clerk in the Atlanta Commissary. The monthly take is $45,000 to $50,000. I ran two poker games at Atlanta. There's no money, it's all done in cigarettes. A guy may owe you forty or fifty boxes. When he leaves, he says who should I send the check to? When I'm in prison, I don't think of the outside at all. Inside is a different way of life. I don't write anybody, not even my folks. Homosexuality? I don't look up on it and I don't look down on it. It's just one of those things. When I leave and I'm out on the streets, I don't think about the inside or even the people. I don't associate with those guys on the outside. That's why it took the FBI so long to find me the last time. No matter where you go, if you've ever been in a major institution, you'll know somebody. Or they'll know your reputation. You take a while to feel your way. Then you pick the people you want to be associated with. I did pretty good in Atlanta. The guy who had the games liked me, so when he left he gave them to me. Now my partner has them.

my

What is the purpose of punishment?

Harold

I knew exactly what I was doing. I did what you might call market research. I knew what I was doing, what the chances were, what the penalties were. I even knew I'd probably get caught eventually.

Scene 4. Graterford Prison

Inside the entrance building, long rows of stiff wooden pews for waiting visitors. Bars completely across the far end of the long room, an electrically operated gate in the middle that also requires a guard's key as an added safeguard. On the other side of the bars, a glass-enclosed control room against one wall, opposite it a set of stairs leading down to the visitors' room. Then, another set of bars with a gate, on the other side of which is a long long corridor with many prisoners milling about. my in leg irons announces to the guard inside the first gate that he is here to see Warden Johnson. As he waits, three men handcuffed to each other are led through the first gate. The handcuffs are removed and the men are searched as they stand opposite the control room. Two are returning from court, the third is a new arrival. They are led through the inside gate, where a man standing by a wooden rostrum checks them in and interviews the new arrival. Enter Warden Johnson. my is let through the first gate, signs a large register and proceeds through the inner gate, where he shakes hands with Warden Johnson. They walk down the corridor and turn into the Warden's office, a sterile institutional affair with a wall full of stiffly posed framed photographs of former wardens. An American flag stands behind the desk. On one wall is a chart with figures denoting the breakdown of the prison population according to the different locations. There are two sets of figures for each location. The larger figures are keyed with a brown star, the smaller figures by a green star. The total count is 1612: 1155 with a brown star and 457 with a green star.

my

What do the stars signify?

Warden

That's the way they tell the race. That's gonna change too. Yesterday was my thirtieth day here. There are places in this prison I still haven't been. The atmosphere here was mostly one of repression. That's got to change. We have a kind of radio station here. It pipes four local stations into the cells. Each cell has a headset and you can switch to any of the stations you want. The one good thing about this place is that each cell holds only one man. Last Friday, I used the station to broadcast to the men in their cells. It was the first time the system was ever used for that purpose. I let them know where I'm at, what I'm into. We covered a lot of their beefs. I have a suggestion box now in each block. I told them I intend to treat them like human beings.

my

[*Turns to audience.*] Warden Johnson is the first black Superin-

[6 6]

tendent in the Pennsylvania Correction system. Two-thirds of the inmates are black, two-thirds of the guards are white.

Warden

I don't think my bein' black has changed their attitude. Maybe the black inmates figure I won't hold race against them. They're right. I think a black warden was long overdue.

my

[*To audience.*] There are five cell blocks. Each has two tiers of one hundred cells on each side for a total of four hundred cells per block. Each cell is about five by nine with a barred window, a cot, an open toilet, a wash basin, and a headset for the radio. There are a few classrooms in which for the most part remedial education is conducted. There are huge factories ("shops") with row upon row of machinery to weave yarn, to make clothes and uniforms, to make shoes. The goods are produced here for almost all state employees and inmates of all state institutions. With the exception of an extremely well equipped dental laboratory, the kind of trade a man learns here is almost impossible for him to find work at on the outside. There is a small carpentry shop and a smaller ceramics shop in which ceramic boats and roosters are made for sale out front to visitors. The library, a tiny room, is being moved to larger quarters, but the selection is pitiful. The books are old, battered, and bland. There are almost no law books. Books and movies are carefully screened by a committee of the Warden or his Deputy, the head guard, and the chaplains. No sex, no politics, no race, nothing controversial and little intellectual. There are counseling and group therapy rooms, but there are only seven counselors for the whole population. There is a huge auditorium and a beautiful chapel built by the inmates. Each is used only once a week, yet there is no inside gymnasium. There is an infirmary and an operating room. The small commissary has a monthly take of $18,000. Inmates are paid between 25¢ and 35¢ a day for their work, except for trustee-farmers, who receive $35 a month. There is a Protestant chaplain and a Presbyterian chaplain. A visiting rabbi tends the spiritual needs of the twelve Jewish inmates. The prison was built in the 1920s. It is immaculately clean. It has 1612 maids.

Warden

There are many things that need to be done. We need more counselors, an inside gym, higher education courses, more work-release facilities. There are only four in the state, and the one in Philadelphia can only take fourteen men. We took the screen down in the visitors' room, leaving only the bars. Soon they'll go and we'll set up a living-room atmosphere, make it as close to home as possible for visits.

my

[*To audience.*] Outside the visitors' room, there is a wardrobe room, where inmates gratefully borrow a pair of pink hobby jeans and a white shirt for their half-hour visit three times a month.

Warden

I know there is homosexuality in here. There's not much you can do about it. There are a lot of things going on here, some you just don't try to know about. It's not a pleasant place to be in, but I want to try to make it as human as possible. Some rules around here have no purpose at all; they've just been done, that's all. I want to check them all. Whatever has no purpose will be done away with. A warden has a great deal of latitude, he's like the captain of a ship. I don't think I'll be here too long, maybe a few years. You could get to like it too much and stay for twenty or thirty years, lots do. But it's exciting work and it's a real opportunity to do something. We won't move too fast, though. We'll submit a complete program for approval by the Commissioner.

my

What is the purpose of punishment?

Warden

I believe the punishment is taking away a man's freedom. That's pretty strong. We have an obligation to society to do something for a man here. And I think we have to take some risks. But I'm not in favor of giving the inmates the power to run this place. I want their input, to know where they're at, what their needs are. But the responsibility to run this place is mine, that's my job. There are men that shouldn't be here, that could just as easily be working on the outside with some supervision. But what would you do, release everybody? [*He presses a button. Enter Sergeant Zaneski.*]

Sergeant

Yessir?

Warden

This is my, Sergeant. Show him around. Anywhere he wants to go.

Sergeant

Yessir.

Sergeant and my exit Warden's office and tour the prison. Since most has already been described, they walk in limbo until they reach the Maximum Security Gate. The "Hole" is a separate low building located at the far end of the compound near one side of the prison wall and overlooked by a guard tower on top of the wall. The Hole is shaped in a U and is completely surrounded by a high fence topped with barbed wire. As they wait for the gate to be opened, the Sergeant speaks.

Sergeant

I been here nineteen years. I came here because there was no work in the mines, and I had a friend working here. It's all right, it's a job, just a job. It's Civil Service, but it could pay better. I don't trust the inmates, but you have to take some chances. I have some working in my office and sometimes I have to leave them alone. But I wouldn't trust one with my wallet. I think I helped a few since I been here. They don't have it bad now, they can even buy TV for their cells.

Runner is walking around a small exercise area near my and Sergeant. He watches them as he walks. The area is surrounded by a fence inside the main fence and is also topped with barbed wire.

Sergeant

[*Continues.*] Sometimes they smuggle in dirty books. I don't know how they get that stuff in, but it's the Hole if you're caught. That's contraband.

A guard opens the gate and the three walk into the building. my is introduced to the Lieutenant in charge, then escorted to one wing by the guard and the Sergeant. There are five small dark cells. The entire front of each cell is barred from floor to ceiling. There is a small walkway in front of the cells and then a wall of floor-to-ceiling bars separating the walkway from a narrow corridor. A Hi-Fi component on a shelf in the corridor is tuned to a rock station. The first cell belongs to Runner, who is back inside the building. The cell is open and Runner stands in the walkway eying the visitor. Of the other four cells, the two center ones are occupied by white inmates—Junior and Biker. They are flanked by two young blacks.

Guard

This used to be Death Row. The schedule here is outside for a half-hour exercise walk each day, showers twice a week. The rest of the time, they stay in their cell. They can order once a week from the Commissary. The radio is on speaker now, but it can be switched into their headsets in the cells. Each inmate gets a half hour a day to choose whatever station he wants. [*Points to Runner.*] This man is a runner. He can come out of his cell. He can't handle food, but he can pick up dirty trays, cleans the floors, things like that. He gets paid a quarter a day. The other wings are about the same, except this one's newer, and they don't get out of their cells at all. They're on Administrative Punishment.

my

[*Turns to audience.*] Capacity in the Hole is 24. Usually, inmates are sent here for fighting. Sometimes they request the Hole to get away from another inmate. After the World Series, it's packed by inmates whose team lost. They can't pay off their bets, so they come here for a month hoping things will blow over. The monotony here makes life among the population seem almost sociable.

Runner

[*To Sergeant.*] Who's he?

Sergeant

A writer.

Runner

Why don't you let the writer talk to the inmates? They want to

[7 0]

talk to him. He can't learn nothin' from you what it's like down here.

Sergeant

[*To Guard.*] It's okay, he said anything he wants.

Guard

[*Shrugs.*] Okay. You each get three minutes to talk to the writer. Who's first?

Junior

I'll talk to the writer. What's your name? Listen, I'd like to correspond with you. I've been down here a long time. They think I'm dangerous, some sort of escape artist. It had to do with a break in Pittsburgh and some zip guns and stuff. I know I did wrong and I'm going to be in for a long time, but I'd like to be with the population, not down here. Would you give me your address? You don't have to if you don't want to. But I've got some ideas that I would like to write to you, not just to vent my spleen on my own problems. People should know about these prisons. They should know what goes on here.

my

[*To audience.*] "Detention in prison was supposed to be a mollification of pain infliction, but it is often more cruel and destructive than beating."—Dr. Karl Menninger. I gave Junior my address.

Biker

I been down here three months, man, and I haven't even been sentenced yet. They transferred me here from Berks County Prison. I got in a fight with some guards. But I don't belong down here because I haven't even been sentenced. I don't know why it's takin' so long. I haven't heard from anybody. That lawyer I had was really stupid. He did nothin' for me. I want to arrange for witnesses. I was convicted of first-degree murder, but I never even seen the victims, man. I think I should have a new trial. I shouldn't have been convicted. I never had a chance to call witnesses.

Inmate

I don't think you can write about punishment until you spend time in here.

my

But I can write about death without dying.

Runner

[*Laughs.*] Right on, writer!

Other Inmate

I'm a writer too. Do you know any publishers I can send my stuff to?

my

[*Turns to audience.*] I gave him some addresses.
my, Sergeant, and Guard move back to entrance. Enter Lieutenant.

Lieutenant

You only hear one side of it from them. They all got some story. That Junior is a tough con. Pulled a stick-up on the Turnpike. They tied up a state trooper to a tree and shot him. Junior was in on about ten and three, but tried a break in Pittsburgh with zip guns and now he's got about twenty. His partner was also in on a short term, but now he's up to a consecutive fifty to a hundred. We took a bomb away from Junior last week, don't ask me how he made it. You get him something from the Commissary, you better make sure to get the empty, he'll use anything. He's a sharp one. The other guy was part of a bike gang that murdered some young guy and his girl-friend. Buried them in a shallow grave. He's been down here for three months because a visitor smuggled a ten-dollar bill to him. I don't know how long he'll be down here. We don't hear nothin', we just keep 'em and feed 'em. That's it.

Scene 5. A Composite

Actors are arranged in a semicircle, each in his own set, facing the audience and my, shackled and handcuffed, back to audience. The small sets are separated from each other by thin partitions. From left to right: David Rothenberg is seated at a cluttered desk at the office of the Fortune Society. . . . "Red" Jackson is drinking coffee at a table in a luncheonette. . . . Detective John Altman is seated in a railroad car. . . . Judge Edmund Spaeth is seated behind his desk in Chambers, feet propped on the edge of the desk, surrounded by shelves of law books. . . . Ephraim Gomberg is seated at the head of a long conference table, but frequently stands or paces as he talks. . . . Turner De Vaughn is seated at a bare desk in a bare third-floor office donated to the BarbWire Society by the Institute of Black Ministers. . . . Harry Bransom is seated at a table in a small Italian restaurant, eating lunch. The stage is darkened, except for a spot on my. As each of the others speaks, he is hit by a small spot which fades out when someone else speaks.

my

[*To audience.*] These are some of the other people who take part in the criminal justice system, or try to pick up the pieces afterwards. David Rothenberg handled publicity for an Off-Broadway play about prisons, got interested himself, and three years ago helped to found the Fortune Society in New York, a group of and for ex-convicts. Ken Jackson, an ex-convict, co-founded the Fortune Society and is a paid staff member. John Altman is a detective on the New York Police Force. Edmund Spaeth has been a Philadelphia Common Pleas Judge since 1964. Ephraim Gomberg has headed the Philadelphia Crime Commission for eleven years. Turner De Vaughn spent time in prison and since his recent release helps run Philadelphia's Barb-Wire Society, which, like the Fortune Society, only newer and poorer, is run by and for ex-convicts. Finally, Harry Bransom works for the Defenders Association in Philadelphia, which offers free legal service in criminal cases. There are others who are not here—bail bondsmen, parole officers, assistant district attorneys, grand-jury members, uniformed policemen, magistrates. And then, of course, there's the family, the ones who get left behind when we put a man away. But the stage could get pretty crowded, couldn't it?

Rothenberg

Our primary job is to educate people about the complete failure of our penal system. Ninety-five per cent of those in prison will eventually be released and most of them will wind up back in prison for worse crimes. The taxpayer deserves more than that for his tax dollars.

Altman

I graduated from the University of Pennsylvania in '65 as a political-science major. I went to work as a cop to stay out of Vietnam. I was always interested anyway. The money's pretty good, good benefits. And there isn't a lot of chickenshit in New York like salutin', except maybe in the Academy. You can even have long sideburns and a mustache if you want. But it's pretty frustrating. The crime rate keeps going up, the prisons stink, judges work from ten to three and quit for golf or else fall asleep on the bench, guys in organized crime keep gettin' off cause the judge has been bought. Sometimes you arrest some politician and you know before you start it'll be fixed someplace higher up. It's like workin' for the State Department and bein' against the war. You can stay or you can quit. I stay, hopin' I can do some good.

Gomberg

When I came here, this became an action-oriented organization, dedicated to determining the quality of our criminal justice system and to improve it. We fought the NRA, the most powerful lobby in the country, to get Philadelphia the best gun legislation. We drafted a program for gang counseling to help put an end to these gang killings. We're Establishment, and we know exactly how to work within the System. We're responsible for a whole new criminal code in Pennsylvania.

Spaeth

A judge has the obligation to consider what is best for the prisoner and what is best for society. They do not always coincide. We have a much better system now of pre-sentence investigation. The law allows for considerable latitude in the actual sentence, but in practice it's not all that simple. The judge is truly faced with a dilemma. On the one hand, to sentence, hoping that it will be sufficient both to deter and to rehabilitate, yet knowing that it will probably do neither, given the actual conditions of our corrections institutions and the overloaded parole system. Unlike Austria, the judge in our system has no control of the prisons, no control over his own sentence after it has been passed. That makes no sense.

[74]

Bransom

I have defended in over three thousand criminal cases. In Philadelphia, eighty-five per cent of the adult cases and ninety-five per cent of the juvenile cases are handled by public defenders. Each man gets about fifteen cases the night before they are to be tried. He usually meets his clients at the trial. At that, he's probably got a better chance than a private defense attorney. They're not very good and they don't know the judges as well. It's just no good, it's a totally destructive system. It's a factory in which we mass produce criminals. I don't understand why there isn't *more* crime, *more* violence. I'm a hypocrite because I do it, but I justify doing what I do because I do so well at it that I do some good. . . . I keep criminals out of jail and on the streets.

Jackson

Where I was brought up, it was no good to help an old lady across the streets. You were looked down on . . . unless you mugged her when you got to the other side. When I went to jail the first time, I was just a small time punk, a sneaky burglar. By time I got out I was a fuckin' maniac. I wanted to kill somebody. I bought a gun and pointed it at people, hoping they wouldn't give me their money so I could beat their brains in. I think I was crazy, to tell you the truth. I went from booze to heroin and back to booze. But AA finally set me straight. When I first went to Elmira I knew how to act, like when you're the new kid on the block. Pick the biggest kid in the crowd and beat him up. That's the way you survive or you become somebody's property. I was pretty good-lookin' then, you know what I mean. I beat one up, then another and another. At first they believed me when I said the other guy started it, but after while they knew the score and sent me to the Hole. Nobody really adapts. You manage to stay alive, on the outside, but on the inside you go to pieces. There's no reality in prison.

De Vaughn

I was teachin' history at the Cultural School. There was trouble with the Muslims, not with me but the school. It was gettin' pretty tough, man. I saw a teacher get beat up one day, so the next day I brought a pistol with me. Two of them attacked me with hatchets, so

I shot one. It was self-defense. They knew it, they wouldn't even testify against me. I was in Holmesburg for twenty-two months waitin' for trial. I was really scared, ya know? They could throw twenty to forty years at me. I was gettin' tight as a drum. Up at five and down to the court till maybe nine at night, tryin' to pick a jury. We went through enough to make four. I couldn't sleep. I saw Doctor Guy to get some pills. He sent a guard that night with some tranquilizers. I didn't want no tranquilizers, just a sleepin' pill. I had a fight with the guard and spent three weeks in the Hole. I don't know Doctor Guy and he may be all right, but if all he can get to do is hand out tranquilizers, he should resign. Sure you get paranoid. That place would make anybody paranoid. It's a pit, a hell hole. When you're down, it's rough man, ya know? I thought I knew what violence was in the ghetto. I thought gang warrin' was violent. I thought war was violent. I just wasn't prepared, ya know, for what goes down inside. Whatever is abnormal on the outside is normal on the inside. I seen cats do things you wouldn't believe, just for cigarettes. Or kiss another cat just for a little affection. There's pressure, man, and tension. There's a duality in man, he's a man and he's an animal. You put enough pressure on anybody, you'll produce the animal. You start to fantasize to make it bearable. After while it gets hard to tell what's fantasy and what's real.

Spaeth

I never met a prisoner that had any self-respect. What little he may have had has been taken away from him. His mail is heavily censored, in some places he can't even receive a book from home. When his wife visits he has to talk to her through a screen, his children can't even visit him. He does menial work if any and gets paid almost nothing. If he's smart when he comes up for parole, he says what they want to hear. And once he's quote paid his debt end quotes, he keeps on paying because we don't let him forget.

Bransom

I wasn't always this pessimistic, but now I'm on Juvenile Court and I'm sick. Kids aren't born that way. We make them criminals. We beat them and lie to them and teach them all the wrong values. We don't spend time with them and we don't show them any affection. Then, when they do something wrong, we do this to them.

Jackson

Prison taught me plenty. It taught me how to beat heads in. There's plenty of time to think in prison. There's nothin' else to do. One guy I know was in for a long time with the same cell mate. Then his cell mate left and a new one came in. The guard came through that night to make his head-count. He passed right by without even an oh you're new. The count was right, that's all that mattered. It dawned on him that he was nothin' but a count. If he died, somebody new would be there and the count would be right. And nobody would miss him. That was his turning point. He wanted to be something more in his life.

Gomberg

My approach is utilitarian, not humanistic. I probably have no compassion for anyone, especially for the criminal. I have no compassion for criminals. But I think I have an understanding for their needs. I believe society has an obligation to them, but even more so to itself, to see that they get placed back into society as law-abiding citizens.

De Vaughn

A man has to know that he's worth something, ya know? He has to know he's a man, that he can still hold a job and be treated like a human being, not an animal. I locked up with a guy for nine months, big guy, really a sweet cat. Went to Temple University. Got busted for havin' two reefers. He used to tell me about his dreams. One day in the mess hall, he just flipped. He beat up four inmates and two guards. It took six or seven just to hold him down. I thought, my God, what would have happened if we were both locked in the cell in the middle of the night and that would have happened? It's scary.

Altman

I've been in a few prisons. They're really miserable. I don't think anybody should be treated like that. Plenty of times I let somebody go, because I knew what it would be like if they were convicted of some petty crime.

Bransom

I'll give you a hypothetical sentence that will sort of sum it up: Looie, you have been tried and convicted by a jury of your peers, selected from the voting lists of your city who happen to be mostly a different color than you because people of your color don't seem to register as much and don't seem to live at the same address very long. You have been found guilty of committing one crime, which you probably did commit although the District Attorney has added some other charges of which you probably are not guilty, just in case you weren't found guilty of the first crime. At any rate, you have been found guilty possibly because the jury thought you were guilty and possibly because they really didn't like you and wanted to go home. So I am going to sentence you and send you away for a few years in an institution where you will be sexually assaulted about five times and have it rammed up your rear by a bunch of homosexuals who have been made that way by the same institution. If there is anything about crime that you do not now know, you will learn it there. You will be administered by a bunch of people who don't care about you, and have not been trained to do the work they do. Well that's about all, Looie. We've done our job. The rest is up to you.

my

What is the purpose of punishment?

Rothenberg

It's all been said. It's all been written. Our job is to make people receptive to the setting up of alternatives.

Jackson

Punishment certainly doesn't serve as a deterrent. It's just revenge, that's all. I'd have separation centers. There'd be one maximum-security wing, if any, for those guys that just couldn't be helped. The rest would be minimum-security. No bars, no walls, no lock-ups. I'd have trained people to help inmates learn to deal with themselves and society. Rehabilitation. Work release. No conjugal visits though, that's degrading. I'd have furloughs. They would be a privilege, I guess. Everything in prison is a privilege for a con, even breathing. He's got no rights at all.

Altman

Punishment doesn't serve as a deterrent, unless maybe you set up a mandatory death sentence for every Class A felony. I don't believe that should be done, but I wish I did believe it because I've seen what people can do with a gun.

Spaeth

That's a very philosophical question. I think Bentham oversimplified.

my

[*Turns to audience.*] An 18th-century utilitarian, Jeremy Bentham, studied the British penal system, then wrote that punishment was not a deterrent if it did not deter, and that most laws prescribe punishments which may well serve as deterrents to the lawmakers, who are usually of the middle or upper class, but which are irrelevant to the lawbreakers, who are almost always of the lower class.

Spaeth

I think that there are times when punishment does serve as a deterrent, as in the anti-trust cases here in Philadelphia a few years ago. Some very high executives went to jail, and I believe that serves as a deterrent to other executives and businessmen. However, I do agree that in the main, punishment does not serve as a deterrent. Murder is most often an emotional act which by definition denies the use of logical thought in considering consequences. Rape is usually the result of a deeply rooted personality problem. Thieves and burglars rarely consider the penalties simply because they don't expect to get caught. Many crimes are committed by people who need money for narcotics, and they certainly are not affected by deterrence. There is a difference, however, between sentencing and punishment. Not all sentences are punishment. This is the distinction that Menninger draws between penalty and punishment.

my

[*To audience.*] In *The Crime of Punishment* Dr. Menninger wrote, "All legal sanctions involve penalties for infraction. But the element of punishment is an adventitious and indefensible additional penalty, it

corrupts the legal principle of quid pro quo with a 'moral' surcharge
. . . the deterrence theory is used widely as a cloak for vengeance."

Gomberg

Operations like the one that John Case has are nothing, a drop in the bucket. There is no reasonable system of rehabilitation in Pennsylvania. We have to change that.

De Vaughn

Most cats don't think about what they're doin' or gettin' caught. If they get caught they expect to get punished, but they don't agree they should be. They can justify what they done. Society forced them to live the way they do because of social and economic conditions. Rehabilitation. That's the word everybody uses. Well prison rehabilitates, all right. It does a good job of makin' a cat what he was, only better. Maybe there should be maximum security for some cats, but even they have a right to be treated as human beings. Every inmate has a right to live a meaningful life, even in prison.

Bransom

I don't believe that punishment serves any purpose whatsoever, so I don't believe there should be any. I think that prisons are thoroughly degrading, dehumanizing, and ineffective. They should be shut down. The courts are a farce, there is no justice in them. It is a thoroughly antiquated system that remains essentially unchanged since Rome in 45 B.C. If anything, it has gotten worse and we have become more destructive. I think it should be completely shut down. How's that for openers? You want some alternatives? One. Eliminate all misdemeanors from prison treatment. Fine them or drop the charges. Two. Drop all crimes which involve self-abuse only from the penal code. Three. Eliminate politics from judicial selection. Substitute one year training at a judicial institute for attorneys with a certain number of years of practice. Four. Eliminate bail bondsmen. Consider the elimination of all bail. Five. Eliminate all prisons—substitute out-patient treatment centers with mandatory psychotherapy, job training, and placement assistance. Six. Provide all legal assistance free through appeal. Seven. Establish special training institutes for prosecutors and defenders. Eight. Total discovery. The judge and jury should have all evidence available to them, not just what the prosecutor wants them to have. Nine. Eliminate all civil penalties such as criminal registration and job discrimination after finding of guilt. Shall I go on?

Epilogue

The small sets have been cleared and replaced with a number of barred cells, benches, etc. The stage is dark except for a small spot on my, who is shackled and in handcuffs. As he speaks, an inmate comes forward and removes the leg irons and handcuffs. Gradually the stage and house lights are brought up, first the one—revealing the entire cast —then the other. The non-inmates begin to give their identification props to inmates, creating new wardens, a new judge, a new lawyer, etc. As my continues to speak, inmates go into the audience and in loud voices make arrests. They lead the "criminals" up onto the stage, where an impromptu kangaroo court has been set up. The judge passes sentences and the new inmates are placed in the cells. This continues until the last line by the cast before the final curtain.

my

On December 10, 1969, the National Commission on the Causes and Prevention of Violence reported to the President: "The typical prison experience is degrading, conviction records create a lasting stigma, decent job opportunities upon release are rare, voting rights are abridged, military-service options are curtailed, family-life disruptions are likely to be serious, and the outlook of most ex-convicts is bleak. The hope of the community that released offenders have been 'corrected' is defeated by outdated laws and community response." So what good is it, this System of ours?

Inmate

You're under arrest for speeding.

Inmate

You're under arrest for cheating on your expense account.

Inmate

You're under arrest for bringing cigarettes across the state line.

[81]

Does it serve any purpose? Our courts are jammed. The backlog is so great that the New York courts will soon dismiss charges on anyone who's kept waiting more than six months for trial. Our city jails are overcrowded with inmates, most of whom haven't even been tried. Riots have become commonplace. Our bail system, which was originally conceived in order to guarantee the appearance of the defendant at his trial, has gone awry and has lately begun to take on repressive and political overtones. Every day, petty criminals are talked into copping a plea—pleading guilty to a lesser offense—in order to keep the system moving by avoiding time-consuming jury trials.

Inmate

You're under arrest for slum-lording.

Inmate

You're under arrest for price-gouging.

Inmate

You're under arrest for job discrimination.

Kangaroo Judge

[*To criminals as they are led to his "bench."*] One hundred thousand dollars bail. Two hundred thousand dollars bail. Thirty years in jail. Twenty-five years in jail.

my

Our reformatories don't reform. Our correctional institutions don't correct. Families without husbands and fathers flounder and end up on Welfare. The whole system costs billions. And it doesn't even work. Well then, what is the purpose of punishment? It doesn't Deter. It only Removes for short periods. It doesn't Rehabilitate. Was Kant right when he said that punishment must in all cases be imposed only because the individual on whom it is inflicted has committed a crime?

Inmate

You're under arrest for Dresden.

Inmate

You're under arrest for Hiroshima.

Inmate

You're under arrest for My Lai.

Inmate

You're under arrest for Kent State.

Inmate

You're under arrest for Jackson State.

my

[*Raises his voice.*] And what are the consequences of punishment? Do any of you give a damn what is happening to your brothers and sisters?

Kangaroo Judge

I sentence you to death! Death! Death! Death!

my

[*Louder.*] Judger be judged! Condemner be condemned! Innocent, you are guilty!

Inmates

[*Banging fists on benches and cells.*] Guilty! Guilty! Guilty!

my

You're afraid to walk the streets at night! You put burglar alarms in your homes and you buy watchdogs and you still go to sleep at night afraid! What kind of a way is that to live?

Inmates

Guilty! Guilty! Guilty!

my

You vote for Law and Order. Whose Law? Whose Order?

Guilty! Guilty! Guilty!

my

You want more cops? Stiffer sentences? Tougher prisons? Fools! It doesn't work! When will you learn? *You* have to do it! *You!* *You* have to go into prisons and work with these people! *You* have to get rid of the grafters and the fixers in the system! *You* have to do something about inequitable laws, about a lousy bail system, about the stigma of the ex-con. *You* have to do something to help save what's left, before nothing is left at all! There is no purpose to punishment!

Inmates

[*Pointing to audience.*] You're under arrest for the crime of Silence!

Curtain

[*September 1971*]

[8 4]

The Maya Bridge

That was before Soledad. Before San Quentin. Before Attica. Before Rahway. But it was after *My Lai. So what else is new?*

It sort of makes you wonder. The Kerner Commission Report got shoved into the basement, Kerner got put in the Tower. The Scranton Commission Report got ignored, Bill Scranton got banished to political obscurity. The Commission Report on Pornography was labeled obscene, and they finally carted poor old Ginzburg off to the Lewisburg clink. The Commission Report on Marijuana said reduce the charge of possession to a misdemeanor and don't enforce it in private. That was the last anybody ever heard of the Commission. It sort of makes you wonder.

It sort of makes you wonder that Medina was on the Cavett Show while Calley was waiting for Nixon's review. Seymour Hersh got the Pulitzer Prize for exposing the massacre at My Lai 4, and then wrote a book that exposed the official cover-up and it hardly sold. Ellsberg made public the duplicity of five different Presidential administrations, and got prosecuted as a traitor. Anderson exposed the connivance of the government, and was vilified as a muckraker. Robert Townsend pointed out that we scream a lot about crime in the streets, but not at all about crime in the suites. And Mayor Frank Rizzo wants the death chair back because it may not be a deterrent, but that's one guy won't kill again. It sort of makes you wonder.

It's all maya anyway. Commissions don't commit, Hearings don't hear. Today's crisis is tomorrow's nostalgia. Bigger wars, smaller populations. Revolutionaries become dictators, dictators become democrats. I went to school with the son of the number-two fascist of Venezuela. The first time he heard someone call his country a dictatorship was when he came to the States. He thought it was a democracy. Maya. Headlines refer to North Vietnam as Reds. It's shorter. Even the Times *said Enemy. They were ours. But we were theirs. Maya.*

The lives of more people were saved when we stopped throwing garbage into the streets than by all of the modern doctors in all of our modern staph-infested hospitals. Modern man needs his modern shaman. But what's the difference? More people are out of prison than in, more people eat than starve, more people screw than rape, more people have than have not. There are more muggers than muggees. Such comforting statistics offer a lethargic security. Maya.

I suppose that's what led me to the Old Man, to Russell. Old causes that burned up desperate juices, Doomsday quotes a hundred years old, scientists who say that it is already too late unless. *The transience of Man is confirmed. The Old Man is my guru. He sees without knowing, knows without understanding, tells without saying. The riddle is in the complexity of so simple a life. Is it possible to reverse the process? Or is Progress immutable? The treadmill goes in only one direction, but always ends where it begins. Maya.*

The Perils of Parity: Part III

The Pay-What-It's-Worth Subscription Plan . . . Revised

With the Pay-What-It's-Worth Subscription Plan approaching the third issue since its inception and still no payment from ninety per cent of its subscribers, the *Treadmill* has had to face its first real crisis. The Two Issue Rule clearly states that a subscription will be canceled if two consecutive issues produce no payment. A decision would have to be made, either to compromise principle or to reduce the circulation by ninety per cent. Obviously the *Treadmill* would need to seek the professional advice of a public relations expert, so I called on B. Arnold III, president of Arnold Associates, "Famous Name Makers Since 1777." I explained our dilemma.

"Your problems are solved," he said. "We'll take care of everything. First, we'll cancel the subscriptions of your nonpaying subscribers. Next, we'll set a price of fifty dollars for each issue. That will get rid of the rest, and you'll fold. Then we'll get stories out on your poor bankrupt publication losing the struggle to maintain high ideals in the crass commercial world of the almighty buck. We'll show how willingly people will throw away the opportunity to decide what something is worth themselves, how easily they give up their rights. Oh, it's perfect! You'll be on the cover of *Time!*"

"But what will I use to pay the bills?"

"Don't worry. When we handled publicity for *Eros* magazine, we got Ginzburg on all the TV talk shows."

"You handled *Eros?* But the magazine folded and Ginzburg is going to jail!"

"So what? He's famous!"

"So is Billy Sol Estes."

"See what I mean? He was an AA client, too. We made them all famous." He gestured to the framed pictures on his walls. The Edsel. The *Titanic*. The Maginot Line.

"My God! Were those your clients? They were all horrible failures!"

"That's not important. What is success? Nothing! Publicity is what counts, and that's what we get! Publicity! We have a hundred-and-ninety-six-year history of making names famous. It's a family tradition!"

"But Mr. Arnold . . ."

"Call me Benedict."

So we have made our decision. The Two Issue Rule is suspended. So is the No Payment In Advance Rule. Pay what it's worth, or pay what you can, or don't pay anything at all. We'll keep it going this way for a while yet. We have our tradition too.

Blandon Guru

I never throwed my line
in another man's water, nur
tuk first shot at somebody else's rabbit,
he said,

'n' I always had my feet
under my own table,
even if all I had on top
was only bread.

A single tear drifted down
the Old Man's hollow cheek and dropped
to the checkered flannel shirt
with the right elbow worn through.
(It's still too new to throw away,
he said.)

He sighed.
I ain't got no regrets, Mister.
I been ready a long time.

Russell

February thirteenth, 1971. The invasion of Laos continues. The three astronauts are back from the moon. Rolls-Royce is bankrupt. California is digging out of an earthquake. Love Story *has just been printed in a paperback edition of four and a half million copies. Marcuse says that the concept of the individual is not obsolete, just premature. Cleaver continues to hold Leary in protective custody. The Senate has scheduled a new round of hearings on the SST, and the Big Four a new round of talks on the Middle East. In Boise, Idaho, a twenty-year-old married college student has been sentenced to four years in prison for a first offense of marijuana possession, and in New York City three detectives have been sentenced to one year each for official misconduct involving an effort to extort cash and narcotics from drug sellers in exchange for not making arrests. Norman Mailer has written an attack on Women's Liberation. Tomorrow is Valentine's Day. Monday is the new Washington's Birthday. The old one was no longer convenient.*

Steady rain. Almost no traffic on the turnpike this early in the morning. The fog shrouds the road, shutting out the landscape, making the hour-and-a-half ride resemble an eerie time warp, the Citroën a bubble moving slowly through the viscous gray. There is time to think of the Old Man, a crude Thoreau living alone in the country, Tessie's father. Tessie. A two-hundred-pound female Billy Budd in her fifties, a young Mennonite girl of sixteen come to work for an Orthodox Jewish family and stayed. The Intellectual Jew and the Old Man who quit school at ten. What could be learned from such an encounter? I wonder if Aquarius was smug when he approached NASA? Well, it would make a good story, this weekend with the Old Man in a time when the world was gone mad, and we who knew knew why.

A right turn off the highway and two miles of potholes to Blandon. Right again between the Post Office and the Inn, and up the narrow rutted hill with no street name or house numbers. Finally on the left a long three-story frame house, part of which a hundred and fifty years ago was a log house already growing old. A knock on the door filled the frame with "goin'-on-eighty" Russell Sholedice, tall and angular with short white hair, glasses the kind that have the see-through hearing aid attached at the left ear, suspendered fatigue pants, and a plaid flannel shirt worn through at one elbow. His teeth are out because they hurt his gums, but he wears them grudgingly to eat, to pray in church, and to visit his girlfriend Gertie. The hearing

aid is a temporary replacement for the one being fixed, and it doesn't always work. Once, in frustration, he interrupts a conversation with, "This thing ain't workin' again. Can't hear nothin' so don't waste your breath." The battery doesn't last long and they're expensive, so he sleeps without it at night and hears nothing. One time a next-door neighbor—the house is divided into two units, and he seems to have a steady stream of new neighbors—blew his brains out with a twelve-gauge shotgun at four in the morning and the Old Man never even twitched in his sleep. "He was a rummy, that one was. Hardly drawed a sober breath."

No sooner in and greeted, I am led on a tour of inspection that includes every single one of his possessions, each of which is taped with the person's name who will get it "after I close my eyes." A stone cellar with two feet of water from the rain, a low-ceilinged living room crowded with too much old furniture, including his favorite reclining chair patched and repatched. Plants at the windows which he protects by lining the windows with cardboard each night. The lamps are all made from something else—a nutmeg grinder, a cherry pitter, a coffee mill. On the walls: I will never leave thee nor forsake thee. . . . Love Never Faileth. . . . Prayer changes things. . . . Christ is the head of the house. The kitchen is warm and friendly with an old gas-flamed Magic Chef, one side of which is a coal-jack stove for heat. An old refrigerator, with squirrels in the freezer section, and an equally old sink with one faucet. "Got running cold water but don't drink it, Mister, it's all yellow. I boil it and put it here in the icebox. If you want a drink, take it from this pitcher and use this big glass next to it. This here one's mine and this other one's Mom's. Been in here since she died." At first he tries to remember my name, but finally gives up and calls me Mister. At church he introduces me as "my friend up from Philadelphia to see how the Old Man lives" with a chuckle.

Upstairs, two small bedrooms plus his own large double bed, which occupies a kind of large hall. Next to his bed is a small night table with a flashlight, Murine, Vicks Vaporub, an inhaler, and throat lozenges. "For my sinus." There is no central heating and the farther away from the kitchen, the colder it gets. "This is your room. Plenty of covers. Here's a flashlight. If you have to piss at night, use this bucket. If you have to go outside to move your bowels, take the flashlight." The outhouse is in the back. In deference to the cold there is a fleece-lined toilet seat, but it doesn't help much at fifteen degrees early in the morning. The other bedroom is loaded with homely looking plants and a hand-made gun cabinet. "Not much of a shot any more, I confess. This here's the twenty-two I used to shoot cats with. Hate cats. Can't stand them. One snuck into the shed and had five kittens onct. Shot the cat and gggttt the kittens." He makes a neck-twisting motion with his hands. "Used to do a lot of gunnin' all 'round here. Had a hound dog onct was really good. Got sick, though. The vet said he was finished. He used to shake and foam at the mouth. Onct I had him out back gettin' exercise. Wouldn't chain him like some folks do. I had him on a long rope so's he could run. Well I found him with his head between the fence and foamin' pretty bad. I got the twenty-two and put it right up about six inches from his head and pulled the trigger. He fell right down. Then I put on gloves so's none of that poison from his mouth would touch me and I dug a hole and I wrapped him up nice in an old blanket and I buried him. I sure do like a hound. But I don't like no cats."

The attic is filled with an incredible amount of junk, all neatly placed. "It ain't eatin' nothin'. Long as it don't eat nothin', I keep it." We go back down to the kitchen, rock in the warmth of the stove, and talk. About noon, he says, "Mister, I'm hungry. Tessie said I wasn't to feed you, so let's go get dinner, all right?" The Old Man eats six meals a day since they removed most of his stomach with a duodenal ulcer. "I was sick for about a year, throwin' up about every two weeks, sometimes it was blood. But I didn't say nothin', Mister, and nobody known. One day I felt sick and went down to the stone cellar. Mom found me there, out cold. I didn't want to go, but they took me to the hospital." Breakfast at six, lunch at nine, dinner at twelve, lunch at two-thirty, supper at five, lunch again at eight-thirty. Lunch is any snack.

We eat dinner at a diner about fifteen minutes away. In the men's room there are vending machines with six different condoms offered, including one with revolutionary custom fit. One machine has a slot marked Instant Pussy and another machine has a slot that says Pecker Stretcher—25 cents. I can't resist, but find myself with only one quarter and a difficult choice. I decide on the Pecker Stretcher. For my twenty-five cents, I get a little plastic box containing a miniature stretcher with a red cross on it and a card on which is printed a sketch of a woodpecker and the notation to place sick pecker on this stretcher and carry to nearest vet. Country humor. After dinner we drive around in the rain and the Old Man shows me Berks County. By now creeks are overflowing and some of the roads are flooded. I impress him by setting the Citroën at high level and driving through the flooded sections, then setting it down again on the other side. He will tell everyone about it at church. He shows me Lake Ontelaunee and most of his favorite fishing spots. We go back to the house and talk some more in the living room. We talk all afternoon, stopping for a lunch of coffee and cake and again for a supper of vegetable soup cooked earlier in the week by Gertie. He hides nothing. Even personal things. He seems pleased by the questions and not at all shy of the camera, after some stiffness in the first roll. Just keeps rambling on. About six or seven, the Old Man begins to lose his voice, and is torn between disbelief and embarrassment. He is known in Blandon for his wind. Not only from his mouth, it seems. With the resection of his stomach came a gastrointestinal involvement with gas and the Old Man produces frequent and extraordinary farts—long rumbling farts —drum rolls of the bowels—announcing the odor as lightning does thunder.

He was born in White Haven, Pennsylvania, about seventy-five miles from Blandon. An Irish father, a Pennsylvania Dutch mother. In the family album there are pictures of both. The father peers out with the dull, stupid stare of a pick-and-shovel railroad man. Squat and obese with a short bull neck and a square, closely cropped head. The mother, taller and meaner. "He died at fifty-seven from Bright's Disease. Mom went worldly, I call it. Couldn't help it, I guess. She had to feed five kids any way she could. She finally went to Philadelphia and lived with a man. Took two of the kids for a while, but brought 'em back later. She married him eventually. He died, she married another one. Got pretty fat after while. I liked both her other husbands. . . . When I was little, I was bad. Played hooky a lot, and I told lies. She used to hit me 'cross the legs with a cherry switch. Then when I'd go to school, I'd get another lickin' from Miss Minnie Deederline for tellin' I was in school when I wasn't. I quit about ten so I could go to work. That's why I'm so slow at writin' and figures.

My daughter bought me a typewriter so's all I have to do is push down the letters, but I can't spell or multiply or divide. Made my boys finish school so's they could do better, but the girls quit school to get married, 'cept for Tessie, who quit to go to work. Between you and me, Mister, I never knew if they had to get married or not and I didn't ask so I let them quit. I worked for the railroad mostly. Spent thirty-five years repairin' cars for the P&R. Not all together though, I left in the middle, that's why my pension isn't so good. I had a bad Irish temper, and I lost it a lot. I'm sorry about that now and tryin' to be a peaceful man. I don't drink or smoke any more. Smokin' was harder to give up than drinkin'. Took me most of a year, and it was terrible.

"During the Depression, when things got bum, I worked for the WPA. Made foreman on a road gang. Got sixty dollars a month, but it wasn't worth it for all the aggravation, everybody complainin' at me. Most I ever made in my life was two-fifty-two an hour. Towards the end at the P&R, I got down in the gumps. Nobody cared nothin' about how good their work was. I got shifted from one place to another. Finally, I came home and told Mom I was gonna retire. The last day you don't have to work, you get to shake hands with everybody and they pay you exactly as if you was workin'. So the foreman, he says, Russell, take a look at that car over there and get them to workin' on it, and I says nope, shake, I'm leavin'. He couldn't believe it. I was older'n most, but I was still the best they had.

"Since Mom closed her eyes, it's been lonely. You'd think those kids would come and visit me or call me or somethin'. We married when she was sixteen and I was seventeen. Her folks didn't go for me much. I never even went into her house. One time we was talkin' out near the cemetery. Her brother sent two friends to sneak up and see what we was talkin' about. I spotted 'em and pulled a thirty-two from my pocket and pointed it at 'em. Ay-yi-yi did they run! When I came down to Fleetwood near here, I sent her money to come and get married. She come. We didn't have intercourse for the first four years. Neither one of us believed in that sort of thing. After we had the first child, though, it was too much, I guess. A baby every eleven months. We had nine. Two died. There was always love in the house. Took 'em for rides and things like that. Mom and I always kissed. It was the last thing we did each night before we went to sleep. She'd roll over and I'd roll over and we'd kiss. We kissed that last night. She wasn't too

well for quite a while. Well, about four in the morning, she was bangin' her fist on the bed. Boom. Boom. We got her to the hospital, but they never even put her in a room. The head nurse, she just kept shakin' her head. She was good to me. I don't think there was hardly a single thing she ever done wrong or mean to me. Wisht I could say the same. I done lots of things to her I'm sorry for, little things maybe, but I think of them now."

Listening to the Old Man talk, reveal his private thoughts, uncover his faults, his weaknesses, is somehow deeply touching. This is no pure, peaceful Thoreau, but this Old Man is certainly more real, more human than the conjured one. He has a strange peacefulness for one

who as a young man had so violent a temper. Sick with his near-stomach-less abdomen, his gas, his piles, his deafness, his sinus, and his headaches brought on by "havin' my head bashed in too often with a sledge iron workin' at the P&R," the Old Man still hunts and fishes and drives his 200,000-mile-old car and visits his girlfriend down the road every night but Monday. And no complaints. "I put my trust in the Lord, Mister." He keeps an orderly schedule, begun when his wife died and from which he never deviates. It keeps him company, like an old friend. Up at five-thirty, he fixes the fire in the stove, reads five chapters in the Bible, washes, "fixes" his diary, does thirty minutes of nude exercises in his socks, eats, shaves, moves his bowels and soaks his rear-end piles in warm water. At seven-fifteen, Gertie calls to see how he is. For an extra dollar a month, he has had an amplifier installed in his phone so he can hear her better. Gertie is seventy-six, and they decided to look out for each other, so the phone is important. The Old Man is full of misinformation, superstition, and myth, but he has an opinion on practically everything and his own unique code of ethics . . . and who's to say he's wrong?

Fishing: "I like to go fishin' with somebody I know, but we don't stay close together. I like it quiet. And I don't want nobody's line near mine. But all my fishin' friends are gone now, and it's not the same somehow."

Politics: "Don't know much about politics, Mister. I was a Socialist in the old days, because they was for the workin' man and I was a workin' man. The Republicans and the Democrats was just out for the money. My way of thinkin', they oughta let some poor people run Washington for a change, 'stead of all those rich politicians gettin' richer."

Women's Lib: "Neither was the man created for the woman, but the woman for the man.—First Corinthians. My way of thinkin' though, women will eventually be runnin' things. Like the Negroes. Colored folks used to want equal. Now they want more."

Man on the Moon: "My way of thinkin', they should spend that money on the poor people. I don't think they really done it anyway. Just made some fake pictures somewhere and put all that money in their pockets."

Economics: "I get two hundred a month railroad pension. It costs me a hundred seventy-five to live, so I get by mostly. Don't want no credit, though. Don't want to owe nobody. But if my machine goes, I'll have to borrow to get another one. Thirty-five years ago my rent was ten dollars, now it's twenty-eight. Don't get no more for the twenty-eight than I did for the ten, 'cept cold runnin' water that's no good anyway. Nowdays, people don't care about their work no more, just their pay. Nothin' works any more. I always said do it right and it'll never come back atcha."

Sexuality: "I don't mind long hair if it's neat, but I don't like men in those tight pants with that thing bulgin' out. And those short skirts make a man so's he can't think of nothin' else. That's why they have so many of those rapes. I had a neighbor onct, young woman, she was standin' nude in her kitchen, washin' whilst her husband sat at the table. It was good she kept herself clean and all, but she knowed I take walks in the morning. She shoulda pulled the blind down."

"Why did you look?"

"She shoulda pulled the blind down."

Violence: "There was always wars, and always will be till the Messiah comes. It's the Devil's work. I had a bad temper, used to fight a lot. In White Haven, there was two words you never used. Son of a Bitch and Cocksucker. Somebody used them words at you, you fought, didn't make no difference how big he was. Don't know why, but that's the way it was. At the P&R, I let 'em know quick they wasn't to mess with me. But I'm not like that no more, I'm tryin' to be peaceful."

Vietnam: "We're fightin' over there so we don't have to fight the Vietnamese over here."

Jews: "In White Haven, there was one Jewish family. One day the boy fell into the mill pond and we all stood around and said drown, Christ Killer. The way I get it, now I may be wrong, the Jews killed Christ and that's why they call them Christ Killers, but now that I been around to different churches, I see different. They don't say that no more. The Jews are supposed to be our brothers. I'd like to go into a Jewish church sometime, if they let me. I been to most all the rest."

Faith: "You got to believe it all, from Genesis to Revelations. My way of lookin' at it, Mister, we're born and we die and we don't know when for neither. I put my trust in the Lord."

We spend the evening at Gertie's house, a cozy warm house with "all the conveniences." Gertie, twelve years a widow, is quiet and good-natured, chuckling when the Old Man's voice squeaks from hoarseness. Occasionally, her hand moves demurely to her mouth to cover a long low belch that harmonizes with the Old Man's farts. Gertie is not too well in that department either. We have "lunch" in the kitchen about eight-thirty, a choice of custard cake or shoo-fly pie, both excellent. Gertie knows her way around the kitchen. Afterwards we sit in the semi-darkness watching Johnny Cash on the television. There is little conversation. The Old Man is talked out and tired. Promptly at eleven we leave, having first taken advantage of Gertie's "conveniences," a protective hedge against a midnight trip to the out-house. Back at home, the Old Man talks for another hour and a half

in his now rasping voice, then reads the obituaries in the paper before turning in.

The rain has stopped, but the howling wind and the chilling cold keep me company under the blankets as I ponder the life of the Old Man snoring in the next room. It is a simple, uncomplicated and unquestioning life. If you do good, God is in you. If you do evil, the Devil is in you. God knows that you resist temptation, but He also knows that the Devil is stronger than you, so will not hold it against you if occasionally you stray from His path, so long as you are repentant. If you live a good life, your reward will be a just one, if not here then later, and if you live an evil life, the opposite fate awaits you, if not here then later. Faith protects your soul, and hypocrisy is only a by-product of the struggle between Good and Evil. Is it Faith then that keeps this Old Man going or has he some instinct for survival? "We are here to serve the Lord," he says, but he has only gotten religion as he has grown older and closer to Death. Who knows? In the end, we will both go out the way we came in . . . without choice.

Up at six, I find that the Old Man has beat me by half an hour and is already well into his routine. Mine takes me to the outhouse and I find getting back to nature damn cold! When Gertie calls at seven-fifteen, they both have a laugh over my discomfort and want to know if everything came out all right, ho ho. The Old Man makes us a breakfast of parboiled eggs, toast, and cream of wheat. We talk some more, or rather what passes for talking, with the Old Man's voice no more than a hoarse whisper and him disgustedly trying to shake it off each time it cracks. By eight o'clock, we dress for church. The Old Man looks like a retired business executive in a shirt and tie, well-cared-for twenty-year-old suit, and a fur-collar coat that was a hand-me-down from a big-city benefactor. It's a beautiful day, the flooding rain gone and the sun shining brightly, God's welcome to His children come to church.

We wait in the car in the parking lot for Gertie to arrive with her daughter and son-in-law. Gertie and the Old Man have been members of the Trinity Church Bible Fellowship of Blandon, Pennsylvania, Donald T. Kirkwood, Pastor, for thirty-five years. We go in together. It's a simple church, no ornaments, no carpet, hard wooden pews with an elevated pulpit up front flanked by an old upright piano for the happy hymns and a new electric organ for the more serious ones. It's bright and it's warm. The pastor, a big man partially bald, smiles effusively as he greets his flock. He is well dressed and well fed and his eyes light up as the Old Man introduces "my friend from Philadelphia. He's a Jew." "Ah, a Son of Abraham! Welcome to our humble church."

Sunday School first, from nine to ten. Our class is held here, the others are in other parts of the building. There are fourteen women in the class and four men. The men sit in the back row. Up front, a chubby woman in a black dress and hat drones in a monotonous voice, "teaching" from the last chapter of Romans, pausing now and then for little ad libs to let everyone know she knows. At one point, she speaks of the Emancipation of Women as a Christian doctrine. I look to see the reaction of the men. They are all asleep.

At ten-fifteen, with the church about half full, Sunday Service begins. Sunday School attendance buttons are given out. Gertie and the Old Man are both called up to receive theirs for "one miss." The Register of Attendance and Offering on the front wall has been updated:

Enrollment *181*
Attendance Last Sunday *136*
Attendance Today *139*
Offering Last Sunday *$37.00*
Offering Today *$38.00*

There are hymns. In My Heart There Is a Melody . . . Under His Wings . . . The Solid Rock . . . His Name Is Wonderful. Jesus Is a Rock, a Redeemer, a Saviour, a Teacher, a Leader, a Light, a Shepherd, a Healer, a Prince, a King, a Lord. The Smiling Pastor is no longer smiling, he has become the Messenger of God as he preaches a sermon on Repentance, part of a several weeks' series on Conversion and Turning Away from Sin to Jesus. This morning, the Son of Abraham gives him added inspiration.

By eleven-thirty, the service is over. The Old Man makes a point of shaking many hands, but no one else makes the effort. He speaks briefly to his friend Harold Schlegel, who then comes over to the Son of Abraham. A smallish man with a gentle smile and shining eyes who says quietly, "My best friend was a Jew. He gave His life for me on the

Cross, and I would give my life if I had to, to Save a Jew." He gives the Son of Abraham a small booklet about two inches square, titled *Messiah the Prince of Peace.* There are quotations from the Scriptures and the last page reads: Men and brethren, children of the stock of Abraham, and whosoever among you feareth God, to you is the word of this salvation sent. For extra copies write: Messiah Booklets, Sonatoga, Pa. U.S.A. Harold says he will try to visit after dinner. The conversion of the Son of Abraham offers a challenging divertissement of a Sunday afternoon in Blandon.

After church, I take Gertie and the Old Man to a restaurant for dinner, a diner he selects out on the main highway. They are both in a happy mood, joshing each other at every opportunity. It's a fine day, they prayed well and have company for Sunday dinner. Seven longhairs leave the diner, boys and girls, two of them black with afros, and pile into a car with New York plates. A ten-year-old boy in the next booth says, "Look at them, you can't tell who's a boy and who's a girl. They must be on their way back to the New York Zoo." His parents smile their approval. So prejudice is nurtured, and so soon after church, too. The Old Man glares out the window and mutters, "Hippies."

After dinner, they pose proudly for a picture. Then, we drop Gertie off and drive home. The Old Man changes clothes, saying that the suit is too young to wear all day. That way, "it'll last a while yet." Harold comes over and later one of the Old Man's daughters with her grandchildren. Harold and the daughter, both smiling peacefully and eyes shining—need one become wary in the face of Love?—do their best to bring Christ to the Son of Abraham, but there's not much time. Harold explains, quoting liberally from the Bible, that the Jews are God's Chosen People and He has warned all to treat the Jews well, so that they too will be treated well. Then, "It'll be here soon, you see. Russia wants Israel because of the Dead Sea, it's worth more than France, England, and the U.S. Minerals, you know. Russia will go to war with Israel, and it will be like boy scouts fighting an army, but God will help Israel to win. No country has every harmed the Jews and gone unpunished. It is God's will." He is speaking rapidly now, leaning forward in his chair, eyes glowing intensely into mine. "The U.S. will help Israel, or the Jews will all leave the U.S. for Israel, and that would

empty Fort Knox, you see. When Israel wins, the skies will open up and God will reveal Christ to the Jews as their Messiah." He is out of his chair now. "When that happens, when the skies open and you see Christ, you remember it was me who told you so. Then the Jews will become the greatest evangelists the world has ever seen, better even than Billy Graham." Harold drops back down in his chair, exhausted from his vision. Harold's Faith is beautiful to behold. It is unshakable. Not that the Son of Abraham would try. Each accepts the stalemate.

Harold, the daughter, and the great-grandchildren leave, and the Old Man and I say good-by. He takes a picture of the Citroën with his box camera and one of me. We shake hands solemnly and he says, "God bless you. Come again." I drive down the rutted street with no name, turn left between the Inn and the Post Office, two miles of potholes to the highway and turn left again. With the sun shining, it strikes me that yesterday's idea of a time warp was romantic. It was no time warp, just another dimension. And the Old Man and Gertie, Harold and the brightly singing voices of Trinity Church, Pastor Kirkwood preaching Repentance in Blandon . . . they're all behind me now. Aren't they?

[*May 1971*]

Patriot Joe Kelly

Is violence less violent if "they" start it?
Is rhetoric more meaningful if less erudite?

Can we be right and carry the wrong flag,
wrong and carry the right flag?
Are we listening if we only hear
what we don't want to hear?

War is Peace, Right is Wrong, Friend is Foe.
The Mad Hatter reigns.

And I will join Socrates.

Who's Who?

He says I am.
I say He's not.
If He's not, am I?

I am until I am not.

March, Hair

BAN THE BOMB/END THE DRAFT/LOWER THE VOTE/
   NO ABM/
POWER TO THE PEOPLE (GAYS too)/SUPPORT WOMAN'S
   LIB/HELP BIAFRA
(but that one's done)

My button's on, my banner's high
My rhetoric's polemical, but pure.
I march for God and Country
. . . and Mankind, oh sure.

I march for CIVIL RIGHTS, HUMAN RIGHTS,
   FEMALE RIGHTS, too
For RED MAN, CHICANO, PANTHER MAN . . . phew!
Oh yes, and I march for EARTH DAY, cough! cough! cough!
So raise the fist, the V is gone.
Get it all together. Right on!

   I'm late!
   I'm late!
   For a very important date!
   No time to stop, no time to talk!
   I'm late! I'm late! I'm late!

   I march!
   I rally!
   I demonstrate, I meet!
   For Justice and Equality, I take to the street!
   I'm a Citizen Activist—very busy, you see
   And I give of myself un-stint-ing-ly.

But . . . (*sotto voce*) . . . it's just a groove to me.

Letter to John Holt

Dear John,

How interesting that you should have written to me about *Ideology and Insanity*. When I first read these essays, I had jokingly remarked that Szasz could be a pseudonym for Holt. (I had, even then, some inkling of your opinion of psychiatrists.) Well, you have asked for my comments.

I agree that psychiatry has managed to suppress individualism, endorse conformity, and serve as a tool of society to repress those who do not voluntarily submit themselves to corrective "therapy" . . . all in the name of science. However, I do not agree that this has been done altogether willingly, without objection, and with premeditation. I think the efforts of Dr. Szasz to discredit psychiatry should have been more objectively selective. There have been too many in the field who do not fit the pattern which he presents as being virtually universal. While it is difficult to find fault with his apparent distaste for the professional elitism that in its condescendingly smug benevolence has exercised control from which there is almost no defense, one wonders at his parochialism. Why should he expect psychiatry, as an institution, to be different from, say, the Educational System, the State Department, the Pentagon, Welfare, the Courts, Corporate Business, Medicine? The case may be made against them all.

Our institutions have grown too ponderous, too resistant to change. They are not responsive . . . it is against their best interests. By insuring society of the right of protection against the individual, we have duped ourselves as individuals into an almost undefendable position. Parkinson's Law is not reversible. Sartre's contention that the individual can maintain control of his individuality regardless of his physical state (i.e., state control, institutional confinement, etc.), becomes less than palatable in a technological society. Or does it? Marcuse thought so, ten years ago. Today he is less sure. What changed his opinion?

For one thing, a militant international student movement which has made a transvaluation of values. For another, Freud. Marcuse separates the man from the theorist (something Szasz seems unable to do!) and ascribes to the latter "certain transcending radical elements." Marcuse says that the concept of the individual is not obsolete, it is premature . . . that the "seeds of revolution lie in the emancipation of the senses [Marx]—but only when the senses become practical, productive forces in changing reality."

Those who would hope to reform our institutions may well be as doomed to failure (though I still think they should try) as those who would seek to tear them down, for the one group can be as easily ingested as the other destroyed. The real hope is for the creation of viable alternative structures which will return priority to the individual. Sometimes these alternatives can be constructed subversively within the institution (e.g., the Open Classroom) while most times they must be constructed separately (e.g., the free clinics or the Federation of Community Schools in Milwaukee).

A new philosophy is emerging, John. As yet it has no permanent name, though perhaps it could be the Pragmaticization of Existentialism. While its negative radical fringe espouses (with diminishing effect) violent revolution, its center grows quietly stronger. It is, I believe, basically nonviolent, humanistic, and contrary to some opinion, counter-nihilist. Its institutions will be accountable to the individuals they serve.

When Szasz wrote "Whither Psychiatry" in 1966, he projected the possibility of a split into two disciplines—"one collectivistic and devoted to enslaving man, the other individualistic and devoted to liberating man." At the time, there was already a third discipline which married the collectivistic and the individualistic—Group Therapy. Gestalt and encounter groups in fact largely do away with the elitist privatism of psychotherapy, replacing it with an honest (and revolutionary) desire to stimulate growth and to involve people in adjusting to each other rather than to "society." Szasz proposed the separation of the psychotherapeutic elements of psychiatry from medicine and similar certification for medical and nonmedical therapists. But the New Philosophy scorns such credentials in all fields, not on the basis of anti-intellectualism, but rather on the basis of anti-elitism. Actions speak more profoundly than sheepskins. Szasz proposed a separate Board of Neurology and a separate Board of Psychiatry. He should have proposed the dissolution of both.

I admire Dr. Szasz for having discerned the failures of his field and for his courage in making them known, but I'm afraid that he has fallen victim to his own brand of "rejection rhetoric" by myopically attacking psychiatry's weaknesses without defending its strengths.

Power

As I Was Dying . . .

As I was dying, I wondered
   if there was any mail.
Would someone write
   to tell me not to go?

"Congratulations we take great pleasure in announcing this rare and distinct privilege you have been chosen nominated selected appointed voted awarded . . ."

Stay
   you are needed.
Stay
   you are recognized.
Stay
   you are loved.
Stay
   you are real.

I don't know
   if there was any mail.
It didn't matter.

An Open Letter of Appeal

TO DONALD VAN WAGENEN, THE NEW SUPERINTENDENT OF PUBLIC SCHOOLS IN THE DISTRICT OF LOWER MERION TOWNSHIP, PENNSYLVANIA, ITS PRINCIPALS AND VICE-PRINCIPALS, ITS BOARD OF NINE SCHOOL DIRECTORS, AND ITS FIVE HUNDRED AND THIRTY-ONE TEACHERS . . . ON BEHALF OF ITS TEN THOUSAND STUDENTS.

We have just made the decision to withdraw our oldest daughter from public school. She will enter private school next fall. And I'm mad!

Why? Because the public-school system has let her down, as it has millions of other children. Because private school costs too much money. Because I am opposed in principle to the "private" school, that sequestered elitist milieu of the predominantly white upper middle class. Because my commitment to improving public-school education is ill-served by pulling my children out. And because it did not have to be. For seven years we have watched the gradual transition from a bright, precocious, and eager-to-learn kindergartner to a disinterested and apathetic sixth-grader; from a turned-on five-year-old to a turned-off pre-teen already wise in the student stratagems for "getting by."

It didn't happen all at once. The signs were there, but we chose to ignore them. Partly because of a naïve faith in a system that "was good enough for us so it's good enough for her," and partly because of an equally naïve belief that a more loving, less restrictive and more intellectually stimulating home life would more than adequately compensate for any shortcomings at school. We were wrong.

How do you compensate for a five-year-old reduced to tears by a teacher who insists that a butterfly must be drawn to look like a butterfly? ("This is trash! You call this a butterfly? This is trash! You should have stayed in bed today!") How do you compensate for a six-year-old being stood in front of the class with a pile of clothes which she has forgotten to take home during the term? How do you compensate for a third-grader receiving an Unsatisfactory in Music for "always singing off-key," or a fourth-grader who has a B in a math test reduced to a C because she forgot to sign her name? How do you compensate for an authoritarian, largely irrelevant and change-resistant system which Mark Twain called "the organized fight of the grown-ups against youth" or about which Ashley Montagu has said, "In the factories called schools the child is forced to engorge large quantities of rote-remembered facts, and then at certain calculated ceremonial ordeals called 'examinations,' he is required to disgorge these facts onto blank sheets of paper, thus leaving his mind blank forever thereafter"?

Can you compensate for teachers who have more respect for discipline than for intellect, more interest in silence and order than in the happy and excited noise of learning, more concern for tenure and automatically self-renewing contracts than for their own ability to teach . . . teachers who even now join their union to demonstrate at the State Capitol as state employees demanding the right to strike rather than demanding a better education for their students? In the past ten years, not one tenured teacher has been dismissed from the Lower Merion School District. Are they all that competent? Not even one inadequate to the task of teaching students who have so often been judged inadequate to the task of learning?

Reverend John M. Culkins believes that "schools are for students; everything else is just a means to an end, to be used or not used depending on whether or not it will serve the growth of students."

Do you disagree? Yet in all of the school laws of Pennsylvania there are but ten short sections dealing with courses of study (half of which are on safe driving and fire and emergency) while over two hundred and fifty sections deal with the raising, acquisition, distribution of, and accounting for money and/or property. One board member told me that "the School Board devotes itself almost exclusively to finances," while the law specifically directs them to adopt text books and courses of study, establish additional schools, appoint or dismiss superintendents, principals, and teachers . . . all in *addition* to financial responsibilities! Has public-school education simply become a big business? And if so, are our children the products or the by-products?

Shall we believe John Holt—"We adults destroy most of the intellectual and creative capacity of children . . . by making them afraid, afraid of not doing what other people want, of not pleasing, of making mistakes, of failing, of being *wrong"*—or shall we believe Louise Bates Ames— ". . . very young children are quite prone to lie, steal, and otherwise misbehave. It takes much time, teaching, and experience before the ordinary child matures to a point where he can tell the truth, refrain from stealing, and otherwise conduct himself in a way that our society approves."

Shall we be inspired by Max Rafferty—"The main goal of education . . . is the equipping of the individual with the arsenal he will need throughout life in his combat against the forces of error"—or by John Dewey—"We may produce in schools a projection in type of the society we should like to realize, and by forming minds in accord with it gradually modify the larger and more recalcitrant features of adult society"?

The private school which our daughter will attend lists these as its objectives: to develop students able to work and learn independently, to have self-discipline and responsibility, the ability to make intelligent choices, to use knowledge freely and creatively, studying subjects that are relevant and meaningful to their lives and interests. Listen to a description of the school: There is a marked emphasis on independent work under the supervision of an advisor-teacher. Most classes are seminars or tutorial. In addition to regular staff, any qualified parent or person in the city can offer a class or seminar in an area of interest. Students work both at school and elsewhere in the city (at universities, hospitals, libraries, zoos, businesses, etc.), and they select their own curriculum. Each advisor-teacher has a maximum of twenty students for whose educational development he is responsible. There are no grades or marks. Students work at their level of competence, and advisors evaluate with written reports on students' strengths and weaknesses.

Each student agrees at the time of admission to meet the minimum requirements set by the Board of Public Instruction, and it is the student's responsibility to work in the required areas before he completes his six years at the school (seventh through twelfth grades). The school is based on a co-operative, not competitive, system—an academic community where students are encouraged to explore and share with their peers individual interests and discoveries, and where students can work free from the fear of being punished for poor intellectual decisions.

What an exciting way to learn! What a thrilling way to turn loose the boundless energy and enthusiasm for education that is so natural in children that it enables them to learn to talk, probably the most difficult of all learning tasks, *without being taught,* simply by being placed in an atmosphere conducive to motivated learning! She who has so often complained to us of boredom in school ("I wish vacation was here") cannot wait for next fall ("I wish there were no summer vacation"). She who has been labeled an "under-achiever," who has "demonstrated very little interest to learn"!

Why does it have to be a "private" school? Why can't it be a "public" school? Because that kind of education costs too much? Nonsense! The average private-school tuition per student per year is a bare two hundred dollars more than the average cost to educate a student in public school. (Probably even less than that if we eliminate the immense bureaucratic waste that our public school system has managed to accumulate over the years.) Not enough teachers, perhaps? Nonsense! Our colleges and universities are turning out B.A.'s, M.A.'s and Ph.D.'s so fast that the Situations Wanted: Teacher ads are overflowing. Parental resistance, then? Nonsense! What parent does not want the best possible education for his child? What parent favors a system of fear and intimidation rather than love for his child? What parent will select tradition rather than relevance as the criterion for his child's education? Only one who is uninformed, who has not had the opportunity to be better acquainted with what is and is not being done, let alone what *could* be done in our Public School System.

We are parents, not educators. While some are concerned, most are not, having placed their faith in an educational system that has, like many of our most trusted institutions, been unwilling or unable to keep pace with the times. Instead of an interested and free exchange of communication among the four participants—administrators, teachers, parents, and students—we have the opposite. School boards who meet in private to determine the destiny of our children. Superintendents and principals who with great autonomy determine policies for which they frequently lack legal authority, yet hide behind that lack of authority in order to evade change they do not seek. A teachers' union that views decentralization and community control of schools as an incursion on their power and an intrusion on their sovereignty. Faculty forums that rubber-stamp their administrators rather than risk their tenure. Teachers who consider their superiors demagogues, the parents their mortal if inferior enemies, and their students as noisy, ungrateful and unmanageable brats. Home and school associations whose primary purpose seems to be to placate parents with two annual meetings—one to see how Junior's doing and the other a May Day outing. Student councils to whom no one pays much attention except now and then to let them liberalize the dress code. And the students? Who listens to students? As Paul Goodman said, "American society either excludes the young, or corrupts the young, or exploits the young."

So they keep coming to school because the law says they must and their parents say they must. And they will be quiet and attentive because their teachers say they must and their principals say they must. And they get the best grades they can, one way or another, because if they don't, they don't graduate and they don't go to college and they don't get good jobs and they don't "get ahead." *But they don't learn.* This country has the greatest number of high-school and college graduates of any country in the world, past or present, and it has the "highest standard of living" in the history of man. But our children are not educated. They are programmed. Or they drop out . . . one way or the other.

Let the reader whose school district is without sin cast the first stone.

[*May 1970*]

"Schools are a kind of temple of worship for 'right answers,' and the way to get ahead is to lay plenty of them on the altar."

—JOHN HOLT

"Our push for early academic education often produces very bright but totally unsocialized persons, people who know a lot, but do not know how to live in a community of others."

—BRUNO BETTELHEIM

[1 1 5]

Boredom is a cover up for anger of some sort.

"Traditional academic learning is coercive and punishing; it suffocates the child and teaches him to hate."

—NATHAN ACKERMAN

"Attendance at boring classes, reading of dull books, writing of required but distasteful papers, taking of acutely painful and humiliating tests—all these cruelties to children are rationalized as good preparation for some life to come."

—GOODWIN WATSON

"A good life today is the best preparation for tomorrow."

—JOHN DEWEY

"One of the most destructive traits of contemporary schools is what seems like a virtual dedication to the extinction of individuality and creativity in the child by treating him, among other things, as if he were a mere anonymous unit in an agglutinated mass of other similar anonymous units."

—ASHLEY MONTAGU

"Our system tends to make people part of the machine, or subparts of the parts—all unified by the self-same program transmitted to everyone through the same education, the same radio, the same television, the same magazine."

—ERICH FROMM

"One ironical consequence of the drive for so-called higher standards in schools is that the children are too busy to think."

—JOHN HOLT

"If we were completely at a loss to state the positive goals of education, we might still insist upon a minimal responsibility: do not destroy what already exists. If you cannot add to the intelligence of childhood, at least do not destroy it!"

—GEORGE DENNISON

[116]

"Learning is in the mind. Going to school is anywhere, anytime, the textbook anything upon which the active mind focuses for study. To educate everybody we must use *all* the hours, *all* the structures . . . museums, libraries, parks, zoos, factories, businesses, courts, municipal buildings and farms, for education in real life not just the isolated brick schoolhouse."

—ATHELSTAN SPILHAUS

"The chief goal of education is to teach the pupil *how* to learn."

—ERNST PAPANEK

Concert

In the shadow of four towers
    spiders dance.
Finger-legs racing over white strings
    weave a soothing web.
Sounds of the concert:
    a dog barks.
    a child laughs.
    a plane drones.
    (damn!)
    lovers whisper.
One deaf old lady
    is too loud.
    (Ssshhh!)

We sit on the grass freely.
Minds wander
    and meet others wandering too.
Together we remember
    when there was nothing to forget.

Drug Education—a Bum Trip?

"No one wants to read about drugs. Drugs are out, didn't you know? They just aren't an IN thing any more."

The remark was made to me by a suburban New York father of two children. He reads *The New York Times*, *The Wall Street Journal*, *Time*, and *Life*. He watches a good deal of television, secs an occasional movie. He considers himself well informed. Two years ago he was concerned about drugs. Now it's Ecology. He is not alone. We are a nation with a strange penchant for losing interest in problems before they are solved.

The father from New York is wrong. Drugs are not "out," they are still very much "in." The problem of drug abuse is bad and rapidly growing worse. Is anybody doing anything about it? Yes. Are they effective? Come with me, and we'll try to find out. Meet some of the "experts" I've been talking to for the past month or so.

Lucille

Under a freshly done bouffant hairdo, Lucille Ferriola's face showed very little emotion. Her voice was quiet and measured, as we sat in the cafeteria of St. Agnes Hospital, where she has run the business office for four years. Her husband is a machinist, a shop foreman. Until June of 1969, she had three fine children. Now, she has two. Her oldest son died from an overdose of heroin.

"When Butch died, I stayed home for two weeks. Then I came back to work. I've never been a religious person, but I talked to the priests and the nuns here, and they felt that God had given me a purpose. You know, God has a reason for everything. I don't know, maybe I just had to believe that so I could take it. Anyway, I came back to work and got active in this drug-abuse education thing. . . . His name was Frank, but we called him Butch. He was a good student, good

[1 1 8]

grades. He played football until he got sick. He played the piano, taught himself how to play the guitar. He was very popular. He didn't have much of a relationship with his father. My husband is a hard taskmaster. He gets mad quickly. But Butch and I were very close. We had talks with each other. We never lied. Like I asked him if he ever used marijuana. He said sure, at Central [Central High School, where he went for two years before transferring to Bishop Neuman Catholic High School], everybody did. I didn't get mad. I stayed calm. I asked him did he know what could happen. He said it didn't do anything for him, that he was more interested in girls and music.

"When he was seventeen, about a year before he died, his best friend came in here with hepatitis. I was really surprised. I told Butch—you know what hepatitis comes from sometimes, don't you, a dirty needle. He said, Oh no, Mom, not him, he wouldn't do anything like that. I decided to get the kids some Gamma G, since his friend had been in our house a lot. One day Butch came to me and said—I think I have hepatitis, Mom. My urine's pretty dark, and I'm tired a lot. Sure enough, he did. We put him in our doctor's hospital. I had been watching him closely since he told me about the marijuana, but now I watched him even more closely. He had a very bad allergy. He got shots every week and took antihistamine pills.

"After it happened, when I looked back, I saw things I had never seen at the time. He'd go out for a half hour or so at night and then come back to watch TV. He used to fall asleep right away, and I would have an awful time waking him up. I'd ask him if he took his antihistamine pills, and he'd say yes. I'd tell him to cut down to one a day, because I had so much trouble waking him. Our doctor watched him like a hawk. He would play tricks on Butch, like when he would come for an allergy shot he'd say I think I gave you a shot in that arm last time, Butch, so he could check both arms for tracks. He was sure that Butch was clean. I guess he fooled us all. When he died, there were two empty bags and two spoons. He might have expected someone else. I think it was the first time he did it alone. Afterwards, I talked to his school friends. At first they wouldn't tell me anything. After while they admitted they were all on drugs. They used to pitch in a dollar apiece for a bag and then pass the needle around. They were on pills, too. They told me most of the school was on something.

"I tried to talk to a parents group at the school, but the priest who was the head of the school was new and didn't want trouble. I told them I hoped the priest was willing to accept the responsibility of another OD like my Butch. That got him, I guess, because they let me come in and tell my story. . . . I don't know why it happened. We fixed up the basement, so he would bring friends home, but you know, after while you can't force them. You have to let them go. One of my neighbors told another neighbor that she knew Butch was on drugs. She didn't tell me, because she didn't want trouble. She should have told me, even at the risk of losing a friendship. Maybe I might have been able to do something, help him. The biggest problem is to arouse the parents. They think it can't happen to them. I tell them it can. It happened to me."

Cold Duck at CCDA

In the heart of North Philadelphia, one of the city's two major "ghettos," is the Community Committee on Drug Abuse. On the third floor of a run-down but warm and clean storefront building, an office Christmas party was just getting under way. For the next three hours I shared warm Cold Duck ("Is this stuff supposed to be chilled?") with some hardworking people who work six days a week at keeping two hundred people alive and away from heroin. CCDA runs a "detox" (detoxification) program. It is one of three methadone centers in Philadelphia. For the past eighteen months or so, it has dispensed methadone to patients every other day. Each pill contains 10 mg, the equivalent of "one good bag." The fee is ten dollars per week, but reduces as the dosage tapers. Methadone is still considered an experimental research drug, and centers are closely regulated by the state. CCDA treats mostly men; nearly half are white and the ages run generally from seventeen to twenty-five. There are two staff doctors, nurses, psychiatrists, office and case workers. Over two thousand heroin addicts were treated in 1970.

Tony: Tall, heavy-set, with closely cropped hair, a Doctor of Osteopathy who has worked at the center for about six months. Professionals are paid a token salary, so they are more like volunteers than employees. Tony believes that drug-abuse education in school only serves to introduce the idea of drug use to kids. He feels that the job belongs to the parents. "Maybe they should handle it in the schools, I don't know. In our day there wasn't so much of a drug problem. We didn't know about drugs."

Charles: Twenty-nine. An ex-addict. Now, a case worker. "I was dealin' for four years before I shot up anything. A whole lot of the dealin' was done by the cops. There was a detective dude who was dealin' across the street from me in an apartment house. He didn't use the stuff, but his sister and his girl were both hooked. I was dealin' mostly bush [marijuana] at the time. He was dealin' skag. He knew I was dealin', I knew he was dealin'. He didn't bother me as long as I didn't move in on him. . . . I was off dope for a year once, but I went back. I went to New York. In three months, I was up to forty-five bags a day. I'd shoot seven when I got up, skin pop eight at lunch. The 'herine' in New York has always been better quality and cheaper than here. [A New York bag costs $3, a Philly bag costs $5.] Addicts in New York spend more time worrying about their clothes, how they look. A lot of them work. I was workin'. I was going to school with the airlines at Kennedy. In '68 there was a big snowstorm, and we were stranded. I was amazed at the amount of dope there was. We'd go behind TWA and cop a bag, go to Eastern and cop a bag. You'd be amazed how many dudes was into dope there, all over the place. I'm clean almost a year now. You know what? I'm high every day, just livin' and knowin' I don't have to worry about where the next shot is comin' from. I'm really diggin' myself, man."

Frank: Twenty-eight. Small, handsome, ex-addict, very charismatic. He is assistant program director. "I started because I was a masochist. I wanted to hurt myself. All of a sudden I heard I was a ghetto kid. I never went without clothes or was hungry. I thought it was a good thing to do. I was fifteen. I gang-warred and drank wine. Then I started trying everything. I thought I could handle it. I woke up eight years later and found I was hooked. Junkie never admits he's hooked till he gets sick. Until then he keeps thinkin'—I can handle it. A dude quits when he's learned to dig himself. We solve it with love, man. We got to have love. Love has become almost mystical. People got to dig each other. Synanon, Phoenix House, Guadenzia—the dudes all groove on that shit—good mawnin', brother, how are you, brother—eighteen months of that and they go out on the street and say good mawnin', brother. Good mawnin'? Shit, what's that? You crazy? Git outta here! They find no love, no identity, they go right back on skag. That's what skag is . . . nothin'! You can forget it all. No problems. No hangups. That's where it ends up. A dude can quit for fifteen years, but make it available, he'll go right back on.

"Sex? I went as long as forty-four months without sex, and I wasn't even in prison at the time. At first 'herine' makes you feel strong. You can go all night and the next day. But after while, you don't want sex and don't miss it. Sex cuts the high. It's climax. Anything with climax cuts the high. I didn't want nothin' to mess with my high. . . . I've gone around to the schools. Once, I was in an elementary school talkin' about sniffin' glue. Then I wondered what the hell was I doin' in that school? It's one thing to educate, it's another to advertise. I think a kid's got to do what he's gonna do. I'm against these experts—social workers and doctors—they never know when to back off. You can overdo it. What do you do if a dude wants to do dope? Tell him not to? I tell a sixteen-year-old kid not to do dope and he says Frank, you're cool. When I'm twenty-eight, I wanna be cool too, but between now and then, I want to do what you done. Maybe another sixteen-year-old dude can do better. The one on dope will say: What do you know, you ever tried dope? He can say: I don't have to, man. See that chick? She's mine. See this, see that . . . mine. I don't need that shit, and I won't get sick without it.

"But look, Tony has cancer, Blackwell has a bad heart, I have Hodgkin's Disease, you have a bad stomach—we would all have something different, but we'd all be sick, right? That's our problem, we're all sick, one way or another. So we have that in common, and we can deal with it. Love. Identity. That's what we need. But the reality is the almighty buck. Every dealer is makin' a bundle. He wants that Cadillac. That's his identity. And it don't make no difference if you're white or black or green. Everybody's out for the buck. There's too much money in drugs. And you can't change the value system."

The Feds

The Federal Bureau of Narcotics and Dangerous Drugs, part of the U.S. Department of Justice, has fourteen regions in the country plus three more internationally. Region III, headquartered in the Customs House in Philadelphia, covers Delaware, southern New Jersey and Pennsylvania. The Bureau functions in law enforcement and in education. I talked with Carl Cipriani, agent in charge of the Training and

Prevention Program, who spends seven-day weeks giving lectures, training sessions, seminars. It's a busy job for this small, haggard-looking man in his early fifties.

"I'm an educator. I started out as a teacher, but I've been with the Bureau for sixteen years. Been in drug education since '66. New Jersey and Pennsylvania both have K-12 programs. It will take five years before we feel it. You have to take a realistic approach. Talk facts. There just isn't any evidence of long-range harmful effects from marijuana. Oh, there are certainly short-range effects—heart, blood pressure, reflexes, eyes, time and distance—but, stop using it and you go back to normal. And marijuana doesn't lead to heroin . . . in the South, only twenty-five per cent start with marijuana. Most addicts there started right in with Dilaudid or heroin. I always include the facts. Using ex-addicts? Oh, they're all right with adults, but I'm against it with kids. They think—'Oh, he's been there and made it back okay'—it's almost like society giving its approval. The kids do gravitate to them, though. I've been on panels with ex-addicts. They get all the questions. My approach is too dry, I guess. I'd place more emphasis on education and less on enforcement. But you don't get many enlightened people in this business. Most of the people who go into police work go in for the power. They have what we call tunnel vision."

Lieutenant Narc

Oh the false illusion of television and movie sets! Philadelphia's Narcotics Squad must surely occupy the dingiest, most disreputable offices in the city, and the squad members (not uniformed) look more like users, though I'm sure the latter is more intentional than the former. The "Boss" (that's what they call him) is Lieutenant Pete Noga, a burly forty-year-old police professional who has been with the force since 1953 and a narc since 1956. One wall of Noga's office has a chart of the drug arrests since 1965.

Year	Arrests
1965	926
1966	1445
1967	1866
1968	3047
1969	3828

In the first eleven months of 1970, there were 6480 arrests (831 were juveniles—under eighteen), but the size of the squad was doubled to seventy in 1970.

Noga and some of his men do a good deal of lecturing to community and church groups, parent groups and schools ("but the kids don't relate to us, they turn us right off"). He thinks that drug-abuse education in the schools is a must, but should be handled by the "medical men" who should emphasize the good that drugs do when medically prescribed. He also thinks that there may be some truth to the theory that drug-abuse education might introduce kids to the idea of using drugs. Noga believes that methadone centers require more controls, so that patients cannot participate in more than one program.

"Junkies are the slickest con artists you ever saw. They'll con your back teeth from you. Every user will produce three more. The worst pushers are users, and most users push. If a kid is abusing drugs, the school should notify the parents. If we're called by the parents, we'll try to recommend somewhere for treatment. But, if there are drugs involved, if there's possession or suspicion, then the police should be called. Mostly, in the schools, it's kids selling to kids. But they don't know what they're buying. See this? Vitamin B. See this? Oregano. They don't know what they're taking.

"I had a girl come down here from New York. She stopped at 30th Street Station [Penn Central Railroad Station] and oiled up with a bag so she could get the nerve to turn herself in. She had two bags on her when she got here. Said she was making a lot of money in New York prostitutin' herself, but couldn't make enough for her habit. Comes from a nice family in the Northeast [white, middle-class section of Philadelphia]. . . . We train men from other towns. Some of these suburban police never made a drug arrest. They figure they got no drug problems. They come here and get trained. We teach them how to spot drugs, pushers, users. Then they go back and make drug arrests."

Surrounding Lieutenant Noga's desk are hookahs of all sizes and shapes. In one corner is a locked cabinet with a glass front. He took out some samples of psychedelia—red, white, and blue cigarette paper for rolling joints, pipes with four stems for group smoking, hash cookbooks, pamphlets on how to grow your own marijuana.

"Kids don't make these. Parents made these. Plenty of parents getting rich on this stuff."

Help

A year ago, Sherri Winters and Shelly Kaplan felt Philadelphia's "freaks" (young street people) were getting too hassled. The "freaks" would have to get together and help each other. So they formed a nonprofit tax-exempt corporation called HELP, a telephone referral service that's trying to grow into a free clinic. If you have a problem—drugs . . . pregnancy . . . draft . . . legal—any kind of a problem—call HELP. I went there instead. They had just moved into new quarters in center city, and hammers were still banging partitions into place. The new cork wall in the foyer already had pictures of runaways mounted on it. Downstairs, there are three desks with phones in alcoves up front, plus a back room with more desks and phones. Upstairs on two more floors, there are rooms for private or group sessions and presumably future examination and treatment rooms. I talked with Rob Rosenbloom, a lawyer and board member of HELP.

"It's a pretty loosely run operation. We have thirty-four lawyers who volunteered, but only five who work at it. I do all the draft counseling. We have two doctors on staff, both residents, plus a nurse who does psychiatric work. Most of the work is done by street people with the professionals on call. We have a great book we made up, with every possible problem that could come up and the answers. The street kids can only work after they have observed for a few weeks. Then, they work on the phone, but they give no opinion or medical advice. Fortunately, no one has checked out on us. Some chick OD'd in Cleveland—died right on their couch—they shut their clinic down. We get no help at all from the city, except they don't hassle us. We operate on a shoestring from donations."

Later, Harvey—one of the street people—was talking to a good-looking boy of about sixteen, well dressed in tweed bells, a short fleece-trimmed vinyl jacket, and a Beatle haircut circa 1960. His hands were in his pockets, he looked down at his feet a lot, and his answers were almost inaudible. His bearded friend in a pea jacket stood nearby. Harvey was saying that of course he was no doctor, but when did he have his eyes examined last? Don't remember. Could somebody have dropped something on him, maybe in some wine or coffee? No, he didn't think so. How much did he drink? A whole bottle. Was it straight codeine or what? Don't know . . . cough medicine . . . don't remember what kind. How long had he been getting these flashes? Since he drank it last Thursday (five days). Had he been sleeping okay? Yeah, he'd been sleeping, but it wasn't like he'd been sleeping. Was he spaced out now? He thought so.

This went on for some time. The boy was frightened. He came to HELP for help. Harvey got him to call his father (who knew that his son had trouble, but wasn't with him). The father gave Harvey the name of his son's psychiatrist, whom Harvey was about to call when one of the doctors came in and took over. The two went upstairs to talk. The boy's friend left. Another kid asked Rob if he was a lawyer. Rob said yes.

"What can they do if you jump bail? I was busted in Jersey in September for drugs. They let me out on bail, and I didn't go back. What can they do to me?"

"Send you to jail. Of course, they might not. I think you ought to see a New Jersey lawyer."

"What about if I make up a story like I was in a terrible accident? And I was in the hospital till now and I could get all this equipment like a brace for my neck and . . ."

"What hospital?"

"Well, I could dream one up and . . . no?"

"No. You get a New Jersey lawyer."

Philadelphia's "Program"

Daniel Falco is Assistant Director of the Department of Physical and Health Education of the Philadelphia District of Public Schools. He is in charge of the Drug Abuse Program . . . such as it is. Danny is in his late thirties, small and dapper in a mod brown suit, two-toned brown shoes, and sculptured haircut. Twinkling eyes, square jaw, and an easy manner.

"Two years ago we got caught with our pants down. The same way we'll get caught with our pants down soon on VD. I was a phys. ed. in one of the districts. Suddenly I get hit with this tremendous promotion. Wow! I'm still reelin' when one day I get a call from a sixth-grade mother whose kid is sniffin' glue. What are we gonna do about it? What are we teachin' the kids in school? I didn't know. I looked at our files and guides—we had practically nothing. I scurried around like crazy. What the hell, I didn't know anything about drugs. I decided to learn. I met with the agencies, doctors, lawyers, community groups. I took a three-week course that summer at Temple University. Then I got on the Greater Philadelphia Council of Narcotics and Dangerous Drugs. I traveled, too. California, Chicago, Detroit. Studied their problems and their programs.

"How much of a drug problem do we have? I don't know. How do you do statistics like that? Surveys? Some kids like to brag they shoot up all the time, even when they don't. Some don't tell anybody anything. Arrests? Reports? They don't even begin to give the picture. One kid in ten on heroin? How do I know? Statistics! All I can tell you is it's bad, and it's gonna get worse before it gets better. It's important to use the right people in the right place. Reverend Bartlett's Teen Challenge is based on religion. Turn off drugs, turn on Christ. They went into a Jewish area and at the end tried to get all those Jewish kids down on their knees to Christ. That's an example of a wrong approach. Mostly, ex-addicts are good. They talk straight, and the kids know it. Also, they can describe the hell of the habit, and they do. It's very effective. Are parent groups effective? Well, they're getting more and more interested, but mostly in the past it's been lip service. They could put the pressure on for state and federal funds. There isn't enough money."

Two of Philadelphia's best pilot programs, funded by Sears Roebuck ($10,000), involved Teacher Education Seminars and a Peer Influence Program using well-trained kids to counsel other kids in the schools on an informal basis. They were so successful that they were planned for expansion this year throughout the district. A plan calling for $210,000 funding was put together and sent to Washington. It was never answered. Neither program was expanded. Danny Falco and his committee of experts took a year to put together a K-12 Drug Abuse Program. The Teacher's Guide, which will soon be distributed to 17,000 teachers and administrators, is 132 pages long including a glossary and up-to-date resources. There's no money to do any teacher training. After a closed-circuit television briefing by Falco, they'll be on their own. Most are not capable of doing the job.

"It's better than we had, a lot better, but it's not enough. Look, I know it's not enough. We're groping, but so is every other city. We're groping because we don't have the answers. Nobody does. We need more answers. We aren't even sure what approach to use. But we better do something, because it's bad. Real bad. They're all concerned now about reading. That's where the money is being spent. Well, I'm concerned about reading skills, too. I'd just like to see them reading about drug abuse, that's all."

Hilda

Hilda is not her real name. ("If you use my real name, I'll lose my job. Even if I don't say anything controversial, I'll be fired. I know it for certain. That's the way the system works. They protect themselves.") She teaches in the Philadelphia School District. Her job brings her in contact with kids in trouble . . . those who get caught. Hilda is an angry, cynical, compassionate woman. She's been at this job for fifteen years. She works at the bottom of the pit we call an urban school system. If there's any good to be seen in the system, it is out of Hilda's range of vision. She wants the whole thing changed . . . now.

"What good is drug-abuse education when you don't solve what sends them to drugs in the first place? Boredom! Boredom turns them off and leads them to drugs. Most of the kids on drugs are truants first. In another few years, you'll only have forty per cent of the kids in school. The rest won't even show up. Then who will you have left to educate about drug abuse? Seven years ago, there were five cases of drug arrests in the juvenile courts in a year, and they were all black. Now, we have two pretrial courts working full time every day. They hear twenty-two cases each. That's forty-four cases. Ten to fifteen are drugs, and they are mostly white middle class. They are generally up for possession. If they were pushing or had a lot of stuff, it goes harder. Mostly, it's marijuana or solvent. We had a lot of cough medicine, for a while. Now, it's glue or paint solvent. They call it 'snuffing.' They rob paint factories and plastics factories for the stuff. I tell you it's awful. Parents don't want to know what's going on. Neither do the teachers. God, it's awful."

Suburbia

The Lower Merion School District is predominantly white and middle class. It encompasses much of Philadelphia's famed Main Line.

The drug-abuse education of its 10,000 students is in the hands of Eugene R. Kessler, Assistant to the Superintendent for Instructional Services. He is a pleasant man in his early forties, with a kind face and sincere eyes. Kessler told me of Lower Merion's program. In 1966 when the district first became concerned about drug abuse, work was begun in conjunction with nearby Lankenau Hospital on a health guide financed under a federal grant. The K-12 Health Guide was completed in 1967, and Health teachers were hired to take over the subject which was formerly taught by regular teachers or phys. ed. instructors. It is 385 pages long and contains 14 pages on alcohol, 8 pages on drugs and narcotics, and 14 pages on smoking. A similar Guide prepared by the State of Pennsylvania is 203 pages long and contains 9 pages on alcohol, 6 pages on drugs and narcotics, and 8 pages on smoking. A six- to eight-hour in-service "drug course" is conducted at Lankenau Hospital for teachers and administrators on a rotating basis that has accounted for about fifty per cent of the current district staff. The course is one of indoctrination and does not attempt to instruct teachers on how to conduct drug-abuse classes.

"We've been at it quite a while, since 1966. Frankly, our kids have had it. They say, 'Enough already on drug-abuse education, we've had it for four years now, and we know all we need to know. Anyway, we don't have the drug problem everyone seems to think we have, and even if we have the twenty per cent they say we have, those kids have been as reached by now as they're gonna be.'—I'm inclined to agree. I think it's time we move on to other important issues like ecology. I also think the answer is in creating a more exciting learning environment. Schools where kids have fun learning. We're trying some of these things in Harriton High School now, and it's paying off. [A Harriton High School senior died in October, reportedly from an overdose of heroin.]

"Maybe I'm naïve in thinking we don't have a drug problem like the others do. But I'm a realist, and I think our kids are just too bright, too knowledgeable, to mess with that stuff. . . . There is no written policy. It has been our custom to notify the parents in the case of suspected abuse, and both parents and police in the case of possession. We don't allow police to interrogate in the school. The School Board has been meeting weekly, attempting to formulate a formal policy on drugs. We've dealt with this since 1966, visited

Shaker Heights, suburban Cleveland, Pittsburgh, Connecticut, and California . . . but the community just started getting fired up about drugs a year or so ago, so I guess we're going to have to continue for a while yet."

Saturday Night with the Narcs

A series of calls with the Commissioner's Office, and Lieutenant Noga got me an okay to spend the evening with the Narcotics Squad. I arrived about 6 p.m. to find six detectives, dressed mostly in hip sports clothes, sitting around a TV set watching the closing minutes of the Dallas-Detroit football game. They told me it would be a slow night since it was the night after Christmas and so cold out that most pushers would be working inside, where you need a warrant for a pinch. They were all in their twenties or early thirties except for Joe, the sergeant, who is a grandfather and with the force for twenty years. The phone rang frequently, but routinely.

One call was from a father who had discovered his son with drugs and wanted to bring him in for a lecture, to scare him. One of the narcs muttered "some father." I asked why he said that, what should the father do? . . . "Bash the kid's fuckin' head in." . . . Joe said only half in jest, "This guy's a writer. Everything you say goes into his head and stops. Use some decent language." I repeated my question.

"I dunno. Maybe take the kid to a doctor. Anyway, we're not a fuckin' nursery. We got enough to do. I got no time for junkies. Can't stand 'em. It's a fuckin' mess. We pinch 'em, they're out on the street the next day, pushin' again. They always get out. Bail's maybe $500—costs 'em $35, they're out again. Police officer spends so much time makin' the pinch, they're out on bail before he's even finished. Goes before the judge, he gives 'em two years' probation. One guy had nine previous arrests for narcotics. His lawyer makes a deal with the DA's Office, pleads guilty, gets two years' probation again. Nine previous arrests for narcotics! That fuckin' guy don't deserve to be out on the fuckin' street."

Joe: "It's a bad problem, all right. You know, it's okay for you and me. We know how to get our kicks. We can handle it. We can go into the corner bar and get a couple of belts if we want to. What can a young kid of fourteen or fifteen do? Where does he get his kicks? I'd sooner see a kid be promiscuous, at least that's natural. Shooting something into your veins, that's not natural. Or popping pills. I even try not to take aspirin when I have a headache. I tell my kids like it is. I take it right down to the nitty-gritty. You take drugs, you're gonna stay small. You won't grow as a person. You'll just end up small. It's awful to see the way these people end up."

Ray: "I don't know how you're going to educate kids to drugs. A lot of kids know as much as you do and half the teachers turn on with pot. Kids start with grass, they graduate to meth [Methedrine—"Speed"], then they graduate to skag.—'Not me, I won't graduate to skag. I just like marijuana.'—That's bull. But I think they'll legalize marijuana. . . . It's the parents' job. They should go into their kid's room. Look around, read the letters she's getting. See what her friends are like, who she associates with. Do it secretly, if you have to. Some of these parents see a needle, they don't even know what it is. Then they say, I respect my daughter's privacy. That's bull. As long as she lives under my roof, I want to know what she's doing and who with. I get parents up here, they fight with you. Won't believe it. 'Not my kid, he was in the car, but he didn't know what was going on.' I remember we had a brother and sister up here. I must have spent fifteen minutes without stopping, explaining to their mother how serious this was, where they were found, what they had, what they were doing when they were apprehended. When I was done, the mother said can my daughter go to her prom tomorrow. Jesus, I just walked away from her. What's the use?"

Joe and two others went out on a raid. Ray went out to eat, leaving Dave and Lefty. Every narcotics arrest in the city of Philadelphia (most are made by uniformed police) is processed by the Narcotics Squad. There is a mountain of paperwork. ("If we could just have four or five clerk-typists in here, we could save the city a lot of money.") They don't like it. They prefer to work alone, operating on the information of their "rats" (informers). As we talked, the father who had called earlier came in with his son. The father was a small, middle-aged man, well dressed, with concern written all over his face. The boy, about fourteen, was taller than his father, also neatly dressed. He looked scared. Dave talked to him. He took him over to a wall full of photos of junkies' arms, legs and torsos. Tracks, sores, abscesses.

"See this? That's what you'll look like. That's where you'll end up, you know that?" The boy mumbled an answer. "You know what this is?" Dave held up a bag of white powder.

"Heroin," the boy murmured.

"You shoot this, you'll be dead before you leave the room. It's rat poison. You think you know what you're shovin' into you? You never know."

Dave continued to speak quietly with the boy for several minutes, then stepped out into the hall with the father for several minutes more. When they left, the father thanking Dave profusely and the boy drenched in sweat, I asked Dave if that sort of thing did any good. He said maybe, that the boy loved his father and had a good job. He had a chance if he could resist his friends. But Dave was not too convinced. None of the narcs are very optimistic. They see no end in sight. They have little faith in methadone programs, claiming that junkies get on a program so they can tell the judge they're trying to kick heroin if they get caught for possession.

Lefty: "I think addicts should be institutionalized. They're sick people. You can go after the pushers, but there wouldn't be a problem if there weren't any users. It's tough to kick skag. They keep coming back. There isn't a pusher or a dealer in Philadelphia that we haven't pinched, unless he's new or really small fry. But dealers and pushers, the law treats them the same. I had a case. Young guy and his girl. They drive to an apartment house. The girl stays in the car. The guy goes up to a second-floor apartment. The girl can see through the window a guy hands the kid something at the door of the apartment. The kid comes back, and they drive to a diner where he takes a spoon and goes into the men's room for a hit. He OD's. Christ, he went down so hard he hit the wall with his head and left some hair on the wall. The girl takes off. I investigate. It takes me five hours to locate the girl. I finally get her, in front of her parents, to agree to testify. She's not a user, she won't get in any trouble. I work up a warrant. It's a damn good warrant. All the facts have been corroborated . . . she identified the guy's car, I got his name from the license. He's a dealer with a record. Now I ask you, should that guy be a homicide? I tried to get Homicide in. No dice. My way of thinking, that guy's a homicide.

"That call I just got? What a lousy situation. A young guy. I know him. He's a user. He had this really beautiful girlfriend. He got her started, too. Then, he got locked up for a month. Now he's out and finds she ran off with two of South Philly's biggest dealers. What a beautiful kid. Seventeen. She looks like she should be on the cover of a magazine. In a year you won't even be able to recognize her. That's what meth does. What a lousy deal. . . . The hospitals don't help much. You can't even get in most of them with an OD. I have a friend in my neighborhood. His kid was on heroin. I know that kid since he was little, he's a good kid. One night, he's out cold on my doorstep. His father says what can we do? I said we'll take him to a hospital. We tried two hospitals. They wouldn't admit him. Said he'd be okay. I finally had to lock him up. My own friend's kid. He got him into Eagleville, but not until twenty-nine days later. It's an awful problem. It's getting worse."

Two Highway Patrolmen (the elite of Philadelphia's uniformed police) came in with a handcuffed prisoner, nattily dressed and replete with sunglasses. One of the officers dumped ten bags onto the counter, each wrapped neatly in foil.

"Please, sir, I found those. Man, I never deal dope. I never even been brought up on anything this big. I found those, *sir*."

"All right, I'll talk to you in a minute," Lefty said.

"But I found those, *sir*."

"I said I'd talk to you in a minute."

They searched him again, removed everything from his pockets and his sunglasses, and placed him in a small, empty, windowless room. They bolted the door. Dave and Lefty started typing forms. Dave made a phone call to check the prisoner's record. ("Damn liar. Five priors, one narcotics.") Then Dave did a field test on one of the bags. Lefty thought it was meth because of the way the bags were wrapped, but it turned the liquid pink—heroin. Lefty looked at it carefully and said it was heavily cut with talcum powder. The two patrolmen had to wait for headquarters to assign a case number. Altogether, between the forms and the wait, it took them an hour. Dave and Lefty, the two-fingered typists, were still typing when they left. Two more policemen came in with a younger man, not so well dressed and without a coat. His eyes were half closed and he walked hesitantly. Again the same procedure, and he was locked in the room with the other. One of the policemen told me the story, as Dave and Lefty started on the forms.

"I thought he was dead. You get to see plenty dead men on this job. He still had a strap on his arm, and his works were next to him. I thought we better call the medical examiner, but then I saw his neck vein start pumpin'. We took him to the hospital, and they gave him a shot of something."

"Has he got some other drug in him? Better call the hospital. If he has something in him besides skag, I can't make him for use, only possession."

They called. He had received 5 mg of Nalline to relieve the respiratory paralysis caused by the overdose. The tedious paperwork continued. It was 10:45. Dave and Lefty had been typing steadily since 9:30, and it would take them at least another half hour to finish if no one else was brought in. It was such a quiet night, they asked me to come back again. I was a good luck charm. I left them . . . typing.

All of this squad was married, most with young children of their own. They are concerned about drug abuse. They see its tragedy every day. Some get hard, most get cynical, but all care. When I first walked into the Operations Room I saw a squad of tough-looking, impersonal narcs. When I left, they were Joe and Ray and Lefty and Dave. They're people. Not the best, maybe, but not the worst either. They have a tough job in a tough part of the world, a sewer filled with dealers and pushers and junkies who will do anything for a bag of white powder. I wouldn't want their job.

Conclusions

If you have spotted some differences of opinion—or even some outright contradictions—you're right. About the only thing on which most experts agree is the severity of the problem and the urgency for effective drug education. It is, however, important to recognize that there are really *two* kinds of drug education competing for the attention of young people. One turns them on to drugs, the other attempts to turn them away from drugs.

In the first kind, the program consists of rock music, hip clothes, love, and an informal life style that is *now*. Its teachers are your best friends, and they have first-hand experience with drugs. Their technique is one of the best—peer pressure. In the second kind, the program takes place in an atmosphere of violence, poverty, racism, and pollution. It is taught in schools that are dull, repetitious, repressive, and *yesterday*. It is taught by teachers that have been poorly prepared to cope with this subject and by parents who are even less prepared . . . pill-popping, liquor-swishing, cigarette-smoking adults, most of whom find it necessary to dictate values, to moralize, and to criticize young people for practically everything. Their technique has been to deny the problem altogether or, in a state of near-panic, to over-saturate it in schools, homes, churches, on radio and TV, in newspapers and magazines. In a mad dash to generate programs, months of committee meetings have generated mountains of paper—mostly worthless, frequently contradictory, and almost always patterned after the same tired format that has already proved inadequate in math, history, and English. Is it any wonder then that the first kind of drug education is proving more effective than the second?

What can be done? For one thing, we could eliminate the duplication. There are so many federal, state, and local agencies, home and school associations, church and civic groups . . . in fact, there hardly seems to be a group of any kind that doesn't have or isn't working on its own "drug program." There is such an incredible overlapping of top-heavy, money-gorging bureaucracies that include among their myriad "responsibilities" that of preparing drug-abuse information . . . if we could just narrow that down to one well-structured and intelligently staffed (including young people at policy level) agency whose *only* responsibility would be to prepare and distribute multi-media resource information, we'd save millions.

We could talk fact instead of fantasy. Encourage honest individuality, not dishonest conformity. Learn, instead of teach. Listen as well as talk. And we could stop being so easily turned off by each other.

Drug education should provide information on the legal, medical, and social implications of drug use and abuse . . . and in terms which each of us can relate to on a personal level. Whether or not to use drugs is a decision each individual must ultimately make on his own. Drug education can only be effective if its aim is to help someone to make that decision. School is as good a place as we have to accomplish these goals, but it can only happen if administrators, teachers, students, and parents share equally and cooperatively in the process. To be effective, that sort of social action cannot be imposed from the top. It must be composed from the bottom. The bottom is the Community, but the Community is everyone or it is no one. Remember,

"If you are not part of the solution, you are part of the problem."

You can't expect the government to solve this one. Nor can you expect it to be solved with great advertising slogans like "Speed Kills," no matter how much exposure they get. No, this is a job you'll have to do yourself. Administrators are Bureaucrats—don't depend on them. The Home and School Association is a Paper Tiger —don't depend on it. Police are not Educators—don't depend on them. Legislators are Politicians—don't depend on them. Doctors are not Sociologists—don't depend on them. But use them all. Use every resource available. And that includes the kids. It's their generation that's on the line. They must have a share in saving it.

If you still think it can't happen to you, talk to Lucille Ferriola.

[January 1971]

The Perils of Parity: Part IV

Report of the Ad Hoc Committee to Develop Practical Alternatives to the Gloriously Impractical Pay-What-It's-Worth Subscription Plan

Sir:

At the request of a Dissident Group of Nonpaying Subscribers, an Ad Hoc Committee was formed for the purpose of developing less equitable but more practical means of subscribing to your publication than the current Pay-What-It's-Worth Plan and its recently revised version which includes the Pay-What-You-Can alternative. Listed below are the Committee's demands including that of a Minority

Report submitted by your mother. It should be added that in view of your tenacious optimism and as a concession to the small but growing list of subscribers actually participating, it has been agreed by a vote of the Committee that you may be allowed to retain your present subscription plan in addition to the new alternatives. The vote was 5-4 with one vote abstaining. (Your mother.)

Respectfully submitted,

The Gnome of Zurich
Chairman

Majority Demands:

1. The Pay-What-It's-Worth Subscription. After receipt of each issue subscribers will forward such payment as they deem the issue worth, with no minimum or maximum stipulated.

2. The Break-Even Subscription. Assuming approximately six to eight issues annually, subscribers will forward check or money order for $8.00 in advance and will be notified of the annual renewal date.

3. The Modest-Profit Subscription. Again assuming approximately six to eight issues annually, subscribers will forward check or money order for $15.00 in advance and will be notified of the annual renewal dates.

4. The Investor's-Special Subscription. A special category subscription will be created for high-risk investors who wish to remit larger sums in an effort to increase the size and the profitability of the publication. These courageous individuals will forward whatever amount they wish. The sum of $15.00 will be deducted from the amount to cover the annual subscription. The remainder may be used for subscription advertising.

Minority Demand:

1. The Exorbitant-Profit Subscription. You people have a lot of nerve. My boy works very hard on this little paper or whatever it is and I think you should pay him a hundred dollars in advance for an annual subscription. Make it more if you can. He's a good boy.

(Editor's Note: I reluctantly accede to all demands. But I think you are all bananas! Not you, Mom.)

The Mitwelt Bridge

Let us talk about kids. Kids and adults and how they get along or don't and why. When do you stop being one and become the other? Sometimes you wish you never had. We all wanted to grow up faster until we did. Fritz Perls said that most adults aren't mature. They just play the role. At the rate some of our kids are dropping out, some of us role-players better do some fast maturing.

Fritz Perls was together. He originated Gestalt Therapy at Esalen. Perls said that there is a common world between you and the other person—language, attitude, behavior, something—and that in this overlapping area of the two worlds communication is possible. He was very together. He called this area of common interest the Mitwelt. Could the Mitwelt between adults and kids be our mutual experience as kids? We seem to have forgotten. We liked being sloppy, why shouldn't our kids? We liked to stay up late, why shouldn't our kids? We liked to pick our own friends, why shouldn't our kids? We liked to win an argument, why shouldn't our kids? We said we'd be different from our parents when we grew up. Why aren't we?

Four kids and I sit in the room and talk about it. Eleven. Televisioned. Cool. Perceptive. What do you like about being kids and what don't you like? *We're kids, but we're people too.* Okay, what don't you like? *School. Arguments with adults 'cause you're always wrong and they're always right. Restrictions. GP should be G, R should be GP, X should be R. Curfew. What difference does it make how late I stay up on a weekend, I don't tell them how late to stay up! They always tell us not to compare them with other parents, but they always compare us with other kids. And we're never good enough.*

But most of your parents were kids once, weren't they? *Not like us. They didn't grow up like us. They had to walk eight miles to school.*

They got straight A's, they studied piano for nine years. (Sarcasm.)
Kids today can say I'll get back at my mother, I'll go on heroin and
that's gonna hurt my parents a lot. Kids are different today.
Lots of parents get mad at something and they take it out on their
kids. Is it possible for kids and adults to be friends? *It's not*
impossible, but it's hard. Most kids wouldn't want their parents for
friends.

When two kids get angry with each other, what do they do? *We*
always make up. We hardly ever get into fights with each other, but
when we do we have to make up because we don't have that many
friends. When times are good between you and your parents, what
makes them good? *No fights. When my mom's not in a bad mood. Yeah.*
Were there ever times when you were angry with an adult even when
you knew you were wrong? *Yeah, well you don't wanna give in, you*
don't wanna admit you were wrong. Do kids and adults have the same
faults then? *Yeah, I guess so.* Are there times when you get really
angry with your parents? *Yes. Yes. Yes. Yes.* What do you do about
that? *Go to my room. Avoid them.* Can't you talk about it? *They're*
always right and you're always wrong, no matter what. And they can
overrule you.

They can overrule you. That's it, isn't it? Catch 22. We can overrule
them. It's always they that need permission. We make compromises,
they get compromised. They ask, we give. Or withhold. We reward our
values, punish theirs. We feed our ego, starve theirs. We expect
them to understand what we never did at their age, and we can't
understand what our parents couldn't at ours. We force them to grow
up, but we complain when they do. With one hand we bestow upon
them the cares of the world, while with the other we slap them down
to wait their turn. And we impose upon them a system that doesn't
work, because they don't have a better one.

Ah, but it's not a one-way street, is it? Sleepless nights and
anguished dreams. Guilt when we don't control ourselves and shame
when we control them. And they're pretty smart, the little bastards.
They know where it hurts. They can make your blood hot or your bed
cold with a few choice words in the right place. They'll make a
federal case out of nothing, or nothing out of something. They laugh
or cry with equanimity. They scare the hell out of you with the

*trouble they can get into, and then tell you you just don't understand
so forget it. There's more than genes between you.*

*What's the answer? To remain in enemy camps? Are we committed
irrevocably to our respective roles? It's complicated, admit it. Don't
make the mistake of thinking it a simple problem. Neurosis is ageless
and hypocrisy works both sides of the street. Still, the rulebook sets no
age for maturity. Nine. Thirteen. Eighteen. Twenty-one. Sixty-five.
Each is an arbitrary selection for an abstract concept. We really can be
friends if we want to. It's in the Mitwelt.*

Perls Pearls

What you were
  you are not.
What you would be
  you will not.
What you are
  you cannot.

. . . unless you see.

Satori.

THE BOARD OF
UBLIC EDUCATION

The Alternative to Public School Is Public School

Some Thoughts on Public School

I'd trade ten Idealists for one Pragmatist. Read less Holt and more Alinsky. (I think John would agree.)

The frustrated teachers who opt for a "more liberal environment" aren't Drop Outs, they're Cop Outs. They care more for their own freedom than for that of the public-school kids they desert. Nobody said it was easy.

Free Schoolers escape to marvelously egalitarian learning experiences with a handful of kids. They frolic in old Victorian houses and organic-growing communes, while forty-nine million just as delightful kids are trapped in public school with no escape. The rationale of the Free Schoolers sounds like the Pentagon explaining the withdrawal from Laos.

Elitism has fallen into disrepute, but a teacher is by condition an elitist. Give me a good teacher and spare me the rhetoric.

If the energy spent developing alternatives were devoted to organizing the community for change, there might be no need for alternatives.

Making the system work for the people is a lot of work for the people. Ask Ellen Lurie. (And read her book.)

Learning can happen anywhere to anyone. Education is simply organized learning. If that is "structure," so what?

Dewey, Piaget, Montessori, Neill. They are guides, not gurus. We have become cultists, and we use children for *our* ends not theirs.

I don't want education to come between me and my children.

The most important goal of a parent should be to help children to love, of a teacher to help children to learn. Sometimes each thinks he has the other's job.

The teacher dropout rate is rising. So is the rate of student dropout. Do you suppose there is a connection?

Teacher dropouts are finding somewhere else to teach. Free Schools, Alternative Schools, Communes. Student dropouts are finding somewhere else to learn, too. Jails, Detention Centers, Methadone Stations.

If some New Schoolers have their way, there will be a whole generation of yogis, macramé-ers, and organic farmers. How will that clean up the Ghetto or the Pentagon?

At a town meeting the local school board president lists, as one of the top priorities of the district, a program for gifted children. Ask her which is the greater gift, verbal or manual skill? Ask her how shall we determine this gift, with the Iowa Tests? Ask her when her car breaks down which is the more gifted, the mathematician or the mechanic? Ask yourself why no one puts her out of office.

You say the schools have not been responsive to the needs of the students? Hell, neither have we! We've been too busy blaming the schools.

Don't start new schools. Subvert old ones.

Don't save the world, save a kid. Maybe he'll save the world.

We have been suckered again. Bussing isn't Education, it's Politics! If we were all the same color and all the same class, we'd still have a sick and irrelevant educational system. The same hacks sell the same snake oil every time they come to town. And we buy it.

It is no longer a question of whether or not the public school is worth saving. There is no alternative, without sacrificing a whole generation. Will you accept *that* responsibility?

Eliminate grade levels. Eliminate standardized achievement tests. Eliminate marks, substitute credit / no credit and written evaluations. Eliminate tracking. Encourage independent study and cooperative projects. Institute a flexible and relevant curriculum selected by a committee of parents, teachers, and students. Eliminate tenure, but not teachers' contracts. Pay them well but set up reasonable standards for evaluation by and accountability to a Standards and Practices Committee of parents, teachers, and students. Utilize the community's facilities and its people. Create an elected Community School Board of parents, teachers, and students with equal voice and vote on all educational activities within the community. Set equal priorities for the education of non-college-bound and college-bound students. A public school belongs to the public. It should be used like the public library. By *all* the people that want to, not just those who are forced by law to attend. If the right changes are made, there will be no more need for compulsory education than there is for compulsory military service. That is the "System" I would like for my children. It can be called New School, Free School, or Community School. But it can just as easily be called Public School. The rest is politics.

We have given up too easily.

TWO POINTS OF VIEW

Dear my,

I think it makes a certain amount of sense to spend some time and energy in trying to reform the public schools, but that is much too small and leaky a basket for me to put all my eggs in. The fact—at least it looks to me like a fact—is that the chances of getting very much done there is slight. There is simply not the human material to work with. So we're fooling ourselves about the kind of people who are in teaching—sure there are a certain number of very good ones, but they're a minority and I now think a very small one in the business. I went to speak at a local teaching training college, and I wish you could have been there with us. It was an extraordinarily revealing and depressing experience to spend a day with a lot of the people and the kind of people who make up the bulk of our teaching profession. The overwhelming impression was of people from whom had been squeezed every last drop of vitality or imagination or joy. What struck me about these twenty-year-olds, as I saw them all around me in the dining room, was how gray their faces were. They were absolutely without color. Lifeless. And in one room we saw an exhibit of materials these teachers-to-be had prepared, to show the kinds of things they might later make with their classes to illustrate various points. Most of these had to do with medieval history, and were models of one kind or another of castles. I was in there with my Associate, Paul Curtis, and he quite sensibly asked if school children themselves had made these. They would have been fairly impressive work for first or second graders, rather ordinary work for third or maybe fourth graders, and decidedly below par work for fifth graders. But these had been done by the students at this university.

my, as the saying goes, you can't make a silk purse out of a sow's ear, you can't get blood out of a turnip. Or, in Latin, *Nemo dat quod non habit*—nobody can give what he hasn't got. There's no sense in asking these poor people to be the kinds of creative or imaginative teachers that we are looking for. It would take a ten- or fifteen-year job of rehabilitation to restore to these people what they've lost—and this under very much more fortunate circumstances than any of them will ever see. It is really foolish to expect very much from these kinds of people. I would add, too, that one of the teachers at the institution, a very nice and lively guy, one of a small handful there who are trying to do a few things, said to me that very considerable numbers of his students tell him, after completing their student teaching, that they find they don't like teaching and really strongly dislike children, but that having spent this much time in their schooling they really can't afford to throw it away and do something different, so they're going to go ahead and be teachers anyway. I do not think that such examples are exceptional.

No, what we have to do, while working with whatever teachers of humanity and ability we can find in the public schools, is at the same time work in as many ways as possible to get children out from under these institutions and these people. We have to drill some holes in the prison walls, make it possible for as many as can to escape. And foolish, too, to say that if all cannot escape none should be able to. Any breach we make in the walls of this really quite remarkably inhumane institution is bound to widen.

Peace,
John Holt

Dear John—

Your letter was welcome and, as usual, thought provoking. Doesn't it come down to this, John? There just aren't enough people who really care about kids. (Even most kids don't care about kids.) If those who do spend their juices on alternatives to public school for the few who will make it through your "breach," what happens to the millions who remain trapped in the system? Conversely, if the same effort could be devoted to subverting the public school system from within—a system already having public support, funding, and facilities—how many more Parkway Schools might there be?

What you suggest—working at both—could be a dangerous dissipation of what little strength is available to do battle with Status Quo. Divided we fail . . . and Skinner wins. I am reluctant to accept that alternative.

Power.

my

THE PARKWAY PROGRAM

The official bibliography runs three pages and only covers about half the articles written. *Time* called it the most interesting high school in the U.S. *Reader's Digest* called it a bold new direction. It's the school without walls, the one where kids wear long hair and smoke and call teachers by their first names and say fuck in class. It studies insurance in an insurance company, art in a museum, home economics in the electric company, economics in a bank, auto mechanics in a garage. There are no grade levels, no marks. Classes meet all over town. Students walk, ride bikes, or thumb to class. The only bussing is the public kind that takes a token. Most important, it is an accredited public high school in the School District of Philadelphia.

This is a look at Gamma Community, one of the four independent units of the Parkway Program. Gamma has its own administration, its own curriculum, and its own headquarters—a run-down three-floor storefront at 16 North Front Street near the waterfront docks of Philadelphia. Gamma is limited to two hundred students drawn by lottery from all eight school districts plus occasionally, very occasionally, from the suburbs. In addition to standard state-required subjects, students choose from a wide variety of electives. A sample: Science for Those Who Hate Science . . . Uptight about Math . . . Paleontology and Fossils (Temple University) . . . Construction Methods and Ma-

terials (City Water Department) . . . Amateur and Commercial Radio (a ham operator) . . . Nutrition (a food-store manager) . . . Growing Old In America (a University of Pennsylvania clinical nurse) . . . Contemporary Black Artists (the Philadelphia Museum).

Parkway began in February 1969 on a planning grant from the Ford Foundation, which has maintained a financial interest although the program is now operated by Philadelphia public-school funds. John Bremer, the British educator who served as Parkway's first Director and chief architect, is no longer Director. Mark Shedd, the Harvard-educated Superintendent who helped push the program through its early stages, is no longer Superintendent. Richardson Dilworth, Philadelphia's former Mayor and leading liberal who served as President of the School Board and did battle with city administration over the program, is no longer President of the School Board. Frank Rizzo, Philadelphia's ex-Police Commissioner and now Mayor, fired Shedd, installed a new School Board President, replaced several liberal School Board members with those more in tune with his policies, appointed a new Superintendent of Public Schools thought to be in sympathy with Rizzo's educational philosophies (though time may prove otherwise). Mayor Rizzo is on record as being opposed to "permissiveness." Parkway is permissive . . . and scared to death.

Parkway has its faults. The theory that students should be responsible for their own education works only when they accept that responsibility. Most do not. Many students flounder when taken from a structured situation to one which is highly unstructured. There is no provision for them. Teachers are ill prepared for this, the most demanding type of teaching—not teaching. Selection procedures for students and for teachers are poor. Parents are badly informed or don't care. Ideological anarchy has bewildered the students and politics has frightened the staff. But it's working. In its own peculiar and awkward way . . . it's working. Kids *are* learning. The atmosphere *is* less competitive and less repressive. School—public school—*can* be exciting.

Parkway's future, now more than ever, is important. Not only to Philadelphia, but to anyone who has a stake in whether or not the American public educational system makes it. That includes 49,-000,000 students trapped in lousy public schools. And you.

Leonard Finkelstein

The administrative offices of Parkway consist of a few desks and cubbyhole offices in a borrowed corner of the Franklin Institute's basement. Taking off his ski parka as we talk, he ushers me into his tiny office. Parkway's second Director is short and stocky with a round friendly face. Mid. forties.

"When Parkway started, interest was very high. Cliff Brenner—do you know Cliff?—had terrific ideas. Really great. Then they brought in John Bremer. From there it went straight downhill. Bremer had a great sense of public relations. He could make everything sound perfect, but there was a big gap between what he said was happening and what was really happening. I've been in the Philadelphia public-school system for twenty-two years. I was a teacher and an administrator and the in-house Nut. They called me in and said Len, see what you can do to solve some of the problems and save this thing. And that's what I've been doing.

"We try to get out to the schools to talk about Parkway, to tell the students what to expect, but it's almost impossible to describe what Parkway is. We have a good cross-section of the city in three of our units. Delta, the new one in Germantown, is more heavily neighborhood. We hear that some teachers are 'volunteering' the kids they can't do anything with—put his name in the lottery without his knowing it. We only have about six or seven Puerto Rican kids. I tried to find out why, so we talked to some parents. They said school is where you sit down at a desk and someone teaches you, that's a school, not where you wander all over town. I don't know how to deal with that attitude.

"Parkway has an image, but it's a different image with different people. Some feel, oh, that's the school for bright students. Others say it's the school for hippies. Or it's the school for tough black kids who can't make it in a regular school. Funny thing is, it's all of those.

"One of our problems is visitors. We have been swamped with visitors who want to come and observe. Everybody wants to start a Parkway. From all over the country. BBC has us as a course in their University of the Air. The UN. Other school districts. Writers and newspaper people. They come here for a day and go back to write about us. You can't do that. You have to live with us to understand what is happening here. But there's just not enough time. We live in a

[149]

fishbowl. And we're flattered by all the attention, but we're harassed by it too.

"We have eight hundred kids, four units of two hundred each. Last night at La Salle they said that's terrible, you should have twenty thousand. Well I'd like that and there's no reason we can't. We could have Alpha, Beta, Gamma, Delta, Tau, Theta, Zeta . . . we could set up units of two hundred all over town. We could set up a Performing Arts Unit, a Senior Citizens Unit. There are loads of models—twenty to be exact—that I have. But first we have to make sure that the ones we have are working.

"How do we do that? Well, first by observing classes. Is it happening there the way it should? And by how the kids are reacting. Are they getting something out of it? For some there's been a complete turn-around in their lives. It's been the greatest thing that could have happened to them. For others it's a complete bust. We are developing some qualitative measures in addition to the subjective ones. But we have to be careful. There's resistance to structure. Like the Town Meeting. That's a disaster. It just doesn't work very well. I know what I want, I know what will work. But I can't just push it in. I have to explain it and get them to understand. I just can't direct it.

"The attitude of the School Board is different for every member. To some, it's the answer to all our educational problems. To some, it's where we send those that can't make it anywhere else. It's not just a narrow experiment that can't grow. We're growing. But the Philadelphia Public School System will never be one big Parkway Program. I'm not so sure I would want to see that anyway. But we have a lot of schools that say this . . . Look, Len, we know you can only take so many students. Show us how to make a Parkway right here in our school. . . . What would you do, would you do that or would you try to set up another unit or would you tell them to send their kids out? It's a tough problem."

Anne McNulty

Administrative Assistant of Gamma Community at 16 North Front Street on a cold but sunny day. Students and teachers moving in and out. No classes here, a zoning restriction. It is most times difficult to tell which is teacher and which is student. Students look old, staff look young, and all dress alike. Except the staff is white and half the students are black. Anne. Pleasant but serious. Forties or so. Short graying hair, a tired face, and a soft little girl's voice. Her husband is a curator of the Philadelphia Museum and her daughter was a Parkway senior in its first year.

"I had been to some of the meetings, heard John Bremer speak. He was a wonderful salesman, very charismatic. But I wasn't really involved. Originally there were supposed to be four quarters with the summer quarter being optional, but the School Board said there was no money. Some of the parents said that wasn't right and said they would find a way to do it. One called me and I said fine I agree, I'll give twenty-five dollars. She said that wasn't exactly what she had in mind, would I make some phone calls. Well I made a lot of calls and raised quite a bit.

"After that they used to call me when they needed some help. When Len became Director he said, Anne, why don't you join the program? So they made me Parent-Community Liaison. Then Gamma's Administrative Assistant became Head. And here I am.

"John was a great salesman, marvelous at p.r. But he couldn't stand red tape. If he had an idea, he would just do it and then tell everybody afterwards. And he wouldn't let anyone else do anything. I don't think we could have gone much further with John here. Len hasn't the personality of John Bremer, but he knows how to get things done in the System. I think each man was needed.

"There's just too goddamn much to do and not enough people to do it. Kids don't always accept the obligations they take on at Parkway. This is not a school that everybody can handle. It couldn't work for an entire district. Some kids go overboard and schedule one class on one side of town and another clear across town with no time to get there. Some kids think this is a great place to goof off—do nothing and get credit and graduate. They find out otherwise. Some teachers use us as a great way to get rid of trouble-makers. They make out multiple applications for one kid. A lot of parents are scared to death for their kid's safety in his school. Will he get knifed? Will he live through the day? So they want their kids to come here because it's safe. No gangs, no knives, no guns. Funny, some of these gang kids really turn around here. I would say about half of our kids are here because they're interested in Parkway as a learning place."

Larry Ellis

Larry Ellis's tenth-grade geometry class meets in a closed-off section of the lobby of the new modern Rohm and Haas Building. Wood panels, thick carpets, towering high sculptured ceilings, glass outer walls. In one corner, long tables are arranged in a square with students around three sides facing Ellis and a blackboard. There are sixteen students. Five are white. Long hair, afros, hooped ears, ringed fingers, cigarettes, coffee, and half-eaten Danish. Three girls play 500 Rummy for the whole period. Ellis is demonstrating that corresponding parts of a congruent triangle are equal.

For the most part the class is attentive. The atmosphere is easy and relaxed. There is a steady click from the gum chewers with an occasional loud *pop* as one of the girls gets a good air pocket worked into her gum. Ellis. Twenty-nine. Tall, long sandy hair, mustache, drawl, dungarees, and a work shirt rolled up to the elbows. He is reviewing material for a test.

Ellis: "Wilson, evry tahm ah ask you if you understand, you say yes. Until the test. Any questions?"

Wilson: "She don't unnerstand, but she won't say nothin'."

Ellis: "Renee, what don't you understand? None of it? Who can explain it to Renee?"

Nobody does, but they go on. Ellis demonstrates with a practical application calling for the measurement of a river wider than the tape-measure available. "What would I wanna measure a river for? That's

not a *practical* application!" . . . "Who wants to know how wide the river is anyway?" . . . "Larry, why not just get a bigger tape measure?" . . . "But, Larry, why would I want to measure the distance?" . . . ("To build a bridge, maybe.") . . . "But, Larry, why would I wanna build a bridge?" The heckling is good natured. They get the point.

After the class, I talk to the three girls who were playing cards. They're still playing. They have an hour before their tutorial in the same room. Tutorial is two hours, twice a week. Approximately sixteen students, a teacher, and an intern. Sort of a "homeroom," but primarily intended to cover basic skills.

Paula: "Ask me some questions. I know all about Parkway. It's a terrific school! Whatayamean, ya got no questions? You're the first visitor we ever had, got no questions! Hey, Bob, what the fuck—oh, pardon my French—whataya doin'?"

Bob: "Whataya wanna talk to her for?"

Paula: "Hey, watch your mouth! Sure this is a great school. Where else can you call the teacher by his first name? Where else would a teacher be dressed like that? Where else could you talk the way you wanna? Sure this is a great school."

my: "Is that what makes education?"

Bob: "Well that means a lot. It's a better atmosphere when it's relaxed like this. It makes the relationship better between students and teachers."

my: "If you didn't have to go to school, would you?"

Card Player: "Not me, man. You're damn right ah wouldn't!"

Paula: "Sure I would. I wanna get ahead in life."

Bob: "I know I would 'cause I want to go to college."

Later, I talk with Larry Ellis in his unheated third-floor office at 16 North Front Street.

"I come from Shelbyville, Kentucky. Went to college at Berea. It's a small liberal-arts school with about fourteen hundred students. There's no tuition, Berea has a sixty-million-dollar endowment. I was kicked out in my second year because I got married. It's really a strange school. It was intended as biracial and at one time it was about fifty per cent black. Now it's about ten per cent.

"I went to Wisconsin for a year and then came back to Berea for my last year. The year at Wisconsin was sort of penance, ah guess. I took my Ph.D. in chemistry at Stanford. Then ah did a couple years of post-graduate work in Zurich. I came back to Berea to teach. It was a mistake. I thought ah could accomplish somethin', but ah couldn't. There's a lot of bleedin' heart liberals down theah, but they don't really do much.

"Berea had great p.r. on how they helped these poor Appalachian kids. But ah did a study on how many graduates continued to live in Appalachia after graduation. Only thirty-five per cent stayed. Then some of us tried to get the percentage of blacks upped to twenty per cent, but we lost by a wide margin. That's when ah recognized ah had changed a lot more than the school in the last few years, and ah left.

"I was out of work for five months. Nobody wanted Ph.D.'s. I went to Columbus, Ohio, and tried to get work but no one was hirin' Ph.D.'s in organic chemistry. I even tried Civil Service, but the government put out a notice that after November first they were no longer hirin' physical scientists. That blew mah mind! If the federal government wasn't hirin' physical scientists, who was? I had a job lined up in a free school, but then mah wife and I separated and ah needed the bread to send to her. I knew Dick Hiler. He was down here and he let me know they had an opening for a math teacher. So ah applied. I started here in January.

"I don't really enjoy the kind of teachin' ah'm doin' in geometry. The problem is that the class is there because they have to be, because it's a state requirement. That puts me in an adversary role which ah don't like. Sometimes ah have to be a disciplinarian. I don't like that. In the spring we'll build a yurk. That's good because it'll be outdoors and they get to do something. Whenever it seems right, ah'll inject geometry, but it'll be practical. I've never read much on education. I just do what seems intuitively right.

"Most of the kids here don't know what the Parkway Program is. A few really make it, but most of them flounder."

Bob

Here's Bob, the boy from Larry Ellis's geometry class, walking up Market Street. We walk together toward his next class. Fifteen. Long hair, good-looking but still suffering from acne. This is his first year at Parkway.

"I really love this program. I was a rebel in my old school. I dunno why, but it always seemed a challenge to rebel against the teachers. I never did what they wanted. It's different here. In my other school you just had to look at them to know they didn't like it. Here the teachers are really dedicated. And they like it. That's why I said that about the atmosphere. They're more human here.

"I still have a tough time getting used to it. I mean, it's all up to me. I have one class, kind of a creative writing class. Nobody knows what it's all about. It really depresses me, that class. But maybe it's not me, maybe the class is just a bummer. The guy's a writer and he just can't teach.

"I don't mind the movin' around. I hitch mostly, but the weather hasn't really bothered me. My father died, so there's just my mother. She doesn't get involved in my school. But that's the way I like her to be in everything I do. There's no gang stuff here at Parkway. I don't think I even heard of a fight. Oh yeah, there was one I heard about. But no real gang stuff. And there's no more drugs than any other school. Probably less. More goes on in the locker rooms or lavoratories in the average school.

"I don't like geometry much. Larry's a good teacher. I have the feeling he doesn't like what he's doing, teaching geometry. I mean, what can I do with geometry? There's a lot in school I don't think I'll ever need. And I think there's a lot of learning that goes on outside of school. But I'd never have the guts to just go off and do my learning out of school. Did you benefit from your education?"

Dick Hiler

Dick Hiler's tutorial meets in the closed-off Skyline Lounge of the Penn Mutual Insurance Building at Sixth and Walnut. At noon. Eighteen floors up by elevator and another on foot. Fourteen students, the last few straggling in ten minutes late. And a young bearded visitor with a banjo who is "visiting alternative schools around the country." And Dick Hiler. Mid-forties. Balding, glasses, thin, quiet. The group is about even in both color and sex. Some are eating lunch. Hiler starts the meeting with an announcement of a parents' meeting on the 28th. "You can come if you want. You may want to check with your parents. Sometimes they prefer that you aren't there so they can ask questions they might not ask if you were there."

[1 5 6]

Girl: "I think we ought to come. That would show them. Do you understand what I mean, Dick?"

Dick: "No."

Girl: "Well, it would . . . like . . . I think . . . well . . . it would show 'em we . . . care."

Other Girl: "My mother and father won't come. I mean, if they won't go to a funeral together, you *know* they won't come to this."

Dick: "Would your mother come?"

Other Girl: "Maybe she would."

Next, a girl suggests that the tutorial go to a Chinese restaurant for lunch. A vote is taken. Three boys opposed. One girl will get a menu in advance to be studied by the group. A boy who works in a Chinese restaurant will bring in a report explaining each of the dishes. The girls will bake cookies and sell them at the Friday staff meeting. There is only thirty dollars in the tutorial treasury. Dick complains that the group is not coming forward with many ideas, that since no one is really working on new ideas he will have to impose some. There is no argument.

For the next half hour, Dick announces: a math test, a book report, a current-events verbal report, would the tutorial favor a speaker from Vietnam Veterans Against the War? (they would), swimming in the Jefferson Medical School pool, would they like to visit Community College? (they would), a poetry reading group and a sensitivity group both to be led by one of the tutorial's girls but—she says—only if they're "really serious," a discussion on Woman's Role in Society, a learn-to-play-chess group. One girl suggests a discussion on Segregation vs. Bussing. Dick wants their logs tomorrow. "It is Gamma policy. No student log, no credit for tutorial." Groans. Math papers are handed out and they begin working on fractions.

The atmosphere is relaxed and informal. Dick is quiet but firm. He commands attention and, it seems, respect. He makes a great effort to get students to participate and sits quietly whenever they talk. The girls participate more than the boys. There is, however, little enthusiasm from anyone.

Later, at 16 North Front Street, I talk with Dick Hiler. His background is "a long one." Several years teaching in public school after Ohio Wesleyan and a master's degree. Friends World College as Director of Admissions, where he "worked my tail off trying to do the impossible. They wanted Staughton Lynd and me to head up the North American Center, but when Staughton got there and saw what it was like, he left." West Africa for a year and a half in a "sort of Peace Corps." Three years with the American Friends Service Committee in Philadelphia conducting social-consciousness seminars. "But I only got those kids for three days. They'd get all inspired for three days, then go back home. It wasn't enough." Then the same in Pittsburgh.

"I started running ten-week tours to Europe and the Soviet Union. That was a little better. At least I had them for ten weeks. But that still wasn't enough. I wanted to be in a position to influence children's lives. I've moved around a lot. I guess I've been looking for the right place. I want to help children gain self-esteem, to believe in themselves. That's more important than cramming a lot of facts into their heads.

"I finally started a school up in Maine, but we weren't near resources, so we went to New Hampshire. We built some yurks on someone else's land again, as we had done in Maine. We had sixteen kids and it was really a wonderful year. But I ran out of money. It happens." He came to Parkway in September, the result of a friend's recommendation. "I wouldn't have traded that year with those sixteen kids for anything. I don't think I could be nearly as effective now without the complete freedom of that year. It takes that kind of freedom to experiment, to work out the ways.

"I don't think most of the staff knows what the Parkway Program is. They think calling a teacher by the first name and dressing relaxed and moving around to different places is the program. And they think it's great. I'm concerned that the kids don't accept the responsibility for their education here."

Parents' Meeting

Dick Hiler's tutorial originally had eighteen students. Two dropped. Two are in Mexico with five other students and two teaching interns, attending Ivan Illich's CIDOC in Cuernavaca. (The cost of $450 each was paid by four. One called Rohm and Haas and talked them into paying. Four have yet to pay back the staff who put up the rest.) Five parents representing four students show up at the meeting. Two students accompany their parents. The meeting is held at the bachelor apartment of Paul Biracalillo, a teaching intern in his last semester at the Pennsylvania Music Academy. The meeting is called for 7:30 p.m. Parents begin to arrive about 8, the last at 9:30. The meeting breaks at 10.

Debbie's Mother: [*Debbie is with her mother. She seems shy but talks a lot. She has a younger sister, twelve. Debbie just started Parkway in the second quarter.*] "When Debbie said she wanna go to Parkway, my friends tol' me at Parkway everybody jus' run around town from one place to the other. My husband say don't look at me, it's your decision, you sweat it out. Debbie says she really likes it. I figure that's somethin' to worry about. If Debbie says she really likes it, she must be doin' somethin' wrong. I never know where she is or whether she's in class or not. At least before she was in a building and I knew where to find her.

"I was gonna take her out of Parkway, but she likes it so much, and she seems to be learnin' somethin', so I guess I'll sweat it out a little longer. But she loves school so much, there *must* be too much freedom!"

Steven's Mother: [*Mother serious and articulate, father a bit nervous but covers with an ever-present smile. Steven is not with them. He likes Parkway, but will transfer to Overbrook, a traditional high school, because he is interested in sports. Parkway has no interscholastic sports, and no provision has been made with the other high schools in Philadelphia for Parkway student participation.*] "Steven was always babyish and immature on one side, suckin' his thumb and all, but mature on the other side. He was startin' to come out of that, but Parkway brought him all the way out. Parkway's been very good for him. But he doesn't tell me very much about what goes on."

Steven's Father [*smiling*]: "What does it be, his first class? He jus' travels around and ah don' even know where or when his classes are. Ah think they got too much time on their hands, even in the regular schools. And the kids got a different attitude towards the teachers, and the teachers got different feelin's too than when ah went to school. Ah don' mean you should discipline them too much, but ah don' think the teachers complain enuff when they don' get respect.

"The police picked up Steve with another boy, goin' to class. Ah didn't even know 'bout it till afterward or ah'd of protested. He wanted to call y'all at the school but they said he could only have one call so he called Her. Ah think the police do a good job but they'd be better off

goin' after somebody else 'stead of workin' on the kids like that."
Hiler explains that the school Director fired off a sharp letter to the
police on the incident and now all students have an ID card with them
because the word is out among other schools' truants, who tell the
police that they are attending Parkway.

Next to arrive are Karen and her mother. Karen is a senior. She has
been working for the Pennsylvania Horticultural Society at the Civic
Center in preparation for the annual flower show. White. Middle class.
Friendly, but they do not participate much in the meeting. The subject gets around to whether or not it's a good time to be young.

Steven's Father [*smiling*]: "Ah thinks this is a great time to be
growin' up. So many things goin' on. The kids learn so much more than
we did. They do so much more."

Debbie's Mother: "But it's a terrible time to be growin' up! It's not
safe. Did you hafta worry about your life when you was goin' to
school? These gangs with knives and guns, I'm afraid to walk to the
store. I don't know whether to be more afraid of the adults or the
kids. If you see a bunch of kids on the sidewalk, do you know whether
to talk to them or run?"

Steven's Father [*smiling*]: "Oh, ah'm not afraid to walk the streets.
Ah'm not afraid of that!"

Steven's Mother: "He's not afraid to walk the streets 'cause he
never *walks* anywhere. But I do and I'm afraid. Most of my kids are
out workin'. It's a sad thing to say, but I can't wait till the last two
are out of school and workin'."

Steven's Father [*smiling*]: "Well, ah still say it's a great time. Not
all kids is like that. But ah don' mind tellin' you ah was against
Parkway at first. Ah tol' Her, ah said what's the matter with you?
There's a school you can see from the house! Ah made a lot of trouble,
but now mah mind's different. Ah think Parkway is a good place for
Steven. Maybe you'll have sports after all."

Hiler begins to discuss the tutorial. It is not functioning well as a
unit because there is considerable racial tension in the group. Steven's
mother asks if there has been anything done to improve these ten-
sions. Karen explains that the ones responsible don't really care. Once,
in Dick's absence, a teaching intern tried to get a sensitivity session
going and it was a disaster. Hiler says that some of the blacks hate
whites and look at them as people who hold black people down, and

there are some white students who can't understand what being black is all about. He hopes for another camping trip where they can all get to know each other better. He is quite obviously frustrated by his failure to affect the situation.

Blake's mother arrives. Black. Middle-aged. Tired. She is Gamma's parent representative on the committee working with the outside firm which is currently evaluating Parkway. She has just come from another meeting. The discussion turns to the fact that there is only one black staff member, Ida Davis, and that perhaps that is the reason for some of the racial tension. Two more were about to be hired, but Gamma got caught in the Presidential wage freeze, and by the time it was over they had taken other jobs.

Hiler: "It is difficult to find black teachers for Parkway. First, because good young men are in demand in industry. Second, because many good black teachers don't believe in a Parkway-type program for black students. They feel that black students should have a more rigid structure with greater emphasis on basics, so they can get a job when they get out of high school."

Blake's Mother: "I think the best thing about Parkway is its diversity. And the absence of classroom ritual."

Hiler: "I think Parkway goes a long way toward giving students a sense of self-esteem. They are learning that we are more competent than we think we are."

Karen's Mother: "I think the experience has been well worth sacrificing the sciences."

Karen: "The science courses are really lousy."

Steven's Father [*smiling*]: "Is the meeting over? Well, ah really enjoyed the meeting. Ah hope you'll ask me again."

Jim Keen

Tall, lanky, soft dark hair, a full turn-down mustache, long brown leather coat. Late twenties. He is eating an apple for breakfast. He gives me one and we go out for coffee. He drinks tea with milk.

"I went to Haverford College. I was going to go on to law school. I had a Congressional internship lined up for the summer, but I got interested in urban education. I come from Harrisburg. I went through high school in Harrisburg, and after that anyone could get interested in bettering education. I was a political-science major but I was always interested in music, so in my senior year I took practically all music courses. When I graduated, I had a major in political science and in music."

Keen worked for the Administration in the Philadelphia Public School System, principally under Rick de Lone, Shedd, Bremmer, and Finkelstein. "I think the image that most people have that John was a dreamer is unfair. There would be no Parkway Program if he hadn't been here. But you know, when John came he said that he would only be here a short while. I think he knew he would have to step on a lot of toes.

"You can't keep politics out of public schools. At Parkway it was a very simple situation. Shedd was in great shape. He had gotten a lot of publicity nationally. If a Democratic administration came into Washington in a couple of years, he probably could have been Commissioner of Education. Suddenly this eccentric Englishman starts to get all of the publicity. It became *his* Parkway Program, not Shedd's. John Bremer set a high-profile style. If he had gone through channels, Parkway wouldn't have gotten off the ground. He came full-time in August 1968. He left in June of '70.

"John never had a contract. He had a three year 'understanding.' It came to a head with the Whitehead. Do you know what a Whitehead is? It's probably the most prestigious fellowship in education. A year's salary—they match your previous year—to come to Cambridge and do whatever you want. You don't even have to teach. John applied for a Whitehead. I have it on pretty reliable authority that when Harvard asked Shedd what do you think, he said no not yet.

"I can't compare John Bremer and Len Finkelstein. You're not comparing two people doing the same job. The job of Director of Parkway is not the same now as it was. But Len was a perfect choice. He was one of the two in-house innovators in the System. When I thought who would be the right man to take over, I thought of Len before I even knew he was Shedd's choice. I was sort of the middle man between John and Len, as the one was leaving and the other was taking over.

"John had some really brilliant educational theories. He conceived of Parkway as being only one of many alternatives to the public-school system, which fully developed would handle 2400 high-school students. Parkway wasn't for everybody. But he did a really poor job of teacher selection. There was a whole committee of about forty interested people screening teacher applications and supposedly making decisions. That was a read fraud. All the time, John was deciding who would teach in Parkway and who wouldn't. His criterion was if they had a lot of energy. If they had their own ideas and wanted to put them to work at Parkway, they were out. The result was we had a poor faculty at Alpha.

"Parkway is a success in some ways and a failure in others. The principal failure is the method of selection of students. The whole idea of Parkway is to have a school where students are there because they want to be, because they're interested. We don't have that. You don't get that by applications made out by a counselor and dropped in a drum. I would make the students do more to get into Parkway, come to a Saturday session at least, to make out their own application. I think we need more effective criteria to determine 'interest.'

"I don't like catalogs and course descriptions. I would place more responsibility on the student to work out with a teacher a curriculum. We still do too much for the student. We take it for granted that he is college-bound, and we don't talk about alternatives. Colleges today welcome a student who's been out of school for a year or two.

"We have no program for orienting a student to Parkway. We take a student from a regular public school, put him into Parkway and say: Swim! We should give swimming lessons. We should have a swimming class for teachers too. Too many of them are traditionalists. Part of a teacher's job in Parkway is institutional contact. I have a contact with the Pennsylvania Music Academy. If a student comes to me and wants to work on something special in the field of music, I have to know who to talk to at PMA and I have to be able to work that out with them and the student. This kind of liaison work is always going on. But it takes time. You can't schedule that. You can't say I'll do that between two and four on Tuesdays and Thursdays. I'm always working to develop new contacts, and keep up the old ones.

"This is a sixty-hour-a-week job. We still have teachers who think of teaching in terms of a class. And we have students who think that way too. Parkway is in a lot of danger now. Too many don't like us. It has everybody on edge, this worrying what people will think. Parkway has become schizophrenic. But I see Parkway's success as having been a dynamic generative influence on American education. If Parkway should close, there are a group of Parkway teachers that would try to continue by utilizing the city's institutions to provide for students what they can't get today in a structured public school. I suppose you could call that a free school, except that I think it goes far beyond the free-school concept."

Bernie Ivens

The elementary-analysis class meets in a small television studio located in the basement of the Board of Education Building. Arriving early, I find several students eating lunch at a long table placed to one side of the studio. The usual questions. Who are you? Who do you write for? What do you write? The usual off-hand way of speaking, an almost deliberate informality. Also deliberately laced with four-letter words to let one know where it's at. An older student with long hair and a thin mustache arrives. Is that Bernie Ivens, I ask? They laugh. No, that's not Bernie. You'll know Bernie, there's no mistaking him. He looks like Jesus. No, he looks like Moses. No, he looks like Fagan, let's call him Fagan when he comes in.

Here he comes. Hi, Fagan. Hello there, Fagan. By God, he does look like Fagan! Tall, long nose, long dark wavy hair, a curly pointed beard. Pea jacket with Free Angela button. Maroon cardigan sweater with a Temple T on one pocket. Open-collar white shirt that sticks out under the sweater and over baggy dark trousers. Class begins.

It is without doubt the fastest-paced hour class I have ever observed. Elementary analysis is an advanced math course. These are mostly seniors who have already fulfilled state math requirements, done well in them, and gone on to this elective. Ivens' style is informal, but he starts at a brisk pace and never lets up. This phase is on analytical geometry, a primarily theoretical exercise. Though Ivens spends most of his time at the blackboard, he has not only the attention but the active participation of everyone in the class. He jokes, chews gum, dances up and down, swears, rocks against the wall, refers to problems as "gruesome," "tough," "really hard."

"All right, I need some hot shots for this one, it's really gruesome. Who knows what the function of x is in this one? Hmm? C'mon! I'm desperate. I'll accept an educated guess. Is it a function or not a function? If you say no, be prepared to back it up. Ya wanna say no? Back it up! Phew! Verrry heavy! Okay, Esther, is it a function? Sock it to me, Es! Hmm? Good. Verrry good! Outta sight!" When the class ends, I can't believe the hour has passed. We talk.

"Are you into math? No? I'm from Philly. Went to Temple. I studied social science. Only they weren't hiring social-science teachers, they were looking for math. I got married early. At twenty. I needed a job. So I took some more math. I already had most of the math I needed. In fact, I took my master's in math.

"I taught at West Philly High. Only I wasn't in too good with the principal. I got in a lot of trouble with him. So I applied here and got it. I was Operating Head at Gamma for about a year. That's an impossible job. I quit it and now I just teach. There is no typical teacher here, everybody's different. They sent you to the differentest. Do I like it? You'd have to know more about me, about my background, to understand my answer. I'm very active politically. Organizing, stuff like that. This isn't a private school, but out there . . . that's where the action is. That's where I really ought to be.

"The biggest failure of Parkway is that there aren't enough teachers. They wanna get rid of some and instead they should get more. It's the biggest problem in education. Look, there are kids here who can't do simple arithmetic, can't read beyond third or fourth grade. I can't teach kids like that! Not unless I can teach them to read and add and subtract on a one-to-one basis. I don't have that much time! Look at Cuba. An illiterate country. They taught them to read and write. Because they had a national purpose! Like in China today. We have no national purpose any more.

"I think that all this talk about what makes a good teacher is just so much bullshit. If you're a good guy and you know your stuff and you like kids . . . that's all you need. As for calling teachers by their first names and smoking and swearing . . . that's crap! That's not education. But it does create an atmosphere that may lead to something else. Change has to take place *in* the public schools."

Bobbi Seiffert

A short visit to Bobbi Seiffert's reading and writing class. In the "Resource Center" on the second floor at 16 North Front Street. Forties. Tall, thin, red hair, large round dark glasses. She taught at a

Summerhillian private school. Now she wrestles with reading and writing at Parkway. Tough job. The "Resource Center" has few resources. A long narrow room with old tables and chairs, a clutter of donated magazines, and a few worn books. One young intern—a woman—is working with a toothpick-sucking senior. Vocabulary. They play draw poker with index cards on which some have the words and some have the definitions. Match a word with a definition, you have a pair. He's winning.

Bobbi is working with a girl from Dick Hiler's tutorial. "She's one of our best students, but she needs someone to push her." Pushing her consists of quizzing her verbally on the Molière book she has just completed. Reading and Writing is an effort at one-to-one tutoring in basic using both teachers and interns. Bobbi's group consists of about thirty students, each of whom is assigned the period twice a week. Assignments are staggered to avoid overcrowding, because of the zoning restriction and the limited number of tutors. This class has about eight or nine students. They wander in as much as an hour late. The worst reading problem—a huge two-hundred pound black student —reads at about second or third grade level. Bobbi works with him until his tutor, who is also late, arrives. All of the tutors in this class are white, all of the students are black. It is a slow and painful process with less than adequate materials. About ninety students at Gamma are involved in some sort of reading work.

"Half the students at Parkway read at sixth or seventh grade level. Our goal is to bring them all up to ninth grade level by the time they graduate. We don't always make it." Since every student applying to college was admitted the first year and nearly every one was admitted again last year, one need hardly inquire which Parkway graduates don't make it to the ninth grade reading level.

Friday Staff Meeting

The Friday Staff Meeting takes place weekly at the Rohm and Haas Building. Students are welcome, outsiders are not. Students and teachers milling about. As usual, difficult to tell them apart. Especially the interns. Except by now I'm beginning to know them. Turbaned Ida Davis. Bobbi Seiffert. Jim Keen. Larry Ellis. Bernie Ivens. Dick Hiler. Anne McNulty. Nancy. Walter with long hair, beard and temper

—all red. Betty Barth, Gamma's Head. She's been away. Late twenties. Hard-looking, pinched nose, tired eyes, long thin bangs. She smokes a lot. But so does everyone else. There are perhaps fourteen teachers and interns, an equal number of students. Including the rummy players from Ellis's geometry class. All seated at long tables again arranged in a square.

The mimeographed agenda is deceptively simple and does not foretell the emotional outbursts that will follow:

1. Office Information—Anne.
2. Movie Announcement—Carmen.
3. Desks—Allen.
4. OSTI Report.
5. Institutional Relations.
6. Tutorial Evaluation and Planning.
7. Priorities and Use of Time.

The first four are quickly disposed of. The fifth opens a can of worms. It is a continuation of a discussion in previous staff meetings. Parkway differentiates between staff offerings on the curriculum and institutional offerings, with the latter constituting classes which meet in the various co-operating Philadelphia institutions and are taught by someone in that institution. This includes the various colleges and universities, newspapers, utilities, city government departments, etc., as well as individual tradesmen, craftsmen, and professionals. The concept is Parkway's pride and joy and reflects considerable organizational work on the part of the teachers. But attendance in these classes has been poor, and Gamma is in danger of losing its hard-won contacts.

A proposal had been made at the prior staff meeting to impose sanctions on students with unexcused absences. Probation for the first, expulsion for the second. This was then discussed in tutorials, together with a list of educational priorities drafted by Hiler and Ellis. Those students that discussed the proposal differed in reaction, from those who thought it harsh to those who questioned the credulity— would the sanctions actually be imposed?—to those who felt the sanctions were a necessary reality. All had difficulty understanding the list of priorities.

Hiler: "I deeply regret that we find it necessary to resort to coercion. If it were the only way, I would agree, but I think there are better alternatives."

Student: "The courses should be better explained in the catalog. I was told to fill up my time from the courses listed. I didn't even know what they were all about." (Parkway students have two weeks after a class begins to decide upon it and may drop the class within that period. Attendance at institutional classes is at present less than fifty per cent.)

Seiffert: "We can't function this way. We're too lax for too long about attendance. Then all of a sudden we decide to do something and we make a handful of kids scapegoats."

Walter: "If there is no action taken on the motion, then I make a motion that the Parkway students no longer be involved in institutions."

Ivens: "I think this is important. What Walter has just said is shit or get off the pot. I think it's important that we all recognize what he said."

Hiler: "Parkway is just not working. It's such a mess, I don't see how any student can make sense out of the Parkway Program."

Ellis: "If you want to know the opinion of someone who has only been here for six weeks and has put a hell of a lot of energy into it during that time, I can tell you that this school just isn't working, and if it doesn't improve ah don't expect to be around next term. Unless something is done, ah think it would be better to shut Parkway down and ah would make that recommendation to the School Board."

There is a tense silence. Then . . .

Ivens: "Heav-y."

Keen: "The way this is laid out, the teachers are the ones that go out to set up these classes. That's why students don't go to them. Students should be active in setting up their own courses, that's my opinion. Now I'll shrink back into my corner."

Student: "We should have a class on how to set up these classes then. I wouldn't know where to go."

Ellis: "We're classing ourselves to death. We are a conventional school without walls. That's all we are, and a long list of classes that don't mean anything won't change that. I don't think the School

Board's gonna close us down, ah think we're gonna close ourselves down! We're gonna self-destruct!"

There is more discussion. The motion is withdrawn. Counter-motions are made. And withdrawn. Some students insist that the whole community is affected and should be heard. Others point out that only ten per cent will participate and the rest will goof off. Nancy reminds everyone of the difficulty in expecting inexperienced students—and teachers—to develop a whole educational system, that it is one thing to work on structural defects and quite another to change the whole Parkway structure.

Ellis: "Are we gonna continue this madness for spring term or are we gonna change? I make a motion that we take a week. Shut down all classes and work this out. The person who started Parkway was an idealist. He's gone and we're left to deal with this mess. If we don't, we're gonna self-destruct."

Keen: "Our catalog may look kinda groovy, but it doesn't mean anything. These are courses that *teachers* want to teach. Students should have the opportunity to create their own courses and find teachers to teach them."

More motions. More counter-motions. None are even voted upon, except the one to do away with institutional classes. It is rejected unanimously. Discussion rambles. Ellis's week is reduced to Hiler's two days next week which in turn is altered to a week at the end of the term to coincide with evaluations. Betty is not convinced. How will these meetings be structured and what's to be done about the ninety per cent that will goof off?

Ida Davis: "This term started a week late. Because of evaluations it will end a week early. The term is only twelve weeks as it is. Now it's ten weeks and y'all wanna make it less? Not all classes are a waste of time. This school's not all bad! My classes are gonna continue to meet for the rest of the term!"

Walter: "Regardless of the vote of this meeting?"

Ida Davis: "Regardless."

Walter: "Then there is no point to this meeting! If we are not to be bound by the decisions of this body, there is no point to this meeting!"

But it continues. The words become threatening—close Parkway down—but no one takes them seriously. It is as if by threatening the worst they can achieve the best. The following week there is a town meeting of students only. They meet to consider Dick Hiler's Proposal for Change, in which he suggests that spring term be spent by students and teachers in tutorial work-study groups, each concentrating on its own area of interest for the term. No one understands the proposal, and the town meeting too dissolves without accomplishing its task. And so it goes. Another crisis passes in the crisis called Public Education.

Overview

Recently, Stanford University let it be known that it was interested in establishing a grant for someone qualified to provide an "overview" of the Free School Movement in American Education. There is no such person. There may not even be such a cohesive thing as a Movement. There are thousands of Free Schools, New Schools, Private Schools, Community Schools and No Schools. No two are alike and each is constantly changing. But Bernie Ivens is right . . . *public* school, that's where the action is. Forty-nine million kids trapped in a system that could be the best instead of the worst. Forty-nine million kids waiting to be turned on. Forty-nine million kids who could be *enjoying* school, who could be *learning*, who could be having *fun* in what they now regard as a prison. *Could* be.

And don't worry about Parkway. It'll be around one way or another long after the idealists get tired pulling it apart and long after the politicians figure how to fiscal-responsibility it to oblivion. It'll be around because its seed has been blowing in the wind and because other Parkways have already started. Good ideas die hard.

PARKWAY SEEDS: THE ALTERNATIVE SCHOOL PROJECT

One year old, the Alternative School is a group effort of five suburban school districts and the School District of Philadelphia. Director of the Project is Allan Glatthorn. Forty-seven. Long sideburns and a dark neatly trimmed Van Dyke. An open-neck dashiki hides stocky shoulders and a barrel chest. He speaks slowly in a low voice. For the last seven years he has been Principal of Abington High School in Abington, Pennsylvania. For the sixteen preceding years—his entire career—he was a teacher and administrator in the same district.

"This began with six superintendents who had an idea. They came to me and asked me to set it up. We wrote our proposal and got a $300,000 Title III grant from HEW. The local districts provide personnel. (One teacher per eighteen students worth $150,000 more.) We started in September. There are three hundred students selected fairly equally from each of the six districts—Radnor, Springfield, Lower Merion, Cheltenham, Abington, and Philadelphia." (There are two units, Alternative East and Alternative West, each located near two or three of the districts. Students' records are maintained at their sending high schools and they will receive their diplomas, on graduation, from those schools. If they wish, they may also participate in the sports, dramatic, and musical programs of their sending schools.)

"We get ninety per cent of our students by lottery. Ten per cent we get by a rigged lottery, so we get some ethnic representation. That's jargon for—so we get some blacks. We have about fifteen per cent black here. We have nine full-time teachers plus some part-time teachers without tenure on an hourly basis. We tried to have a screening committee made up of teachers, students, and parents, but actually I ended up making the selections. I tried to look for teachers with good expertise, teachers who were really competent and had something to offer. There were plenty of radicals who just wanted out from the System. I didn't pick them.

"Our cost per student is fifteen hundred dollars. I hope to reduce that. Our grant is for one year with a two-year renewal. After that we have to raise the money locally. I don't think it will be too big a problem, but I don't know. I'm not very good at politics. We have our own School Board . . . one teacher, one student, one parent, and one superintendent from each of the six districts. It's a pretty big Board.

"I get some parents who are against the idea of the school. They don't buy it at all. Others say I buy your rhetoric, Allan, but will it get my kid into college? We've done very well so far on college admissions. The results aren't in, of course, but I would say that we had nearly sixty kids apply, and over thirty have been accepted so far. Twenty-some haven't heard yet and only one is 'still looking.' About ten per cent of the school dropped and went back to regular school. It just didn't work for them. I don't know if it was the school's fault or theirs.

"I have six young and energetic superintendents. They're all in their early forties and willing to experiment. But is this just an escape valve or do they think of it as something to be expanded? I don't know. Probably the former. There was a lot of pressure in these schools for an alternative. Now most of the people who were behind the pressure are here and there's less pressure on those schools to change.

"We have not had a lot of success in attracting non-college-bound students. Our courses are mostly academic. I set out to try to establish an intellectual community. Of course I can't determine what the school will be like. The students and the teachers come together and they decide what kind of a school it should be. But I really would like to have a school that was both [intellectual and non intellectual].

"We have drawn much and learned much from the Parkway Program, there is no question about that. I would like to see ten or eleven units like this one. Maybe not all the same. That's what I keep suggesting to the six superintendents. But I don't know. . . ."

[*April 1972*]

The Perils of Parity: Part V

Memo to:	my
From:	The Gnome of Zurich, Chairman, Ad Hoc Committee to Develop Practical Alternatives to the Gloriously Impractical Pay-What-It's-Worth Subscription Plan
Subject:	Swan Song

Your response to our last communication, in which we requested a feasibility study and marketing plan for new subscription prices, was viewed by the Committee as somewhat less than reassuring. That at your staff meeting, "Pasha the Cat purred demurely and Shofar the Dog barked concordantly, thus demonstrating the Staff's concurrence with the present policy," hardly addresses itself to the problem of your current deplorable financial condition. Notwithstanding your antipathy for economic determinism, surely even you must realize that to continue to pay out more than comes in can only result in an unsatisfactory conclusion to your venture. The Committee wishes to make clear its position, since it continues to be held accountable by the many interested parties which it represents. Under the circumstances, the Committee again requests that you discontinue the Pay-What-It's-Worth Subscription Plan, and institute a more acceptable plan encompassing both a fixed rate and a regular publishing schedule. An additional recommendation is being prepared by your mother for Committee approval which will deal with the acceptance by the *Treadmill* of paid advertising of consumer products and services, exclusive of hemorrhoid preparations, depilatories, and feminine-hygiene products.

Respectfully submitted.

Memo to: The Gnome
From: my
Subject: Tag. Not It!

I know the Committee means well, and I'm sure you're right. But I can't keep the color inside the lines and my push-pulls aren't neat like the other kids'. I never could remember to shoot fouls like the coach said or to stop peeking behind doors that said Do Not Enter. (There never was anything there, that I could see.) I know people are lazy. Some procrastinate. And some free-load. Well, that's their problem. They still should have the right to pay what something's worth to *them* not the producer, and *after* not before. Over twenty per cent are, and most of the rest will. However, you may inform the Committee that I have talked to the Staff. In the event it should become necessary for me to resign, they have both agreed to stay on . . . without pay if necessary. Pasha sleeps a good deal in the typewriter case and Shofar does like his play, but deep down like Archie there's ink in their blood. They'll come through. Tell Mom no advertising, but if we ever decide to do a Benefit, she can play "Sleepy Lagoon" on the piano.

my

A Report on the Use of Behavior Modification Drugs on Elementary School Children

Background

On June 29, 1970, the *Washington Post* carried a story from Omaha, Nebraska, concerning the widespread use of "behavior modification" drugs to calm hyperactive children in the elementary schools of the Omaha School System. Similar reports have appeared in the media since then with increasing frequency. On September 29, the House Committee on Government Operations Right to Privacy Inquiry, chaired by Cornelius Gallagher (D–N.J.), held hearings on federal responsibility in promoting and encouraging the use of these drugs. On the same day, Dr. Edward Sewell, the Director of Medical Services for the Philadelphia School System, acknowledged in a radio interview that the drugs are being used to treat overactive youngsters in Philadelphia schools.

Although the transcripts of the Gallagher hearings are not expected to be released until mid-November, Gallagher is highly critical of the government's involvement. In a letter to Secretary Richardson (HEW), Congressman Gallagher points accusingly at poorly administered HEW-granted research, sloppy FDA investigation of the Omaha program, and the belated funding of follow-up studies of 150,000 children treated with the drugs under a three-million-dollar grant of the National Institute of Mental Health. The Nixon administration expressed its concern on October 12 with an announcement by Dr. Edward Ziegler, Director of the new Office of Child Development, that he would soon convene a "blue ribbon" panel to warn pediatricians and educators against the overuse of "behavior modification" drugs to calm overactive children.

Thus, the recent chronology of a situation which began over thirty years ago with the research of Dr. Charles Bradley on the use of amphetamines in the treatment of some "disturbed" children and which has currently reached a popularity of such proportions among educators as to cause respected writers in the field of education such as Nat Hentoff and John Holt to sound the alarm of 1984 some fourteen years early. The problem is extremely serious, and it concerns us all, for, superimposed on a failing and largely irrelevant authoritarian educational system, its frightening implications feed the paranoia of repression. Sensationalism has crept not only into reports of usually reliable media but also into articles and letters of those usually more objective in their criticisms. The result has been that a good deal of confusion has been created. The situation calls for cool heads and informed parents, and it is in that direction that this report makes its effort. For those who would retrace my laborious steps, a bibliography has been included at the end of this report. For those who do not, here are the salient facts as briefly as is possible.

The Condition—What Is It?

A federal study group which set out several years ago to define the condition found thirty-eight different terms to choose from. They selected "minimal brain dysfunction (MBD)." The alternatives include: "learning disabilities," "psychoneurological insufficiency," "hyperactive-child syndrome," "minimal cerebral dysfunction," "hyperactivity," "hyperkinetic impulse disorder," and most popularly "hyperkinesis." Here is a description by M. A. Stewart in the *Journal of the American Medical Association:* "Typically a child with this syndrome is continually in motion, cannot concentrate for more than a moment, acts and speaks on impulse, is impatient and easily upset. At home he is constantly in trouble because of his restlessness, noisiness and disobedience. In school he is readily distracted, rarely finishes his work, tends to clown and talk out of turn in class and becomes labeled a discipline problem." Richard Jenkins writes in the *American Journal of Psychiatry:* "The hyperkinetic or hyperactive reaction is widely recognized in child psychiatry. It is disproportionately frequent before the age of 8 years and tends gradually to become less frequent and less prominent thereafter. It usually disappears by the middle teens."

Some clinicians hold to the theory that brain damage is involved, a theory which gained some popularity shortly after the 1918 epidemic of encephalitis in the United States. Most, however, conclude that only a small percentage are brain-damaged, choosing to interpret such signs as clumsiness, squinting, and speech difficulties sometimes accompanying the syndrome as resulting from functional disorders of the brain rather than from structural damage. Hyperkinetic children tend to be of average or above-average intelligence. They have been described by teachers with such phrases as "troublemaker," "fidgety," "unmanageable," "disruptive," and "can't sit still." Psychiatrists have estimated that perhaps four per cent of all elementary school children are hyperkinetic. Educators have estimated between fifteen and twenty per cent.

The Diagnosis

What has been described in the medical literature is a known disorder. But, how is it known? Most if not all of the characteristics of hyperkinesis closely resemble the actions of highly charged but far from abnormal children who find it difficult to sit still for hours on end, listening in silence to "lessons" which hold no interest . . . who would rather play than eat or study . . . who resist authoritarianism by which they have yet to be fully programmed . . . and who spent their most productive learning years learning how to walk and talk amid playful noise which they must now forswear. Psychiatrists who have worked with the disorder are firm and unanimous on this point: while parent and teacher observations and questionnaires are helpful, an accurate diagnosis is completely dependent upon a series of complex psychiatric and neurologic examinations. Many psychiatrists with whom I talked had never personally diagnosed a case of hyperkinesis, and some could not recall ever having seen one. Information disclosed in the Gallagher hearings revealed that in many cases the diagnosis was being made by teachers, administrators, school nurses, school doctors, and family physicians. Cases were cited in Ohio, New Jersey, California, Hawaii, Arkansas, Nebraska, and elsewhere.

The Treatment

Over thirty years ago, Dr. Charles Bradley of Rhode Island discovered that "disturbed" children improved in behavior when he gave them stimulants called amphetamines. For some reason yet unexplained, these stimulants have a paradoxically calming effect on hyperkinetics while tranquilizers serve to stimulate the hyperactivity. The drugs which have been most commonly used are Dexedrine, Benzedrine, and Ritalin (an unrelated drug with similar effect).

Others somewhat less popularly used have been Deaner, Aventyl, and Tofranil. The United States Food and Drug Administration on September 30, 1970, labeled "dangerous" both Tofranil and Aventyl. It has also urged physicians to exercise extreme caution in prescribing Ritalin (Sweden banned its use) because of the danger of addiction and because its side effects include marked anxiety, tension, and agitation.

By far the most popular drugs used are the amphetamines Dexedrine and Benzedrine. They do not always produce the desired results. Sometimes they stimulate after all. Sometimes there are undesirable side effects such as nausea, vomiting, insomnia, and loss of appetite. In 1967 in Canada, Dr. Philip Ney discovered a case of amphetamine psychosis produced in an eight-year-old boy as a result of amphetamine treatment for hyperkinesis. It was the first such case. As hyperkinetic children approach adolescence, symptoms begin to disappear (with or without treatment, apparently). Also, as the children approach adolescence, amphetamines begin to lose their paradoxical effect and there is danger of building a dependence on the drug. Because of these problems, because the amphetamines serve only to mask the symptoms, and because of increasing drug abuse among teen-age users of amphetamines, most psychiatrists tend to be conservative in their use of these drugs in the treatment of hyperkinesis.

"It is important to keep in mind that the drug is no substitute for more intensive therapy. It is useful only as an adjunct to adequate psychotherapy. It is self-evident that the drug does not remove the sources of conflict which led to the difficulty."

—H. Bakwin

"There is a definite need for psychotherapy for the child and work directly with the parents. . . . Disturbed behavior in children should not be treated indiscriminately with amphetamines."

—M. Laufer, E. Denhoff, *and* G. Solomons

"There is a particular need for patience, steadiness, understanding, restraint and kindly repetition in the training of the hyperkinetic child."

—R. Jenkins

"Drugs are useful in the symptomatic treatment of hyperkinetic and perceptually handicapped children, but their administration should be preceded by a careful clinical evaluation. On the basis of present evidence, short term trials of drugs are justified as an adjunct to remedial education. . . . The use of central nervous system stimulants and mood-modifying agents for prolonged periods should await further evaluation by long-term controlled studies."

—J. G. MILLICHAP

Summary

The discrepancy between the four-per-cent estimate of experts in the field of psychiatry and the fifteen- to twenty-per-cent estimate of experts in the field of education is more than disturbing. It is frightening. In Omaha an estimated three thousand to six thousand elementary-school children are on drug therapy to "improve classroom deportment and increase learning potential." There are only sixty-two thousand students in the entire Omaha system. Although many are poor and black, Assistant Superintendent Don Warner says, "It's all over the city. There are at least some kids on these drugs in just about every school." Orabelle Poll, chairman of the Academic Freedom Committee of the American Civil Liberties Union of the state of Washington recently wrote, "In a casual investigation, we on the academic freedom committee haven't yet found an elementary school that doesn't have some of its children tranquilized." She suggests an ACLU-sponsored panel of teachers, parents, psychologists, doctors, and civil libertarians on the disadvantages of controlling grade-school children with drug therapy and the possibility of finding alternatives.

Dr. Edward F. Rabe, professor of pediatric neurology at Tufts University School of Medicine, says, "Educators often are talking about any child with learning disabilities, while pediatric neurologists are talking about a child with signs of neurological deficits and learning deficits." And R. G. Buddenhagen has written in the *American Journal of Mental Deficiency* that "Behavior is socially adaptive (or maladaptive) only on the merits of its acceptability to a given audience . . . a subjective judgement is required in the last analysis to determine which behaviors are acceptable and which are not." Finally, Dr. Sidney Berman, president of the American Academy of Child Psychiatry, cautions that these drugs "should not be used indiscriminately, as people use drugs as a way of circumventing the real problems they are confronted with."

Conclusion

It should be obvious that the key to the problem lies in the diagnosis and who makes it. While I am sympathetic to all and in accord with most of the educational views of John Holt and Nat Hentoff, I believe that their use of this problem for yet another attack on our educational system is counterproductive. Nor do I believe that the intimation of quackery within the psychiatric profession is reasonable or justified. The weight of medical information on the subject overwhelmingly supports the thesis that the disorder is both real and prevalent. However, the line between a normally energetic and undisciplined youngster and an abnormally hyperactive one is too fine for someone unqualified to draw. The category of unqualified "experts" would include parents, teachers, school nurses, school doctors, school administrators, family physicians, and most pediatricians. *Parents must be made aware that the diagnosis is a complex one which requires psychiatric and neurologic examinations, and that anything less constitutes a serious threat to the physical and mental well-being of their child.*

As to the use of amphetamines in the treatment of hyperkinetic children, there is sufficient confusion among the medical researchers regarding the merits of this treatment to suggest that all concerned proceed with the utmost caution. *To date, there has been no study made on the long-range effects of amphetamine use among young children with hyperkinesis.* This fact alone ought to convince us of the wisdom of using alternatives such as psychotherapy and remedial education.

Freud has written: "The future may teach us how to exercise direct influence, by means of particular chemical substance, upon the amounts of energy and their distribution in the apparatus of the mind. It may be that there are other undreamt-of possibilities of therapy." In the field of psychiatry, that prediction is now a practical reality. However, the social and political implications have yet to be resolved. We all have a vital and selfish interest in that resolution. The use of behavior modification drugs on elementary school children is a case in point.

Bibliography

1. Maurice W. Laufer, Eric Denhoff, and Gerald Solomons: "Hyperkinetic Impulse Disorder in Children's Behavioral Problems," *Psychosomatic Medicine,* 1957, 19, 38–49.

2. Harry Bakwin: "Benzedrine in Behavior Disorders of Children," *Journal of Pediatrics,* 1948, 32, 215–216.

3. Richard L. Jenkins: "Classification of Behavior Problems of Children," *American Journal of Psychiatry,* 1969, 125, 1032–1039.

4. Herbert G. Birch, ed.: *Brain Damage in Children: the Biological and Social Aspects.* Baltimore: The Williams and Wilkins Co., 1964.

5. Philip G. Ney: "Psychosis in a Child, Associated with Amphetamine Administration," *Canadian Medical Association Journal,* Oct. 21, 1967.

6. Gabrielle Weiss, John Werry, Klaus Minde, Virginia Douglas, and Donald Sykes: *Studies on the Hyperactive Child, V: The Effects of Dextroamphetamine and Chlorpromazine on Behavior and Intellectual Functioning.* Department of Psychiatry, Montreal Children's Hospital and McGill University, *Journal of Child Psychology and Psychiatry and allied disciplines.*

7. C. Keith Conners, Leon Eisenberg, and Avner Barcai: "Effect of Dextroamphetamine on Children—Studies on Subjects with Learning Disabilities and School Behavior Problems," *Archives of General Psychiatry,* October 1967.

8. J. Gordon Millichap: "Drugs in Management of Hyperkinetic and Perceptually Handicapped Children," *Journal of the American Medical Association,* November 11, 1968.

9. "Minimal Brain Dysfunction," *Medical World News,* 30–36, May 22, 1970.

10. Mark A. Stewart: "Hyperactive Children," *Scientific American,* 94–98, April 1970.

11. Richard L. Jenkins: "Behavior Disorders of Childhood," *American Family Physician,* May 1970.

12. John S. Werry: "Studies on the Hyperactive Child—IV. An Empirical Analysis of the Minimal Brain Dysfunction Syndrome," *Archives of General Psychiatry,* July 1968.

[1 8 2]

13. "Quackery"—letter from John Holt to *The New York Review of Books*, August 13, 1970.
14. "Hyperkinetic Children"—letter from Dr. Carlos Carrillo to *The New York Review of Books* with an answer from John Holt, October 22, 1970.
15. Excerpts from Nat Hentoff's column in *The Village Voice*, October 8 and 15, 1970.
16. Letter to Honorable Elliot Richardson, Secretary, Department of Health, Education and Welfare, from Honorable Cornelius E. Gallagher, Chairman, Right to Privacy Inquiry, House of Representatives Special Studies Subcommittee of the Committee of Government Operations, October 12, 1970.

[*November 1970*]

Moon Age Compendium

I'm afraid to go out.
I'm afraid to stay in.

I'm afraid of being knifed/shot/robbed/mugged/maced/busted/
   beaten/raped in my sleep
     or on the street
      or on the first tee.
I'm afraid of The Bomb. nerve gas. germ warfare. multiple-warhead
   missiles. mace. napalm. rats. cancer. syphilis . . . (but not very)

I'm afraid of niggers.
I'm afraid of Mister Charlie.

I'm afraid to be alone, I'm afraid of crowds.
I'm afraid in the city
     or the suburbs
      or the Army.

I'm afraid of white black red yellow and brown
I'm afraid of long hair,beards,crewcuts,rednecks,Commies,Chinks,
Socialists,
Fascists,
Birchers,
Crackers,
Hunkies,
Liberals,
Leftists,
Anarchists,
Jews,
Wasps,
Catholics,
Pigs,
Panthers,
and Narcs.
I'm afraid of SDS,SANE,NAACP,SWP,FBI,CIA,CID,YAF,YSA,
KKK,VC and VD . . .
    (but not very)

I'm afraid to say yes.I'm afraid to say no.
I'm afraid to conform.I'm afraid to be different.
I'm afraid of polluted air,polluted water and fluoride.
I'm afraid of my boss,my landlord,my neighbors,my dentist,and the
    friendly neighborhood fuzz.

I'm afraid of starvation,cyclamates,cholesterol,and The Pill.

I'm afraid of the dark.

I'm afraid to sit on strange toilet seats.

I'm afraid of The Establishment, The System, The Media, The Rich,
    The Poor, The Military-Industrial Complex, The Bureaucracy, The
    Proletariate, The Bourgeoisie, The Computer,
And all those goddammiddleclasspotsmokingaciddroppingspeedfreak
    hippies.

[1 8 4]

I'm afraid of Inflation,Deflation,Recession,Depression,Aggression,
                                                    Repression,
                                                    Oppression,
                                                    Suppression.

I'm afraid of being knocked up.
I'm afraid of knocking somebody up . . . (but not very)

I'm afraid of fags,pimps,fairies,queers,lesbians,peeping toms,perverts,
    drug fiends,deviates,degenerates,Victorians,Mid-Victorians,
    Moralists,Puritans,dirty pictures,dirty words and pubic hair . . .
    (but not very)

I'm afraid to lead to follow to be first to be last to be up front to be in
    back to join not to join to be included to be excluded.

I'm afraid to wave the flag.
I'm afraid not to wave the flag.

I'm afraid of Imperialists/Colonialists/Totalitarianists/Marxists/
    Maoists/Leninists/Pacifists.

I'm afraid of things the way they are, but I'm afraid of change.

I'm afraid of myself,
        for my family,
            for my friends,
                for my fellow man . . . (but not very)

I'm afraid of Life.
I'm afraid of Death.

I'm afraid to love.

I'm afraid to hate . . .
(but not very)

                                        I'm afraid to sign my name

[1 8 5]

Fun House

(To be accompanied by a kazoo)

I want to go to the
Fun House, please
Where the clown goes
Ho
Ho
Ho
He starts every morning
Where he leaves off each night
And his laugh just tickles me so.

I've grown so tired
Of talk, you see.
Of nothing works
And
Nobody cares
And
Christ what a miserable life!

They say
There's no reason to smile
Any more,
Folks are feelin' so tense.
What with air polluted
And bucks diluted,
Nothing makes a whole lot of sense.

What was it we thought
We'd have, do y'think?
Some happy utopia, no less
Where we'd all live long
And painlessly.
(Not like our current mess.)

But the war goes on,
Whichever one it is,

And there's too many cars on the road.
Too much bad
For not enough good.
The world is a stuffed-up commode.

Well life is a drag
But death is a pain
So what do y'think we should do
When there's no more hope,
God is still dead,
And the Devil rides a B-fifty-two?

Why, let's all go down to the
Fun House, friends
Where the clown goes
Ho
Ho
Ho.
Where no one boos,
There's no bad news,
And nobody
Ever
Says
No.

Oh, I want to go to the
Fun House, please
Where the clown goes
Ho
Ho
Ho
He starts every morning
Where he leaves off each night
And his laugh just tickles me so.

A Handbook on Death

                              then
            laugh, leaning back in my arms
            for life's not a paragraph

            And death i think is no parenthesis

                                   —*E. E. Cummings*

Introduction

Mors omnibus communis. Dum vivimus, vivamus.

It is said that man cannot be free in life unless he is free from the fear of Death. We laugh at macabre undertaker jokes, sigh at romantic poems about lost lovers, thrill to films with titles like *Diabolique* and *Psycho*, and are mildly titillated by the newspaper accounts of plane crashes and grisly murders. Yet all the while, we avoid serious discussion. Too morbid. Serious talk brings it too close to home—the deaths of our loved ones, of the most loved one of all . . . Ourself. Shudder and turn away. Change the subject. Give a nervous little laugh and say oh yes I'll think about that later. And when later comes, it is too late and we make others think about it for us and in their grief (or guilt) arrange for us what we should have arranged for ourselves.

Clouded by myth and superstition. Hidden behind euphemisms. Passed away. Departed. Eternal sleep. Just reward. Not buried, interred. Not a grave, a final resting place. Not undertakers, funeral directors. Not gravestones, monuments. Not a body, mortal remains. Not ashes, "cremains." And we've made the whole thing become so commercial with our "grief therapy" and our "final memory picture" that we not only have to keep up with the Joneses in Life, we have to keep down with them in Death. Well, now we grow older and live longer and we're still scared of dying. There is a death every 16-½ seconds in this country. We just don't want it to be us. Transplants and artificial organs are having a race with the Bomb. Science vs. Science. What is Death. The Ethics of Death. The Morals of Death. Abortion and Transplants. Euthanasia and Cryogenics. Genetic Manipulation and Is God Dead. The lawyers, doctors, and clergy argue on these intellectual matters, but what about us? We're still afraid! What about that, Buddha? What about that, Confucius? What about that, Muhammad? Moses? Jesus?

If you fear Death you must find your own answers. These Dialogues on Death are with people who live with it every day. They are interesting, often fascinating people. Most of them are groping for the answers too. One or two have found them. Perhaps they may be of help. Don't turn away because the subject is distasteful. It needn't be. That's the point.

Dialogues on Death

1

"I don't fear Death, but I certainly don't want to hurry it along."

Dr. Maurice Linden is a fifty-five-year-old psychiatrist with a more than passing background in Geriatric Psychiatry. He looks like Broderick Crawford. Strong round face, deeply tanned, partially bald, burly with big square shoulders, a bull neck, short muscular arms, and a too-big belly. His office is on the second floor of the Jefferson Unit of Philadelphia State Hospital at Byberry. We sit in semi-darkness; a whirring fan behind me competes with his rapid low voice. His left hand toys continuously with the horn-rimmed glasses on his desk. Between us there is a large cheap ceramic ashtray with two green snakes coiled around the edge and meeting head to head. Each has one red eye. He apologizes for keeping me waiting.

"I just had to close my eyes for a few minutes. It's too busy, my schedule. I don't get enough rest. Days, nights, weekends. Too much. And I have my own private practice. But that's what makes medicine worth while. I recall a patient of mine. She was a dear and beautiful person. She had been in analysis for some time when she developed cancer of the uterus. It was inoperable. She was aware of the mass inside her and that her chances were not good. We talked a good deal about Death. They were no longer analytical sessions, they became philosophical discussions about a wide range of subjects.

"I told her that I felt that life had been good to me, that I had had many rich and rewarding experiences. That I realized that Death comes to everyone and that if I should have to die, I was quite ready. In that way I introduced the idea to her. I tried to keep her hopes up. I told her that there was still a chance, that I had heard of cases where the cancer was sloughed off.

"Later, I met with my patient's family. I explained that she was anxious that they not be dependent upon her, that they be able to care for themselves. I said that I interpreted that to mean just the opposite, that she wanted them to be with her and to care for her and love her. I was very close to her. I think I loved her as much as anyone in the family. I even talked to her doctor. I was quite put out because he was withholding certain drugs that could alleviate some of the pain on the basis that she would become addicted. My God, if you can't make an addict out of a dying patient!

"Aging is depressing. One begins to lose things—youth with all of its vitalities. Youth is a possession, Old Age is not. They begin to think it would be better to die. It's a passive suicidal wish. Others manage not to be depressed. There are compensations for Old Age. Wisdom, for example. I can always tell. If I ask a patient where he expects to be in ten years, what plans he is making, and he answers, Well, I have this cottage at the shore I'm going to fix up and I'll probably be living there—then I know he's still pretty vital and has adjusted to some degree. But if he answers, Oh, I don't know, or, I may not even be here by then—well, I know he's depressed.

"There is also the aspect of guilt which plays a very strong role. Guilt about how they have treated other people, guilt about leaving loved ones behind. But one thing about Old Age I learned many years ago. There is no such thing as Old Age. No one ever admits that they are old. I have this group at the Naval Hospital—all old men. They're really decrepit, in bad shape, some so far gone they can't even hold their heads up. A real bunch of old geezers. I say, if there's an old man in the room, hold up your hand. Nobody holds up his hand. Most of them are in their seventies or eighties, but if I ask them how old they feel they usually say fifty or fifty-five. You see, you look at yourself in the mirror and you can see you're aging, but you're not growing older inside. It's just the physical you, not the you that's inside. As you grow older, there is this coming apart of the Psyche and the Soma.

"Now I've grown older. I'm fifty-five. And I can appreciate many of the aspects of Old Age. I'm slowing down, I tire more easily, I have less vigor. But my ego is essentially unchanged. I still have the same values to a degree, the same desires. We develop this strong love of self, this self-adulation is narcissism. A little bit, of course, is important. I think it was Rabbi Akiba who said, 'If I don't love me, who will?' But this narcissism makes us believe that the world simply cannot continue without us. After all, reality is when we're here. If we are not here, where is reality?

"I witnessed my father's death. He developed cancer from stomach ulcers. He was in the hospital on the Coast. I went out to see him. We joked a lot. That was the way in my family, to kid around and joke back and forth. They wanted him to stay in the hospital longer, but he insisted that we take him home. He said get me a hospital bed at home. He wanted to be able to look out the window at his lawn and his car. So we got him the hospital bed and he stayed in the back room— it was once my room—looking out the window at the lawn and the garden he cared for. And his car. He had a Packard and he loved it even though he couldn't drive it any more.

"Nobody told him what was wrong, not even the doctor. Finally, I had to leave to go back East. He was still fairly strong and I had to leave. I thought I'd be strong and just go in and say good-by, but when I went in I just collapsed. I fell across the bed, crying. He patted my head and he said, 'Don't worry. Everybody has to die, sooner or later. It's as simple as that.' He was consoling me! After he died, we found he had been reading all of my medical books. Every section on cancer had been worn. He knew all the time.

"There is really not a great deal of preoccupation with Death among old people. They don't seem to have the fear we would expect. Many grow tired and look forward to it. I'm growing older and more tired. I have depressions. I don't fear Death, but I certainly don't want to hurry it along. But I'm not afraid of it. I don't think I believe in a Life After Death, but I've never met anyone, not even an avowed atheist, that didn't hold at least some small prospect of the existence of God. The nearest thing to soul of which I can conceive is this Life Force that's deep inside us. Freud called it the Id. But I don't believe in soul in the traditional sense. Yet matter cannot be destroyed. We are created from matter and after Death, we return to matter in a different form. I don't know."

2

"I wouldn't go to a funeral if my life depended on it."

Alden Whitman is the chief obituary writer for *The New York Times*. He looks more like the owner of a bookstore in Princeton than an obituary writer, but then what should an obituary writer look like? In six years he has written the obituaries of T. S. Eliot, Martin Buber, Adlai Stevenson, Helen Keller, John Steinbeck, Ho Chi Minh, Bertrand Russell, and many more which you can read in his *The Obituary Book*. Fifty-eight. Small. Twinkling blue eyes peering over half-glasses perched on his nose, the lower half of his face covered with a squarely trimmed beard which barely reveals an impish grin. A pipe and a bow tie.

"I don't deal with Death. I write about people's lives for the break-fast-table set. I do forty or so obits a year—about one a week. I write them in advance, sometimes years in advance. I write mostly about men over seventy, except the President, the Vice-President and other officials. The toughest obits to write are scientists or philosophers, because there is so much to their lives. These are more like biographies that I do.

"I often visit with important people before I write about them. I'll be leaving soon for a 'ghoul tour' in Europe. It's not for historical material. That's all available in files. You try to get anecdotes, of course, but mostly you try to get a feel, a sense of the man. I've written about many people that I've known, some that I've known intimately. I'm not really affected, it's my profession. But if it's someone whom you dislike—like Franco, who did so much harm to the people of Spain, who was such a dreadful man, or Hess—well, you can't help getting a little subjective and some hatred may come out in the writing. Or, if it was someone whom you liked, who you had a high regard for, then some of that warmth may also come out. If it's a house obit—someone you've worked with and know well, it may be too tough so you let someone else do it.

"You don't like to do an obit after the fact. You end up doing a job in a day or two that should have taken weeks. You try to avoid that. Some people write in with their own obits. I like that. We file them until they may be needed. We have a pretty extensive file—oh, there must be a couple of thousand or so accumulated over a period of time. I sat at a copy desk for twenty-five years. I got bored. The position opened up and I took it. I've been doing it ever since. You try not to make them all alike. That's the challenge of the job, to come up with ways to make them different.

"I don't think much about Death. I don't go to funerals, they're barbaric. I wouldn't go to a funeral if my life depended on it. It's been a lifelong policy. I think the Jewish funeral is a much better way to deal with grief. A quick burial and sit Shiva with the family to take their mind off the grief. Or the old Irish wake is a good idea. I'm an atheist and I hold no brief for the After-Life. In my will I direct that I should be cremated as quickly as possible. Cryonics? I think Cryonics is a farce.

"I haven't written my own obit. I've never even thought of it. That would be the absolute height of narcissism."

3

"We were twelve hundred that arrived together at Auschwitz. Four survived."

Her name is now Marie Schwartzman. In November of 1941 it was Marie Zansznica. Three months later it was 35056. She was sixteen years old in Paris, the second oldest of seven children. Her father and mother had come from Poland after the First World War. He was a clothing designer working for the French government to redesign the Army's uniforms. When the war came, he joined the Foreign Legion to avoid the Polish draft since he was still a Polish citizen. He was in the south of France when Paris was taken by the Germans.

"Nobody thought it would happen. We had the Maginot Line. It would protect us. And the French government—we were French—it would protect us. Refugees from Germany used to tell us what they were doing to Jews in Germany, but no one wanted to believe them. The Maginot Line lasted two days. And half the French government was selling out to the Germans. When they took Paris, it was already too late. My mother was under forty, but she was alone. My father was away. She didn't know what to do. At first it was all right, but soon they started to round up the Jews.

"We lived across from a church. My mother used to get shots—hay fever, I guess—the nuns used to come to give them to her. They said, let us take the children. Then when you come back, we'll return them. She said no, if we were to die, we would die together. There were always rumors before a round-up—don't sleep at home for a few nights, there's going to be trouble. Sometimes the French police would tell us when they knew. My father came home. Even though he was still in unoccupied France, he wanted to be with us.

"I adored my father. I would wash his feet for him, anything. My mother and I weren't getting along too well at the time. He opened a small business. One day he was leaving for work. Outside, two Germans and a French policeman stopped him and asked if he knew Monsieur Zansznica. He was too honest. He said, I am Monsieur Zansznica. They told him to get a blanket and some things for a few days. When he came in, he told me what to do, who owed him money, things like that. Then he left. We never saw him again.

"One day, a friend told us they were coming for three of us, the three oldest. My older sister was about nineteen and worked in a hospital as a nurse. After me, the next youngest was another sister, about thirteen. The youngest was my little brother. He was two and a half. We had a house in the country. We went there for a while, but it started to get rough there too and we were running out of money. By this time, the French were becoming anti-Semitic. It was the result of the propaganda—the Jews have caused all your problems. The Jews are the reason you are hungry. The Jews. The Jews. If you know of Jews still free, it is your duty to turn them in. You will be rewarded.

"We went back to Paris. I was playing the piano. My mother told me to stop, that there was no sense in telling everyone we had returned. I said, it's only two o'clock in the afternoon, no one will hear. At two-thirty the Germans came. They only wanted the same three.

We hid my younger sister behind a closet. It was very frightening. We spent the night in the police station. Then they said come and meet the rest of the family. They had gone back for everyone else.

"We were taken to a camp outside of Paris where we stayed until February 1942. Then we were taken by train to Auschwitz. We were separated in the train. We had the baby, but my mother was in the other car with the milk. It was very bad. At Auschwitz we were separated into files of five. My mother and brothers and sisters were in front of me. My oldest sister was carrying my baby brother. They were loaded into the trucks. It was very frightening. There was so much noise. The SS were shouting and they had dogs and clubs and they were hitting everybody. We were all so tired. They asked my sister if my brother was her baby. She answered wrong. She said yes. So they put her on the truck too. I never saw them again. I learned later that the trucks were for the crematory. For many years after, I refused to believe it. I blacked it out. Then one day, I believed it.

"I was at Auschwitz from February '42 until May '45. I was very lucky and I had a lot of help from people I often didn't even know. I hated it. Inside me I would get so mad when I would see one human being degrade another that way. One time I got so mad, I started to the fence to throw mud or something at the guard. He pressed the button and I saw sparks as my fingers touched the fence, so I stepped back. Then he shot me. It wasn't bad—in the foot—but it got infected and I had a bad time.

"The facilities were very bad. The food was terrible. There was no water. The Germans were not organized at first. Everything was very confusing. We did work, but it was foolish kind of work. I was on a road. Pick up one stone here, put it there. Later, pick the same stone up and put it back. There was typhus and we were quarantined. There were two kinds of typhus. The one who came from lice and the one who came from water. We had both. There was no medicine for the Jews, no hospital. The inmate doctors would help you if you paid some bread, some rations. Otherwise, they would do nothing.

"Finally, I was selected for the crematory. Tauber was the head of the camp. At the formation, I kept telling him—I won't let you kill me. You won't kill me. I'm not going to die. I'm not!—We had to take our clothes off and get in the trucks. I moved to the front of the truck. Tauber got in next to the driver. I kept shouting to him, over and over—I'm not going to die! You're not going to kill me! I won't die!—As we walked into the gas chamber, he threw a blanket over me and motioned me out." (Marie testified at Tauber's trial at Nuremberg.)

"I was assigned to Block 25. That's where they put you when you're sick. In three days, if you're not better, you go to the crematory. I was one of the . . . like maids . . . to clean the Block. The dirtiest work. I got typhus and I was very sick. But I had help. When Tauber came in the daytime, the others said I was sleeping because I worked all night. If he came at night, they said I was sleeping because I worked all day. Finally he said he didn't believe it. Tomorrow, she goes. The next day, I crawled to the door. I couldn't walk. But I stood at the door and opened it to let him in. He looked at me and said nothing.

"I had a very strong will to live. The ones who wanted to survive, did. The others gave up. The Germans had . . . well, not respect, but perhaps understanding for the ones who felt like that. It was easy to die if you wanted to. Some committed suicide on the wire fences. Or if you got really tired, you could just stop. On Sundays, we used to have exercise they called it. Running up and down the road, only nobody could run. If you wanted to die, you could just sit down and refuse to go further. Then they would shoot you.

"We had the famous Dr. Mengele. You've probably heard of him. He was replaced by Dr. Rhode. He [Rhode] was a wonderful, wonderful man. He closed down the crematory. He opened a Jewish hospital. He died, I think, and Mengele came back. I was in a potato kommando. It was a very bad kommando. It was cold and underground. I think I would have died in that kommando. But a friend said she would put me down for the hospital and I became a nurse. I was sick, but the doctor made believe he didn't know. Once I was under the bed and I made believe I was cleaning. I couldn't get up.

"Sometimes I was ready to die, but most of the time I had a very strong will to live. The first few weeks were the worst. Sometimes they made the women strip and go up and down in front of the men who they lined up to watch. At first, I was very upset. I was only sixteen. But afterwards I even walked over to talk to them. It didn't make any difference, they didn't care. Everyone was in bad shape. Was I pretty? I don't know. How could you be pretty there, with your hair cut off?

"Toward the end, they brought in the Hungarian Jews. For some reason they left them alone until late in the war. Half a million of them. The three crematoria were working day and night. The crematory kommando revolted. They refused to work. They were replaced and then they went to the gas chambers. I was in Briginka, the little camp between two of the crematoria. The job of my kommando was to sort the packages of the people who went to the gas chambers. They used to tell everyone—take your jewelry, take all of your belongings —then they would take it away anyway. It bothered me, the work. I used to faint. Or I used to sleep a lot. Anything to blank out what was happening. After while, they put up a fence so we couldn't watch.

"We were evacuated. The Germans were afraid to be taken by the Russians. We were packed into railroad cars. It was very bad. People were dropping right and left. There was no water. We slept on dead bodies. When our food was gone, we took the food of the dead. The worst was no water. We were in those cars for three weeks. Finally, we arrived at Ravensbrueck. I was very frightened. Ravensbrueck was where they conducted the experiments. I would have drawn the line on two things . . . the prostitution and the experiments. I would have died first. We arrived on February 11. I know, because it was a co-incidence—the same day I arrived at Auschwitz. There was much confusion. The attitude of the Germans changed. Now we heard about their orders and duty. But we left and started walking. I wanted to run away, but a soldier said where would you go? I was liberated on May 6 in Lux.

"What I have told you is nothing. There were things that happened that no one would believe. They would say it couldn't happen. I can't even wear a low-cut dress in the back from the marks of the dogs. We were twelve hundred that arrived together at Auschwitz. Four survived. After I was liberated, it was very difficult. I had no one. I had no money. No job. I was sick for eighteen months with tuberculosis. At first I stayed only with others from Auschwitz. All they talked about was hate and revenge. They would always say to others, oh, what do you know, you weren't there. But I did not feel that way. I knew I must break away from them or go mad. So I made new friends and I stopped talking about it.

"I was not afraid of Death. It was just that I wanted so to live. I thought I was too young to die. Now, sometimes, I am very tired. I see things happening like before. Vietnam and all the killings. Drug addicts. It's such a senseless waste of life. I think if I had to go through it now, again, at my age, I would not make it. I don't have the strength. So many people then just gave up. Especially the young. I was very lucky.

"I have no fear. Except in my sleep. I used to have such nightmares. I would wake up screaming horribly and literally tear my hair out. Then I would not sleep for two or three days. It's not so bad now. I am not afraid. What could possibly happen? So many things happened to me then, nothing could be worse. Over and over, I asked why. Still I have no answer. You cannot blame just the people who did it, yet how can you blame everyone? I do not believe in God. How could anyone after that? And I do not believe in Life After Death.

"When I am dead, I want to be cremated and throw the ashes away, maybe somewhere to help flowers grow. I do not think of the crematoria then and cremation now in the same way. They are separate. I am not afraid of dying. Even if it was cancer or some other painful death. I have known so much pain that a little more now would not bother me. I could take it. Then I would sleep and never wake up."

4

"You could make a million dollars if you wrote an exposé on the cemeteries. They make Capone look like an amateur."

"I'm no coward, but I'm not independently wealthy either. If you use my name they'll make trouble. They can do it, too. Let them try to guess who it is, if they want to. If the things I have to say make some of them sweat . . . good. They deserve it. Maybe some of them will stop charging for foundations when there are none. Maybe some of them will give the Perpetual Care they're getting paid for, and put the money in a trust fund like they're supposed to. Pennsylvania needs a Cemetery Commission like some of the other states to watch over the interests of the individual lot owner. He's getting taken! I could tell you plenty."

So said this monument dealer, who for obvious reasons wishes to remain anonymous. And though it is a sad commentary, we shall honor his request. He is neither a small dealer nor is he new to the business. It has been in his family for several generations. He says that only some of the cemeteries with which he deals are guilty of the unethical and often unlawful practices of which he speaks.

"Most of the people in this business are terrible businessmen. You can make good money in it, but most of them were just stonecutters and they didn't know about business. They would take an order for a stone from somebody in his forties, charge him what it was, and forget about it. Now the guy lives another twenty years before he dies. The price of the stone has doubled or tripled, but the stonecutter didn't figure the increase when he originally charged."

(This business does 1500–2000 monuments a year in a range of $200 to $2000, with the average about $400. There is an additional charge of as much as $120 by the cemetery which usually insists on providing the foundation for the stone. Granite is usual. Marble wears poorly, especially in a cold climate.)

"Mitford's book attacked the wrong people. You could make a million dollars if you wrote an exposé on the cemeteries. They make Capone look like an amateur. The old days of the small, family cemetery is gone. Now it's the big boys and the promoters. A fast buck, that's all they want. Some of the things they pull are outrageous. But they got away with it because they've got a captive audience. The undertakers can't do anything. I talked to one undertaker who was having a disagreement with a cemetery. So the cemetery called and said, that funeral you got lined up for Tuesday? We can't handle it. You'll have to make it Wednesday. He said, I can't do that! Well there wouldn't be a grave on Tuesday. So he sweated. He really sweated. In the end, he gave in. He had no choice.

"They sell bronze markers for a hundred-fifty bucks on Pre-Need. They're sports. They give two-three years to pay. So what? They get the use of the money for twenty years before the marker's needed. The cost increase in ten years doesn't even match the first year's interest on the money. They charge a hundred-fifty for a disinterment. It's a racket. They use machines now, not hourly laborers. I talked to an operator who told me it takes one-fourth the time it used to. Or the Gardens, that's a joke. The father's already buried in a site, now the mother dies. 'Mrs. Goldman, have you seen our Shalom Gardens? It's so quiet and peaceful. It's surrounded with shrubbery and has genuine rocks from King Solomon's Mines in Israel and no monuments for vandals to turn over. We won't even charge to move your father to the Gardens.' Before they're through, they've sold a $1500 deal and freed up a gravesite that originally cost $50 or so and now sells for plenty more. For what? The ground cost them twenty dollars or so based on their acreage and the lousy bushes cost a couple hundred dollars.

"The crematory, that's a racket too. You can make a fortune with those urns on a shelf. And don't believe they burn those caskets. I wouldn't swear to it because I've never seen it with my own eyes, but some of those guys are supposed to be my friends and they wink at me. I know they lower the body down in the casket, but when it gets below the floor they remove the body and give the undertaker back the casket. They don't burn those caskets.

"I don't see many tears in my business. Usually it's a year or so after and they're over the shock. I like to deal with the middle class. Some people in this business deal with one kind of trade—Italians or Jews or Colored—but I deal with them all. The Italians and Poles go for the most elaborate. Lately, I've been getting a big Colored trade. I like them. They spend well and there's no fuss. I get along well with the Jews because they know I'm no bigot. People don't have many arguments over monuments. They usually know what they want. But the young people lose respect for the old people. I've learned one thing in this business: don't rely on your children. Don't grow old and expect them to be understanding.

"Some people make fun of the monuments I have on display. They laugh or joke or lay down in front of them to make fun. But let somebody die and they're here the next day or so, buying the biggest they can afford. I don't know why people go in for so much show. I think it's guilt and remorse. A guy can't dig his wife up and talk to her. Maybe he treated her rotten. Maybe he beat her, cheated on her. So he feels guilty and buys a big monument.

"I had a guy once, a machinist. His wife died and left him $5000. So he wanted to have a tomb he could visit. I said that was possible. But he said he wanted to see her and touch her. I said, but the thing is sealed . . . you can't do that. He said he'd written to Russia to the Communists to see how they did it with Lenin. I told him that must cost thousands and thousands for pumps to keep that stuff circulating and they can't touch him anyway. So next he decided he wanted a sculptured angel on a base over the grave with her wings spread like so. Well, we do that. But he said he wanted the face to be that of his wife. Then he wanted to run a wire from the cemetery office to the gravesite so he could have an illuminated halo that would go on over the angel at night. People get wacky sometimes, after a death! Fifteen years later that guy hasn't even put up a wooden cross at his wife's grave. I don't know what happened to the $5000. He used to play the horses a lot."

(We were interrupted by an old man and his son. They wished to purchase a stone, but there was considerable discussion over the inscription. The old man was Jewish and spoke with a thick accent. First there was a problem over his wife's Hebrew name. He said in English it was Sophie, in Hebrew it was Sheva. But he couldn't spell it. They looked it up in a book of Hebrew names. Was he pronouncing it correctly? Was he a Litvak or a Galitz? Was it S or Ch? Finally, they found it. It meant Life. "She lived, all right," said the old man. "Look, my name is Swartz. S-W. That's the way the guvment said, that's good enough for me. But she spelled it Schwartz. S-C-H. People asked why. Whatsa matter, ain't you married? I told 'em . . . we was married. But this is a double marker. If you spell her S-C-H and you spell me S-W, people will ask wasn't they married? It's not right. So her name got to be Swartz with a S-W. Okay?")

"I don't think much about Death. I'm not very religious. In my business, Sunday is the busiest day, so I never went to church. I have a will, but I don't specify what I want. My wife and I have an understanding. No viewing. We don't believe in that nonsense. A simple casket and burial under ground. I don't see cremation. It's like burning a dead cat or burning the garbage. I just can't see that. But I don't think too much about it. Except I'm starting to see a lot of friends dropping by the wayside. I don't believe in a Life After Death. You know what they say. Nobody's ever come back to tell about it."

5

"The first autopsy I did as a Resident was the girl I took to my high-school prom . . . It was quite a shock."

Dr. Marvin Aronson is Philadelphia's Chief Medical Examiner. Medium height, balding, a faint red mustache on a round face, an old pipe clenched between his teeth. He is very heavy. His hands are constantly busy as he talks, tamping his pipe or cleaning it or lighting it or clipping his nails. He is a great fan of Sherlock Holmes and plans to write mysteries based on the many plots that he has already outlined. Dr. Aronson is a forensic pathologist, certified by three Boards.

"I came here thirteen years ago. I finally decided to go to work at thirty-four after spending a lot of time learning medicine. I only intended to stay a year or so, but I liked it so much I stayed. With my experience, I could go on to a job on the outside that would pay forty or fifty thousand more than I make here, but I like this too much. We investigate deaths that are known or suspected to have been unnatural. We have a staff of sixty-five, five of which are professional. We're caught in a budget squeeze, but no worse I guess than others in the city. Our budget for next year is about $220,000 which means a salary cut of fifteen per cent.

"We were promised to go on computer, but it never happened. No money. In the basement there are literally a billion facts and pieces of valuable information. There's no one to correlate it. Give me three million dollars and two years and I'd have it all on computer. If they'd have done it when I suggested, it would have only cost a million. There are tremendously important clues there to the solving of diseases and the social violence of man. But I'm the only one who believes it.

"We examine about forty-five hundred bodies a year here. About eighteen hundred to two thousand of them are autopsied. Most of the autopsies we do are intended to confirm our opinion on the cause of death. Attorneys around here have gotten pretty sophisticated. They know a gunshot wound may not be sufficient to cause death. Many times the autopsy exonerates the accused. Once we've taken jurisdiction of a body, the decision to autopsy is ours. We do not need the family's approval. However, where there are borderline cases and the family requests through the funeral director that there be no autopsy, we try to co-operate.

"At one time, many of the bodies that came through here were unclaimed and had to be buried at city expense. I think the cost for that is now around seventy dollars, but we have very few—maybe five or ten a year—and I would guess that whoever gets the contract next year will want more. Seventy dollars doesn't go very far today. A lot of our work is investigative, and by tracking down families, we've saved the city a lot of money. Easily the cost of the investigator.

"I keep my own statistics. As of the first of the year, I have done 3,719 autopsies. It doesn't change my attitude if I know the dead person. Of course I wouldn't want to autopsy my father or my wife or my children. I've got a whole lot of cousins, some of whom I wouldn't mind autopsying, but if it was somebody who I knew really well, I'd have somebody else do it. I'm the Chief and I have a staff to do things like that. You see, you arrive at certain conclusions at an autopsy, and I wouldn't want someone to think that my conclusions were influenced by my former relationship with the person. That would be the reason, not the emotional impact.

"I autopsied two people that I actually knew pretty well. One was the first autopsy I did as a Resident, but I didn't know at the time who it was. It was the girl I took to my high-school prom. She committed suicide. The job had already been begun, so that when I got there her face was covered. And she had married, so I didn't recognize her name. When I finished up and saw her face, it was quite a shock. The other one was a fellow student in medical school. He had committed suicide much later and of course I hadn't seen him in a long time. Funny, one thing I realized at the time of the autopsy was that he was a fairy. I was surprised that I hadn't known he was a fairy in med school. Of course, he may not have been a practicing homosexual when I knew him.

"One thing that really affects you is kids. I don't care how much experience you have, whenever it's a kid it's as if you're just starting. It gets worse when you have your own kids. That's why I tell my kids —yes, your father is different and that's why there are rules in this house that are different from anybody else's down the street. I'm sorry, but that's it. —My kids aren't allowed to have a balloon in their mouth. They're not allowed to have cap pistols. They're not allowed to swim alone. I've made them have a great deal of confidence in the water. It wasn't easy, it had to be subtle so I didn't instill fear instead. But I wanted them to know that if they were ever in a situation, they could remain afloat for a long, long time.

"When I was about six, my grandfather died and I was very close to that situation. About a year later, I had reason to see that these old people with their payyes and yarmulkes were a bunch of hypocritical old bastards. That was when I became a seven-and-a-half-year-old Atheist. Now, I've come around again to believing in a Supreme Being. I'm not formally religious, but I think I've developed a sense of Life . . . that we all play a part in the Medium of Life, like a bacterium relates to a culture medium. There are two unique circumstances in Death. The first is that it is universal. We all die. The second is that no other animal but Man knows this and makes plans for, or at least contemplates, his own death.

"I think about my death from time to time. I don't think my work has in any way influenced my views. My wife knows, I've talked about it many times, that I would want my body turned over to the Anatomical Board for dissection by medical students. If for some reason my body is unsuitable, then I would wish it cremated and thrown to the wind or somewhere where it won't cause pollution."

6

"Whoever tell you he can talk with the Dead is a liar!"

My long search for a Spiritual Medium led me finally to a dingy store front in a run-down section of town. The sign out front read: Spiritual Advisor—Palms Read. The door was open and I walked in. I was in a small darkened room about eight feet by ten. My eyes grew accustomed to the darkness and I saw an old Gypsy woman seated at one end of a low sofa. At the other end of the sofa, a small child was sprawled in sleep. There were two more children sleeping on another old sofa across the room. Through a partially curtained doorway, I could see into another much larger room, at the end of which a young woman stood cooking at a stove. The smell of herbs and cooking oil permeated the whole place.

The old Gypsy gave me a toothless grin and patted the sofa next to her. I handed her my card.

"I'm looking for a Medium," I said. "Someone who can be in touch with the Other World."

She answered, but I had difficulty understanding her. She became exasperated, finally yelling over her shoulder in a broken voice to the woman in the other room. The language was unfamiliar. The daughter came out and asked what I wanted. I told her. She shrugged.

"Nobody around here can do that. Mostly, they read palms. My mother here knows about Spirits." She walked back to the kitchen. I tried again.

"I'm looking for someone who talks to the Spirits."

She pointed to her ear and said, "I can't hear so good." Then her hand fluttered to her chest. "I just got back from the hospital."

"Are you feeling all right?"

"Are you a doctor?"

"No."

"Are you a newspaper writer?"

"Yes."

The old Gypsy took a deep breath. Then she surprised me with a loud clear voice that I had no difficulty understanding. "Whoever tell you he can talk with the Dead is a liar! Some people would die just to be able to talk to the Dead. When God take them, they don't talk no more. Whether to Heaven or whether to Hell, the Dead Man don't talk. Whoever tell you he can hear him is crazy in the head."

She sank back weakly on the sofa. As I left, she was still patting the sofa next to her and showing her gums in another toothless grin. One of the three children whimpered in his sleep.

7

"We have a joke around here. When someone says that doesn't look like so-and-so when she was alive, we say yeah but you ain't never seen her dead before."

The Baker Funeral Home is one of Philadelphia's better-known black funeral homes. I waited in a dimly lit entrance hall. It was early in the morning. The doors to Chapel A were open and I looked into the large high-ceilinged room. There were three sections of metal folding chairs, about twenty rows of ten to a section. Up front, surrounded by a great many flowers, was an open casket in which I could just make out the figure of a black man. The face was covered with a white cloth. In the hall a table held a stack of white mimeographed papers, programs from the memorial service of the night before. It included several hymns and the announcement of the interment scheduled for that morning. Wendell Baker arrived and we went into a small office adjacent to Chapel A. On the way he turned on the air-conditioning in the chapel. A tall man, good-looking, with his hair cut short but worn in a natural, mustache and goatee. He is thirty-six and cool.

"We're very busy here all the time. We have about six hundred cases a year, eighteen this week. Everybody wants the weekend. We just can't do everybody for the weekend. We get very few cremations, I don't think ten in the last ten years. This business is built on customs and traditions and social mores. The black people are very emotional about their funerals. The Italians are too. They probably spend the most. But the black people and the Italians and the Jews, they don't believe in cremation.

"About fifty per cent of our cases have been autopsied. It's not true that undertakers charge a hundred dollars more to embalm after an autopsy, but sometimes we have to charge more. What they didn't tell you and what they don't tell the family is what goes on sometimes. It makes it harder to do the job of embalming. Also, they don't tell the family why they do autopsies. Every doctor wants an autopsy to con-firm his diagnosis. Hospitals need them to authenticate their records. I can see an autopsy sometimes, for science, but not on an old person. Most of the old people die of heart trouble. Why do an autopsy on an eighty-year-old? Sure we try to talk the family out of an autopsy.

"Embalming is for sanitary purposes. You wouldn't want an un-embalmed body around in the summer, no sir. Why, we have air-condi-tioning and a big exhaust fan that operates from the roof—that's the hum you hear—but even with all that, you can smell it when you pass my Preparation Room. Wow, you wouldn't want to have unembalmed bodies in the summer! We have a joke around here. When someone says that doesn't look like so-and-so when she was alive, we say yeah but you ain't never seen her dead before.

"I went to Morgan State in Baltimore where I studied economics, and I went to Eckles embalming school here in Philadelphia. They closed. Nobody new going into the business. Couldn't make a go. I didn't want to join the business as a kid, because my Daddy's pretty strict and he wouldn't pay much. Now I see him from a different per-spective. He's got a fine reputation. He started this business in 1928 [sic]. My mother said he was crazy—people was jumpin' out of win-dows and blowin' holes in their heads, gettin' out of business. He saved three hundred dollars in the Depression and came home and said, I'm goin' into business. Once he accused me of not workin' hard enough. On the way home, I told my mother and she said, Son, in the old days your Daddy had three jobs. Many a night he'd come home, plop down in a chair and sleep for two hours, then go back to work. So I guess he had a right to tell me I wasn't workin' hard enough.

"There's no trouble any more with racism in the cemeteries. Again, there are traditions. Most black people want to be buried with the rest of their family. I don't think there'd be any trouble from a cemetery if an established firm like ours wanted ground for a black person. But the white and black firms work pretty well together. We're all in the same business. There's no block bustin' in cemeteries. We're workin' together to try to hold down the outsiders comin' in and drivin' prices down. You can't get a corporate charter in Pennsylvania any more, so a big outfit like this Texas oil company comes in and buys someone to get the charter. Then they go into the finance business and they go into the cemetery business and they start lowering the prices.

"One of those outfits bought an established place in a black community and they want a black man to front it. It's white-owned, but they get a black man to front. That's the way it was mostly in the South. There was a few black millionaires in the business down South, but mostly it was white-owned with a black front. My conception's changed since I've traveled down South. You might have to work hard for Mister Charlie, but one thing was you always knew where you stood. There's no b.s., Mister Charlie calls a spade a spade. If you're doin' somethin' he don't like, he tells you. Not like up North.

"When Death is business, I don't have any trouble. I'm cool and I handle it. But if it's my own family or someone I know well, I get as emotional as anybody. I'm very religious, but in a philosophical way. I had polio when I was eighteen months old and I had rheumatic fever when I was four. I had something like St. Vitus Dance at the same time and the doctors didn't hold no hope for me. I've been shot and stabbed. I been run over by a bus, a truck, and a car. I've had every childhood disease you can think of. I think about Death, all right. I think about the Man up there watchin' over me.

"Some people say they don't see me at church. I'm a Trustee. Well, I'm there. I don't have no Day of Rest, just a piece of one. I go over, check the money and do the books, then run back for a quick lunch, see my kids and get back to work. I do a lot more churchin' than those hypocrite deacons who get up there and pray for five minutes, then go chasin' after some woman.

"I think more about dyin' than Death, I guess. I have a will, but there's nothin' in it about what to do with me. I haven't thought much about it. I'd want to be buried above ground, though, I know too much about what goes on underneath the cemeteries. Maybe in a mausoleum. But I don't personally go for all the pomp and circumstance. That's what people want and it's my business, but I wouldn't want it for my family."

8

"I could sit down next to a casket and eat my lunch and it wouldn't bother me. Unless it was someone near and dear, and then my attitude hasn't changed in forty years."

Charles Clark is the Director of West Laurel Hill Cemetery, one of Philadelphia's finest. He is also a director of the Pennsylvania Cemetery Association and the American Cemetery Association. He was extremely suspicious and the interview began badly. He seemed certain that I was intent on an exposé à la Jessica Mitford, and I had difficulty convincing him otherwise. He said that her book was unfair and did not give a representative cross-section of either the cemetery business or the undertaker business, that West Laurel Hill was a very ethical place and had never cheated anyone. West Laurel Hill was founded as a private nonprofit corporation in 1869. It consists of 187 acres in which 95,000 have already been interred. Burial sites begin at $55 for charity cases and go up to $5000. When I suggested that perhaps under the circumstances we should conclude the interview, his attitude changed and we had a nice chat. Clark, in his sixties, was conservatively dressed in slacks, a sports jacket and a bow tie. Balding, glasses, a faint pencil-thin mustache.

"I came here in '31. I was in the insurance business, but I hadn't weathered the Depression. I told the Director here that I had no money and if he wanted me to be able to maintain payments on my plot here, he'd have to give me a job. He said he'd never heard that given as a reason for a job before, so he hired me. The first week I didn't have enough money to buy coveralls, so I cut grass in a bowler and a Chesterfield coat.

"I don't think we ever had an application for a grave made by a Colored family before the Civil Rights legislation was passed. We still have only ten or twenty Colored here. But we were always nonsectarian. As early as '38, our attorneys said if you have an application from a Colored person, you better sell him.

"Some cemeteries are definitely unethical. We don't let them into our association. We have a reputation to protect. These promoters— they offer free dishes if you purchase a site—or they offer a free grave to a Veteran, then charge twice the going rate for a site next to it for his wife. These are the ones that make a bad name for the rest of us. It's bad publicity. But I think we have the best relationship with the undertakers of anyone in the business.

"Our crematorium was started in '38. The first in Philadelphia was about the turn of the century. The first in the country was built much earlier in Washington, Pennsylvania. Anyone can be cremated in our crematorium. We do have certain requirements. The body must be delivered in an acceptable container. One delivered a body in a pouch. We wouldn't accept it. Our men have to handle the body then. But it doesn't have to be an expensive casket. One manufacturer makes an acceptable container out of rigid cardboard. As for embalming, that's a legal question. The law says you must embalm after forty-eight hours.

"People have a mistaken idea on what cremains look like. It's not a fine powder. Within the ashes are bone fragments sometimes six inches long. Bones are calcium and that's not combustible." (In her book, Jessica Mitford claimed that the heat was kept deliberately low enough to insure that these fragments would be present, so as to dissuade people from scattering ashes.) "They have the idea that they can just spread the powder around, but they can't. The law says that cremation is not the ultimate disposition of the body. If the ashes are unclaimed or the family has signed the release authorizing us to dispose of the cremains, they are consigned to under-the-ground burial. We wait until we have two or three hundred, then we put them under ground with no marker. Or they can be interred in a regular site or an urn garden. We also operate a Columbarium, where we will sell shelf space. We do not provide an urn, but we do sell them. Otherwise, the cremains are placed in a cardboard box and mailed to the family."

(Later, on visiting the crematorium:) "These two caskets are awaiting cremation. The wooden one will of course be consumed, but not the metal one. We can't have a high enough temperature to melt down the metal. We use 1700 degrees Fahrenheit. We'll remove the lid of the metal casket and lean it on one side. Afterwards, it has to be cooled and removed, then carted away. It's really more work, but some people seem to need that elaborate a show."

In the "shipping room," several boxes were ready to be mailed. Certified parcel post or occasionally by air or truck. About twelve inches cubed, the boxes were wrapped in a white paper with a red seal on the top. I picked one up. It weighed about five or six pounds. Clark brought me an open box yet to be wrapped. It was filled with grayish ashes with little bits and pieces of off-white bone.

"Cryogenics? It's very expensive. How long are you going to have to keep the body frozen? Even when we set up trust funds for Perpetual Care, we have trouble. Costs go up, interest fluctuates. Then there's the problem of space. Where will you put all of the bodies? And how about damage from the freezing process? Even if there was no damage, say you have a nineteen-year-old you freeze just before the last breath or just after the last breath, and you bring him back even twenty years later. What's going to happen to him? Everybody is twenty years older, but he's still the same. No, I think it's just a fad. If Forest Lawn isn't in it—and they're out for the buck—then I don't think it's got much demand. I was out at Forest Lawn two or three times. I don't see that sort of thing. This latest is even worse than their Last Supper area. Now they've got the Crucifixion, a whole panorama. Then they open up a gift shop connected with it. That kind of commercialism is a desecration.

"When I first came here, I had to turn my back when a funeral passed, I was that emotional. Now, I could sit down next to a casket and eat my lunch and it wouldn't bother me. Unless it was someone near and dear, and then my attitude hasn't changed in forty years. But I'm here to serve people who need me, regardless of how I feel. My wife and I both believe in cremation. And no funeral. I think it's a desecration. Rows of mourners lined up looking in the casket—doesn't he look nice, he almost looks alive—nobody looks nice when they're dead.

"I studied as a boy for the ministry and I was a Sunday-School teacher, but I don't go to church any more. My wife was Episcopalian and I was divorced, so when she married me she was thrown out of her church. I believe in God, a Supreme Being, but I don't think some native in the far Pacific, who hasn't discovered Christ, is damned. He has a God—maybe the Sun or the Wind or something. I'm not certain I believe in a Life After Death . . . but I'm not certain there isn't one either."

9

"When I die, I want the full treatment. After all, I'm in the business. I can get it wholesale."

A large pink stucco building, fronted with tinted glass. The huge raised letters over the door spell Goldsteins' in script. Inside, elegant draperies, thick carpets, plush sofas, and paneled walls. It could be the lobby of a small resort hotel, except for the small prayer books tastefully placed on a corner table. The first page reads: Goldsteins'—A Family Staff for Sympathetic Family Service. There follows, in addition to the prayers, the pictures of eleven members of the "Family" and several pages of copy concerning the impressive facilities including modern lighting, engineered air-conditioning, high-fidelity sound systems, and special humidity and temperature controls. Bennett Goldstein, 39, was modishly dressed. Sculptured hair and tinted glasses. We talked in his large paneled office on the walls of which hung framed diplomas of various members of the family.

"Goldsteins' was started by my father and my cousin in 1944. She was a figurehead. It was actually my father and my uncle. They worked for other funeral directors before that. My father worked for an Italian. They did livery work. I started in '49. I always wanted to be an undertaker, even when I was a kid. I went to Central High, then to Eckles mortician school. It's closed now. Eckles ran off with his secretary. My uncle and my father are still active, but it's my show now. This place was my idea. I wanted to be the top banana. We are the largest Jewish funeral director in the city, probably the state. We handle about eleven hundred funerals a year. They go all the way from no cost for indigents to as high as $8000. The average is $1200. Our 'season' is from November to March. From the first frost, that's the busiest time for us.

"We're different from the others. We're a family operation. We give family service. We know most of the people we service. Probably ninety-five per cent know one or another of us. Many of the other funeral directors are family-owned too, but usually they are neighborhood funeral homes. It would be hard to get into a business like this, with an operation this size. You'd have to have a half a million dollars or three quarters of a million to invest before you'd even begin to make anything.

"About ninety per cent are embalmed. Only the real Orthodox Jews don't get embalmed. We don't charge extra if someone's been posted [autopsied], but some do. The problem is that when we embalm, we need the neck veins and arteries. But they often cut them and it makes it very difficult. Also, it's usually a young first-year resident. Sometimes, he postpones [the autopsy] until the next day. In the Jewish religion, burial is supposed to be the next day.

"We don't have too many cremations. The trend is to immediate-family viewing, then a closed-casket funeral. I think they realize that these open-casket viewings for the general public are barbaric. I've had some strange requests. One wanted cremation and the ashes scattered over Valley Forge. Another wanted ashes scattered in the Bahamas. I was going there on a fishing trip, so I took the ashes along. I took care of the Valley Forge request also. The most unusual request came from a woman who refused to attend her father's funeral. Then, a week after the burial, she had the body disinterred, reembalmed with a special fluid—I don't even know how they did that, I've never heard of a complete reembalming—then the body was shipped to the Cryonics Society in Long Island. She had to buy a special capsule for about six or seven thousand dollars. The capsule was placed in liquid nitrogen about 270 degrees below zero. The Perpetual Care was about nine thousand dollars. The whole thing is ridiculous. I don't think there are more than about six or seven frozen bodies in the country.

"You get pretty used to Death in this business. You handle it pretty matter-of-factly unless it's someone you know. My cousin was murdered by her boyfriend last New Year's Eve. That was pretty rough. It's always rough when you're close, no matter how long you're in the business. But you go away every five or six weeks for a few days. Get the place out of your system. Then you come back and you can work.

"I'm scared of Death. I don't think I'm afraid of dying. I always tell my doctor, if there's something the matter with me, don't tell my family, tell me so I have time to put my affairs in order. When I die,

I want the full treatment . . . a bronze casket, a sealed vault in the family plot, but only the religious service. After all, I'm in the business. I can get it wholesale. I want to go in style. I'm not very, very religious, but I go to synagogue on the High Holidays and maybe eight or nine Friday nights. I believe in God. And I believe in a Life After Death. Sort of. Well . . . it's a nice thing to believe in."

INTERMISSION

Thus far, these dialogues have dealt mainly with the physical aspect of Death. There remains the spiritual, and the dialogues that follow will touch upon that aspect. One is with a rabbi, one is with a priest, and one is with Charlotte Jasper who talked with God. Some who have read the manuscript thus far have suggested the need at this point for levity, the subject of Death having weighed heavily upon them.

The amount of humorous material connected with Death is minimal, and even that generally has more irony than humor. Like the one about the Chinese funeral director who practiced the ancient custom of placing food at the gravesite after each of the funerals he serviced. One day, an Italian friend in the same business jokingly asked when was he going to stop leaving food on the graves for his customers to eat? The Chinese funeral director smiled and said, "When you stop planting flowers for yours to smell."

But perhaps the best humor on the subject may be found in some of the old churchyard epitaphs. Once, they were traditional. Now, in most private cemeteries, they are no longer permitted. Creeping commercialism has determined that it encourages people to linger in cemeteries longer than necessary, creating some sort of human traffic problem for the efficient marketing experts that are taking over the business. Most now limit inscriptions to names and dates and innocuous endearments like Beloved Mother. Many have done away with tombstones altogether, substituting bronze plaques in "memorial gardens." For those in need then, here is a brief interlude in the form of some humorous lines from the days of the now obsolete graveyard epitaphs.

Here lies the body of THOMAS WOODHEN,
The most loving of husbands and amiable of men.

His name was WOODCOCK, but it wouldn't rhyme.
  Erected by his loving widow.

At rest beneath this churchyard stone
Lies stingy JEMMY WYATT;
He died one morning just at ten, and
Saved a dinner by it.

Some have children—some have none—
Here lies the mother of twenty-one.

Life is a jest, and all things show it,
I thought so once, but now I know it.

Here I lie, at the chancel door,
Here I lie, because I'm poor:
The farther in, the more you pay,
Here I lie as warm as they.

What I was you know not—
What I am you know not—
Whither I am gone you know not—
  Go about your business.

OWEN MOORE is gone away
Owin' more than he could pay.

Sacred to the memory of Anthony Drake,
Who died for peace and quietness sake;
His wife was constantly scolding and scoffin',
So he sought for repose in a twelve-dollar coffin.

Beneath this stone our baby lays
  He neither cries nor hollers
He lived just one and twenty days
  And cost us forty dollars.

Whilst BUTLER (needy wretch!) was yet alive
No gen'rous patron would a dinner give;
See him, when starv'd to death, and turn'd to dust,
Presented with a monumental bust!
The poet's fate is here in emblem shown,
He ask'd for bread, and he received a stone.

Here sleeps in peace a Hampshire Grenadier,
Who caught his death by drinking cold small beer;
Soldiers, be wise from his untimely fall,
And when ye're hot drink strong, or none at all.

Here lies the body of barren PEG,
Who had no issue but one in her leg;
But while she was living she was so cunning
That when one stood still the other was running.

> As I was, so be ye;
> As I am, ye shall be;
> That I gave, that I have;
> What I spent, that I had;
> Thus I end all my cost;
> What I left, that I lost.

Here lies the bodies
Of THOMAS BOND and MARY his wife.
She was temperate, chaste and charitable;
> But
She was proud, peevish and pashionate.
She was an affectionate wife, and a tender mother:
> But
Her husband and child, whom she loved,
Seldom saw her countenance without a disgusting frown
Whilst she received visitors, whom she despised, with an endearing
  smile.
Her behaviour was discreet towards strangers;
> But

Independent in her family.

Abroad, her conduct was influenced by good breeding;
　　　But
At home, by ill temper.

She was a professed enemy to flattery,

And was seldom known to praise or commend;
　　　But
The talents in which she principally excelled,

Were difference of opinion, and discovering flaws and imperfections.

She was an admirable economist,

And, without prodigality,

Dispensed plenty to every person in her family;
　　　But
Would sacrifice their eyes to a farthing candle.

She sometimes made her husband happy with her good qualities;
　　　But
Much more frequently miserable—with her many failings:

Insomuch that in thirty years cohabitation he often lamented

That mauger of all her virtues,

He had not, in the whole, enjoyed two years of matrimonial comfort.
　　　AT LENGTH
Finding that she had lost the affections of her husband,

As well as the regard of her neighbors,

Family disputes having been divulged by the servants,

She died of vexation, July 20, 1768.
　　　Aged 48 years.
Her worn-out husband survived her four months, and two days,

And departed this life, Nov. 28, 1768.
　　　In the 54th year of his age.
William Bond, brother to the deceased, erected this stone,

As a weekly monitor, to the surviving wives of this parish,

That they may avoid the infamy

Of having their memories handed to posterity

With a PATCH WORK character.

The One remains, the many change and pass;
Heaven's light forever shines, Earth's shadows fly;
Life, like a dome of many-coloured glass,
Stains the white radiance of Eternity,
Until Death tramples it to fragments,—Die
If thou wouldst be with that which thou dost seek!

—SHELLEY, *The Triumph of Life*

The young may die
  but the old must.

    —LONGFELLOW

All our knowledge merely helps
us to die a more painful death
than the animals that know
nothing.

      —MAETERLINCK

Death is the veil which those
  who live call life;
They sleep, and it is lifted.

—SHELLEY, *Adonais*

[220]

Death is nothing to us: for that which is dissolved is without sensation; and that which lacks sensation is nothing to us.

—EPICURUS, *Principal Doctrines*

. . . That's what dying is: The last, hopefully the best, of all ego trips. Dying is one's last, best chance to know the mystery of oneself. Surely the most meaningful experience in one's life.

—MAGGIE SAVOY, former Woman's Editor
for the *Los Angeles Times*, from
unfinished notes for a book on dying,
written while in the final stages
of terminal illness.

Those who welcome death have only tried it from the ears up.

—MIZNER

Death is Nature's expert advice
to get plenty of Life.

—GOETHE

If you have lived one day you have seen all. One day is equal to all the other days. There is no other light; there is no other night. Death is not to be feared. It is a friend.

—MONTAIGNE

THIS MONUMENT IS A MEMORIAL TO
CHARLES S. STRATTON, A NATIVE OF BRIDGEPORT,
WHO GAINED WORLDWIDE FAME AS TOM THUMB IN
THE EXHIBITIONS OF P.T. BARNUM. THE LIFESIZE
STATUE WAS ERECTED BEFORE TOM THUMB'S DEATH
ON JULY 15, 1883. IN 1969 VANDALS SMASHED
THE STATUE. IT WAS RESTORED BY THE BARNUM
FESTIVAL SOCIETY AND MOUNTAIN GROVE
CEMETERY ASSOCIATION WITH FUNDS RAISED
BY PUBLIC SUBSCRIPTION.
NOV. 19, 1969

Death hath set his mark and seal
On all we are and all we feel,
On all we know and all we fear.

—SHELLEY

It is not the consciousness of death but the flight from death that distinguishes men from animals.

—NORMAN O. BROWN, *Life Against Death*

And this is the will of him that sent me, that every one which seeth the Son and believeth in him, may have everlasting life: and I will raise him up at the last day.   —JESUS CHRIST, *John 6:40*

A man finds himself, to his great astonishment, suddenly existing, after thousands and thousands of years of nonexistence: he lives for a little while; and then, again, comes an equally long period when he must exist no more. The heart rebels against this, and feels that it cannot be true.   —SCHOPENHAUER, *The Vanity of Existence*

For what thou art shall perish utterly,
But what is thine may never cease to be.

—SHELLEY, *Queen Mab*

I am glad God saw Death and gave Death a Job taking
care of all who are tired of living.

—CARL SANDBURG, *Junk Man*

And so I did sit between the City of the Living and the City of the Dead. Yonder I sat thinking on the never-ending strife and ceaseless movement in the one and the quiet that reigned over and the peace that dwelled in the other. Here, hope and despair and love and hate; poverty and riches, belief and unbelief. There, earth within earth that Nature turned over and in the stillness of night created therefrom first plant, then animal life.

—KAHLIL GIBRAN, *In the City of the Dead*

Men fear death as children fear to go in the dark: and as that natural fear in children is increased with tales, so is the other.

—BACON, *Essays: Of Death*

[229]

10

"There are even caterers now who cater the meal at Shiva. And there's laughing and joking. It all lacks dignity."

Rabbi Sheldon Freedman at thirty-three has been an Orthodox Jewish rabbi for nine years. He is the spiritual leader of Philadelphia's Adath Zion Congregation, a Conservative synagogue. He is also chairman of the Funeral Standards Committee of the Philadelphia Board of Rabbis. Stocky. Modishly long sideburns, conservatively cut hair. A plain dark suit. Coming in from the outside, he replaces his gray straw hat with the traditional black yarmulke. His cluttered study is lined with books.

"Death was always a hang-up with me, perhaps because I lost my father very suddenly when I was eighteen. He was not yet thirty-nine. I've always felt that what a rabbi says is terribly important at the time of a funeral. He can give some sense of meaning to the person's life for those who are still living. But it is a time which is not repeated, so the things which the rabbi does not say, he will not have the opportunity to say again. Often the rabbi did not even know the deceased. He may try to talk to the family, to see what he was like. Or he may just have the basic information—he was sixty-five, he was a father, his children's names and so forth—and he makes up the rest. And then there are burying rabbis who may do six or seven funerals a week. They do a splendid job, but it's usually canned.

"For the first five years or more, I wrote everything down, word for word. Now I don't do that. The eulogy or Hesped is very important in the Jewish tradition. The Jewish funeral is really for the dead not the living, and the Hesped is his right. In fact if the children should request no eulogy, they are to be ignored. Only if the deceased requested no eulogy can there be none. The purpose of the Hesped was to glorify the deceased, but also to make the assembled mourners cry —I don't do that—not to cry too much, but to cry. There were even professional criers—Kononim—hired to mingle with the mourners and to cry during the Hesped. The eulogizer was to be the first to be paid from the estate, before debts, taxes, or inheritances.

"The traditional Jewish funeral is a very simple affair. As chairman of the Funeral Standards Committee, I have had to do battle many times with funeral directors. They are very kind, very considerate, very solicitous . . . but very commercial. They are in business to make money. If they embalm, then they can have an open casket, use a cosmetologist, sell an expensive casket. I had one case where the family was told that the law insisted on embalming after twenty-four hours. That's not true. It is required only if the family does not object on religious grounds. In this case the death was on a Tuesday and the funeral could not be for several days and the weather was very warm. But they did it. They can do it when they want to.

"Years ago people would sell their household possessions in order to dress the body in the most magnificent clothes possible, far above what they could afford. Then they would go without food. In fact, that's where the tradition began of having neighbors prepare the food for the mourners. Finally the rabbis decreed that no matter whether a poor man or a king, all should be dressed in a shroud. And the casket should be a plain one. We don't still use a bier, which was used in Biblical days. Cremation is not allowed because the Bible says that you shall return to dust in the earth. Jewish cemeteries are consecrated ground, but there was provision for a Gentile member of a mixed marriage to be buried near the fence.

"The Jewish religion definitely believes in a Life After Death. Some say it is not covered in the Bible, only in the Midrash, but it is alluded to in the Bible, definitely in David's Psalms. The Soul in Jewish tradition—it's not in the Law—rises in stages. The first day, the third, seven days, a month, and a year. And it is judged along the way. In fact, each day in our prayers, three times a day, there is mention of the Hereafter.

"I've had different people relate unusual experiences. One was an old man in his seventies with a diseased spleen that had to be removed. He was not a well man anyway, and the doctors told him he had only a ten-per-cent chance, but the spleen had to be removed. He said all right. Well he survived and when I went to see him he said, Rabbi I've been to the Other Side. I said, what do you mean? And he said, there were some people who kept pulling me and telling me I must go with them, but I refused and said I was not ready to go, that I wanted to live yet a while, and they let me. He swore that it happened, that he didn't make it up. That was his story.

"Another man, young yet in his forties, had a serious heart attack.

He almost didn't make it. He told me that he talked to God and that he told God he was not ready, that he still had much to do, and that God gave him a number of years more. That was his story. He had a complete transformation. Sold his business, grew a beard, moved to Baltimore to a Yeshiva. His wife cooks for the Yeshiva. His children go to school at the Yeshiva. A complete transformation.

"The traditional Jewish funeral is a continuity with the past and is prescribed by Jewish Law. But the commercial aspects have begun to turn it into a party, and I'm against that. There is such guilt on the part of people—why didn't I tell him how much I loved him? Why did I argue with him? Maybe I hastened his death.—So now they decide he will have nothing but the best. An expensive casket, a vault, a huge monument, flowers. Then someone who has attended this funeral has to arrange one for their father and naturally they have to show that they loved their father as much as the other people loved theirs. It becomes competitive. There are even caterers now who cater the meal at Shiva [week of mourning in which the family is visited at home by friends and relatives]. And there's laughing and joking. It all lacks dignity.

"I don't think much about Death. I'm a fatalist. I don't believe I'll live a long life. Perhaps because my father died early, and his father. I am a great believer in an ethical will. I have two children—twenty months and five years. From time to time I write them letters and deposit them in sealed envelopes. I want them to know their father, what I believe in, what I would hope of them. It may be that this is a way of extending our lives a little, but I think it means more than that. If I should die now, what would my children know of their father?

"Certainly it's a natural thing, but Death is a tragedy, a calamitous event. I cannot minimize Death. You can adjust to the death of a loved one. You can adapt to the loss of an arm, to the killing of people in a war, to the Hydrogen Bomb . . . but it is no less a tragedy. It is said that scar tissue is the strongest type of skin. Perhaps the scars of Death make us stronger that live."

11

"I believe God gives us a moment of choice . . . to go willingly or unwillingly and when it is my time, I hope to go willingly."

Twelve years ago, when the Right Reverend Monsignor Charles Mynaugh was appointed Director of Radio and Television for the Philadelphia Diocese, the Church of Saint Stephen had a congregation of over three thousand families. Today, in spite of the population increase in the parish, the congregation is down to eight hundred families and he is their priest. The parish is predominately black, but the congregation is about half white. Msgr. Mynaugh is fifty-five. Thin gray hair, aluminum framed glasses, a friendly if not robust face. We chatted at the Rectory on a warm summer afternoon.

"There are really very few prerequisites in a Catholic funeral. We make no great demands. People think of us as stern dictators, scowling and saying you must do this, you must do that. We are in opposition to cremation because it flaunts the concept of Resurrection. It says: I do not believe in the Resurrection and to prove it I will have my body cremated and scatter the ashes. Well that's wrong. But I'm sure that there are other areas of the world where Catholics are cremated. In Europe in some places, there is no more room. As for suicide, there's no problem to be buried in a Catholic cemetery. We just don't make a public thing of it, a public ceremony. I've had some over the years and the families are quite thankful not to have a public ceremony. We cannot grant a Christian burial to someone who has been in public scandal. If I should run off with someone, that would be a scandal, and we would not wish to appear to sanction such an act. As for autopsy, embalming, viewings, wakes . . . this is all custom. The Church has nothing particular to say about these things.

"I was fortunate to have been chaplain at an Old Age Home for three and a half years—Sacred Heart—and there were 180 people from about sixty to a hundred years old. Most were well and lived happily. Some were senile and some were sick. I helped many to face Death. I would say it was split down the middle between those who looked forward to Death and those who feared it. I would tell them that the end of their life on this earth was nearly at hand, but that it was God's will. I told them to think of the many good things they had accomplished in their lives. Not to dwell on the weaknesses and the mistakes. We all have them, and God had already forgiven them since we had administered the sacraments. That God was a loving and merciful God. It was almost always of help.

"We service Temple University Hospital and do the same thing. Of course there are so many more—about half the patients are Catholic —and we don't get to know them in the same way. We try not to make it mechanical, although sometimes it turns out that way. Sometimes the family requests that we come. It's funny though, they always tell me to just make believe I dropped in, so the patient won't be upset. I tell them that's ridiculous. If I'm to deliver the sacraments, I can't have just dropped in, after all. Most of the patients are glad to see me. Damn glad!

"This business of Last Rites. We used to call it Extreme Unction. Then it was called Last Rites. I don't know where that came from. Now we call it the Sacrament of the Sick. Yet the prayers have always been the same, they've never changed. We ask for forgiveness, but we ask for the patient to be cured. We anoint the Oil of the Sick to the five senses—eyes, ears, nose, mouth, hands, and feet if possible—to help them get better! But you still have nurses who ask if you've delivered Last Rites.

"Once I had a patient I had seen several times. Finally the family asked me to come to deliver the sacraments. When I entered the room there must have been a dozen people around the bed. The doctor asked me to wait a little bit, so I stood against the wall. A head nurse came in and, seeing me, said that they didn't want the patient to be disturbed or to worry. I pointed to the crowd and said if that didn't disturb the patient, I certainly wouldn't. I think people who are dying are receptive to me, but I wouldn't describe their participation as active. It's a wonderful thing to be able to help in such a time. It's a very Christian thing.

"We say that as long as there is organic life, the sacraments should be given. But if I deliver the sacraments to someone that has been dead for an hour or so, I have a hang-up on the part about praying for cure and anointing with oil. I skip it and shorten the prayers. It's mostly for the peace of mind of the survivors, anyway. I pray for the soul, of course, but the rest is of no help to the person who is dead. Some people wait to be baptized until they know they are ready to die. They know about the innocence of one who has just been baptized, so they're afraid to be baptized too early. They don't use it as license, of course.

"Most of the concepts and laws come from the Judaic Laws. Especially the hygienic ones—the quick Jewish burial—it gets hot in the

Middle East, you know. As for the eulogy, that's a regional thing. There was a statute in this diocese against eulogizing. I guess one could get carried away and practically canonize someone. The homily is supposed to use the themes from the readings of the Scriptures and to apply them to everyday life. The homily is like a eulogy and is a definite part of the service, but if someone asked me to omit it, I would.

"I find the whole idea of Cryonics, of freezing and preserving bodies, abhorrent. But I do sympathize with the idea of Death with dignity. I think that once there is no longer hope, life should not be prolonged. I've had arguments with doctors over this keeping of patients 'alive.' They keep the body going, but what about the person? I've seen some of the apparatus in the Intensive Care Unit—pumps to pump blood, pumps to pump air—these contraptions. For what? I tell them if there's no hope, to stop. I see no ethical or moral difference between not connecting the plug and disconnecting the plug. No difference.

"I come from a large family. There were nine of us. I'm the youngest. I was present when my mother died. She was ninety-seven. And when my brother died. He was next to youngest. I did not feel differently about helping them than anyone else, because I feel so strongly. I would like to think that a Catholic is better prepared to accept Death. The security the Church offers, the special relationship that a priest has with his parishioners. It's a wonderful and Christian thing.

"I think a lot about Death, not just since my brother died, but for the last five to seven years. I wouldn't say I'm totally without fear. It still is a mystery, you know. I have this concept of the Spirit of Choice. I believe God gives us a moment of choice . . . to go willingly or unwillingly. And when it is my time, I hope to go willingly. As long as I try to make the right choices day by day, then I hope to make the right choice when it's time to die. If I still have work to do here, that's God's problem isn't it? He makes the decision."

12

"He said: Do you believe in Me? And I said: No. I don't know how many times He said that to me. . . . Finally on the tenth day He said: Do you believe in Me? And I said: Yes, I believe in You. And I woke up. They hadn't expected me to pull through, but I did."

Charlotte Jasper is an attractive forty, deeply tanned with blue eyes and a shag haircut with blond streaks. With the exception of her right arm which is somewhat distorted with lumps from the wrist to the elbow, it would be difficult to know that she was sick. Upstairs in the front bedroom of the Jasper home, a nicely furnished half-a-double in a neat residential area, is a kidney machine that keeps her alive. Charlotte has been very near Death twice during her ten-year bout with an incurable kidney disease. On both occasions, she saw God. And God saved her.

"It started with a strep throat and the infection went to my kidneys. It doesn't always do that, sometimes it goes to the heart. Or it can just clear up. I was pretty bad. I didn't even know what nephritis was, never heard of it. The kidneys can't get rid of the poisons. The kidney functions like a filter, only mine didn't work and my body filled up with fluids. My blood was full of poison.

"My husband went everywhere trying to get me on a machine. He went to anybody and everybody. I felt even worse for him than I did for myself. He tried so hard. The machine was very expensive. At that time, there were only two in the city. They cost as much as twenty or thirty thousand dollars. Everywhere he went, he struck out. Meanwhile I was really sick. They tried different things. Put a hole in my stomach to drain it that way, but that was no good. How many holes can you put in your stomach? Then they put—a loop it was called— a loop in my stomach. I felt awful with that, itchy and wet where the pads were on my stomach, like I was a baby in diapers. Every night I had to mix this solution and have it enter my stomach through one tube and come out the other. I was up half the night . . . all night, actually. I think if I'd of had to have that loop my whole life, I couldn't have taken it.

"Well I was really bad. The doctor told my husband I had about a month to live. He works for Food Fair, so he went to them for help. That was strange too. He says it wasn't his words that came out of his mouth. He didn't know where they came from, it was like a record. The big executives there had to decide. Then one day, for no reason, he was transferred to manage another store. Next door was a bowling alley owned by one of the Friedlands. They own Food Fair. He didn't have anything to do with Food Fair directly, though. He came into the store one day and Marty told him about me. What a marvelous,

marvelous man! He called Lou Stein, who was president. Mr. Stein told him they were considering the matter and Morris Friedland said: Who do you think you are? God? So they did it. I still don't know how much was involved, but it was a wonderful thing. Like a miracle.

"I was so bad, I went into a coma. I was in the coma for ten days. That was when it happened the first time. I saw God. His face was like the sun. You know how they draw the sun with the points around it to denote the rays? Well His face was the sun. I don't know about the body. It may have been a woman's body, like a nurse. But it didn't make any difference about the body. And the face didn't matter much either. I always thought God didn't want you to see His face anyway. But I remember His voice vividly. It was a nice, clear, man's voice. Not a booming one like in the movies. He said: Do you believe in Me? And I said: No. I don't know how many times He said that to me. Each time I said no. For a long time before I went into coma, I kept saying: What did I ever do that You should do this to me? I guess that's why I kept saying no.

"Finally on the tenth day He said: Do you believe in Me? And I said: Yes, I believe in You. And I woke up. They hadn't expected me to pull through, but I did. It was very vivid at the time. I remember I was very awed that I had spoken with Him and He had helped me. Now as time goes by, I'm less sure because I ask myself what did I ever do to deserve such treatment? Why should God treat me like I'm special? I haven't done anything for anybody. People all do things for me! Yet I know it was Him and I know He did it all for me. But I don't know why.

"Then last year, I had pneumonia and I was pretty sick. No, that was two years ago. I didn't go into coma, but I was pretty bad. A man on the machine in the hospital also had pneumonia. I may have caught it from him because we were on the machine together, side by side. Well he died and I didn't. I was so sick I didn't care if I lived or died, but I lived. And he died. Why?

"Last year I developed bronchitis. They gave me codeine to stop the cough. We didn't know at the time, but my body couldn't get rid of the drug and it was building up in me. I was always groggy. When they couldn't give it to me orally, I got a needle. Then I went into coma again for three days. That's when I had the second dream. I felt I was already dead. In fact, I could look up and see the lid of the coffin.

Then . . . it had to do with the sun . . . I was behind it but it wasn't hot. You know how you're supposed to burn up if you get near the sun. But it was cool.

"God was talking to some people there. He was dressed in white like a doctor. He was discussing me. I couldn't hear everything. This was less vivid than the first time. He was saying: What shall we do with her? Shall we send her back? Then He said: I think we'll send her back. And I came back, real fast-like. And I woke up. And I was better. I was still pretty sick, but I got better and here I am. I talk about it, but not to just anyone. You have to be interested. I mean it was a very real experience, and I don't want people poking fun at me.

"My parents came over from the Old Country—Russia. My father was learned in the Talmud. He was like a mayor in his little village in Russia, because of his learning and all. But he didn't go to synagogue much. My mother bought kosher food, but we didn't keep two sets of dishes. My husband is more religious. He has a lot of Faith. His father wanted me to keep kosher, so I do, but we don't go to synagogue often. I get fidgety now if I sit for a long time.

"I was always afraid of Death. I believed in God because I was afraid not to believe in God. But I always felt you could only be special to God if you had a lot of Faith and I never did. That's why it's all so strange. I mean, first I said what did I ever do to deserve this sickness? Then I said what did I ever do to deserve this special treatment? I'm no longer afraid of God. I love God. When I light the candles on Friday nights and I say all the prayers, then I tell God that I hope that He has a good week. I mean, He does so much for us, that's the least we can do for Him. I know there is a God. There must be. Look around you. If we were built like a rock, then maybe you could say different. But when I look at someone and see how their eyes work and their hands and their bodies . . . it's such a miracle. It has to be God's work.

"I have these five girls who come in. They're terrific! You ought to interview them, they're a scream. Five psychiatrists. I go on the machine every third day. We get up at five in the morning and my husband puts me on before he goes to work. There are two tubes with needles that have to go in my arm. One carries the blood to the machine to be cleaned and the other carries it back. That's another thing, I have such big veins. I'm lucky. Some people have a lot of trouble, but I don't. They made a fistula here under the skin. Tied the vein and artery together. It takes six hours and the girls sit with me and joke. Afterwards, I'm really drained and tired. I like to be alone then, because I haven't the strength to do anything. I lose five or six pounds in that six hours. It knocks you out. The next day, though, I'm completely different. I feel terrific!"

Charlotte showed me the machine. "We don't have normal vacations. We can only go away for a day or two, then I have to go back to the machine. There's a real story there, about the trouble people have had to get a machine. Now they have production lines, so it's a little easier. This one costs about $5000, but there are smaller ones now that are more portable. In the beginning it was really terrible. We spent everything we had, even borrowed on the house. Finally I had to go to my neighbor. We didn't want to, but we were down to the bottom. She was wonderful. She said don't worry about a thing. They started a Charlotte Jasper Fund to pay some of the bills. We still owe the hospital about $6000. The Fund has a little bit left in it and they're paying off the hospital slowly. It's an expensive proposition. Without money, people just have to die.

"That machine keeps me alive, I would die without it so I have nothing against it. But that's because I have a family to take care of. If I was young and single, I don't think my attitude would be the same. Some say they'd rather die. I've seen kids on the machine. It's terrible. What have they to look forward to? The longest anyone has been on the machine is eleven and a half years, but that's because that's how old the kidney machine is.

"Lately I've been thinking about transplants. The kidney seems to be the easiest to transplant, but the rejection is the problem. My husband says that when the time is right, we'll know it. He has so much Faith. I'm still afraid of Death. I mean, you don't know what it's like. I mean, can you see when you're in the coffin or what? But I'm not afraid of God. I just don't know why I was so special. I never did anything for anybody."

Buryography

(What to know before you go)

To be useful, a Handbook on Death should not only try to make the subject of Death less fearful, but it should also answer some basic questions . . . questions about which, frankly, I too have been curious. How much should a funeral cost? Must a body be autopsied? Is there such a thing as a simple burial and how can it be arranged for in advance? If I wish to be cremated, may the ashes be scattered? Whom would I contact to arrange for freezing after death? How would I go about donating my eyes? My body? What rights do I have over my body after death? What are the rights and/or obligations of my survivors concerning my body? Have I any right to privacy after I am dead? How can I be assured a "Death with Dignity"?

The answers to these questions and others which you may have come from many sources, a good many of which are legal and vary from state to state. Unless otherwise noted, the answers below relate to Pennsylvania. You can easily check your own state's requirements in any good law library. By all means consult an attorney for legal advice.

Q. How much should it cost?

A. The range is wide, starting in the low hundreds and ending up in the thousands, depending on the needs and purse of the buyer. In 1960 based on U.S. Census figures and exclusive of flowers and transportation, personal expenditures for death expenses averaged $1160. Since then prices have gone up. With some exception, the question can best be answered with a question: How much do you want it to cost?

Q. Must a body be autopsied?

A. Unless the body has been given over to the jurisdiction of the Coroner or the Medical Examiner, an autopsy may only be performed by written authorization by the deceased during lifetime and by the surviving spouse after death, or by the surviving spouse, or if there is no spouse or spouse is not available then the next of kin or any other relative or friend assuming custody of the body for burial.

(Purdon's 35:1111) Unauthorized autopsies are generally considered misdemeanors.

Q. Is there such a thing as a simple burial and how can it be arranged for in advance?

A. Of course there is. Funeral directors sell inexpensive caskets as well as expensive ones. Cemeteries sell inexpensive plots as well as expensive ones. Cremation is relatively inexpensive. Monument dealers sell inexpensive markers as well as expensive monuments. In most cases there need be no embalming. There need be no viewing or elaborate and costly services. You can arrange these matters simply and with each of the people involved. Or your church or fraternal organization may have already set up the mechanics for such an arrangement. There are an increasing number of funeral and memorial societies throughout the country. These are volunteer groups of people who have joined together to obtain dignity, simplicity, and economy in funeral arrangements through advance planning. Membership is open to all for a modest fee (usually under $20) and there are various types of services from which to select at lower costs than you would probably be able to arrange for yourself.

For a list of these societies, write: The Continental Association of Funeral and Memorial Societies, 59 East Van Buren Street, Chicago, Illinois 60605.

Q. If I wish to be cremated, may the ashes be scattered?

A. In many states, scattering is prohibited. In others the prohibition is indirect, relying on statutes which deal with the dumping of refuse, etc. In still others the statutes are not as clear as they might be on the subject, for example Oklahoma: "The residue resulting from cremation . . . may be disposed of in any manner desired or directed by the person or persons charged by law with the duty of *burying* the body." (my emphasis.) (Oklahoma Statutes Annotated 1-332. Laws 1963 c. 325, art. 3.) In California scattering is permitted by boat or air not less than three miles from the nearest shoreline, within fifty days of cremation and after first filing with the local registrar. (West's:7117.) Usually, cremated remains are interred in either a normal gravesite, an urn garden, or a columbarium. If you wish, the cremated remains may be signed over to the crematory for consignment to unmarked mass burial under ground (there may be a small additional fee) or the ashes may be mailed to the next of kin.

[241]

Q. Whom would I contact to arrange for freezing after death?

A. If you have the money—it's expensive—and the interest, write: Cryonics Society of New York, 9 Holms Court, Sayville, New York 11782. There are additional Cryonics Societies in Oak Park, Michigan; Santa Monica, California; Menlo Park, California; Costa Mesa, California; and Indianapolis, Indiana.

Q. How would I go about donating my eyes?

A. Many cities have hospitals which maintain eye banks. Call your local hospital. If they do not have an eye bank, they will know the location of the nearest one to you. There is no disfigurement to the body after removal of the donated eyes. Anyone can donate, regardless of age, color, sex, or condition of eyesight. It is interesting to note that most states go out of their way to protect your wishes in the matter including accepting a will or written instrument regardless of the validity of the will in other respects.

Q. How would I go about donating organs or my body?

A. Forty-four states have adopted the Uniform Anatomical Gifts Act which stipulates that any person of sound mind, eighteen years of age or older, may arrange for a donation. If you do not wish this done, you must so stipulate or your survivors can make the donation, "unless the decedent was a member of a religion which relies solely upon prayer for the healing of disease." The gift may be made by will (effective at death without probate) or other document (a card designed to be carried on the person). Temporal bone banks have been started in various sections of the country. For more information on them, write: The Deafness Research Foundation, 366 Madison Avenue, New York, N.Y. 10016.

Most states have created an Anatomical Board consisting of medical and dental school faculty members and the state Secretary of Health. By contacting the Anatomical Board in your state or any medical school, you will be able to obtain the necessary forms. Some states will pay to have a body shipped in from out of state, others will only pay to have a body transported from within the state. Bodies are used primarily for instruction in medical schools, following which they are interred in ground owned by the Anatomical Board, with a simple ceremony. Bodies are acceptable even if the eyes have been donated to an eye bank first. Most states will honor your wishes, but these wishes should be clearly indicated, both in a will and informally to your next of kin.

Q. What rights do I have over my body after death?

A. Generally, your wishes will be respected, so long as they do not violate the law. One exception would be if you would place the decision in the hands of someone other than your next of kin and if there should then develop a conflict between the two. Otherwise, the court will, whenever possible, protect your wishes. In New York: "A person has a right to dispose of his own body, and his wishes in that respect are paramount to all other considerations." (Abbott: Sup. 1945 Penal Law 2210.) In California: "One possesses a proprietary interest in his body, sufficient to enable him to make a valid direction as to place and manner of interment, which directions, if they be reasonable and appropriate, may be judicially enforced." (New California Digest: Henderson Estate 1936.) It is clear, however, that in order to exercise these rights, you had better advise all concerned as to what they are . . . not only in a will which is often not read until much later than would be necessary, but also to relatives and friends who may be trusted to carry them out.

Q. What are the rights and/or obligations of my survivors concerning my body?

A. With the exceptions already noted (your expressed wishes, etc.) your survivors have the same rights to your body as you do, provided you have not exercised your rights beforehand. The order of priority generally is: surviving spouse, adult children, parents, brothers or sisters, adult grandchildren, aunts or uncles, cousins, and then more distant relatives and finally friends. The laws also state that it is the legal duty of the next of kin to dispose of the body. In California not to do so constitutes a misdemeanor and carries treble damages. (West's: 7103.) If there is no next of kin, some states still hold the "householder"—the one who owns the house in which somebody dies—responsible. If there is no money and no relatives or friends are willing to assume the expense, then burial is at public expense. (Purdon's 35:1092.)

Q. Have I any right to privacy after I am dead?

A. Cemeteries are rarely if ever held responsible for the bodies interred. If there is grave desecration, the offender if convicted is usually guilty of a misdemeanor. As for the right of privacy, it usually dies with the individual unless the invasion can be proven to violate the rights of the living, that is, violate their memory of the decedent. In this case, since recent Supreme Court decisions have broadened those earlier decisions restricting the right to privacy of public figures to now include even private individuals, it would be difficult to win such a suit.

Q. How can I be assured a "Death with Dignity"?

A. There is no assurance, but one can improve the odds by accepting the idea of Death and by making the arrangements noted above for a simple burial and memorial service. In addition, there are those who believe that medical science has a moral obligation to comply with the wishes of their patients and that this is violated by prolonging a patient's life when there is no reasonable expectation of recovery. One such group is the Euthanasia Educational Fund, which in addition to various other literature on the subject, has produced a Living Will. In essence it states that in the event there is no hope, the signer wishes to be allowed to die and not to be kept alive by "artificial means or heroic measures." The document is not legally binding, and so far Florida is the only state with legislation supporting this concept. Florida's law is quite unspecific, however, and reads more like a supporting resolution. For more information, write: Euthanasia Educational Fund, 250 West 57th Street, New York, New York 10019.

Resources:

1. *The Law of Cadavers and of Burial and Burial Places.* Percival E. Jackson. Prentice-Hall, 1950 (second edition).

2. *The Law of Death and Disposal of the Dead.* Hugh Y. Bernard. Oceana Publications, 1966.

3. *The American Way of Death.* Jessica Mitford. Simon & Schuster, 1963.

4. *The High Cost of Dying.* Ruth Mulvey Harmer. Collier Books, 1963.

5. *The Prospect of Immortality.* Robert C. W. Ettinger. Doubleday, 1964.

6. *A Manual of Simple Burial.* Ernest Morgan. The Celo Press, 1968 (fourth edition).

7. *The Right to Die with Dignity*. The Euthanasia Educational Fund, 1971.

8. *The Pursuit of Death: A Study of Shelley's Poetry*. Benjamin P. Kurtz. Octagon Books, 1970.

9. *Pennsylvania Cemetery Laws*. Compiled by James S. Bowman. Keystone State Association of Cemeteries & Cemetery Association of Pennsylvania, 1964; rev.

10. *The Psychiatrist and the Dying Patient*. K. R. Eissler. International Universities Press, 1950.

11. "Fear of Death." H. Segal. *International Journal of Psychiatry*, 39: 178–181, 1958.

12. *Geriatric Psychiatry: Grief, Loss, and Emotional Disorders in the Aging Process*. Edited by Martin A. Berezin and Stanley H. Cath. International Universities Press, 1967 (second printing).

13. *On Death and Dying*. Elizabeth Kubler-Ross. Macmillan, 1969.

14. "Do-It-Yourself Burial for $50." Anton Nelson. *The Last Whole Earth Catalog* (pg. 225). Portola Institute and Random House, 1971.

15. *The Tibetan Book of the Dead*. W. Y. Evans-Wentz, ed. Oxford University Press (paperback), 1960.

[*September 1971*]

The Perils of Parity: Part VI

Memo to: Dear Readers
From: Shofar the Dog
Subject: Fringe Benefits

It was one thing to watch the Boss get ripped off. At least we still had our two squares a day and a place by the fire. But lately Pasha the Cat has been sleeping on *The Wall Street Journal* and the other day he asks the Boss, "Boss, what about fringe benefits?" Well I guess it was one of those bad days. You know, when money goes out and nothing comes in? Anyway, the Boss throws a Saul Alinsky book at us and says, "Get your own fringe benefits. I'm broke!"

So Pasha goes to sleep on Alinsky and I go out to dig up an old bone. I think better when I'm busy. We get together later and have a meeting. It's a short one because Pasha's patience isn't what it used to be, what with this battle against the fleas which he says I gave him but I swear I couldn't have because I've got this special collar that kills them dead. Pasha says we need some security for our old age, that nobody gives a damn for old cats and dogs and we gotta start looking out for ourselves. Independence, Pasha says, is something that every self-respecting journalist needs. So Pasha makes a deal with the Boss. Anything we can bring in over and above cost of printing and postage, we get to split fifty-fifty. Pasha says he'll look out for our half because I'm nothing but a canine hedonist. I wish he'd stop sleeping on the *Random House Dictionary*.

Pasha says the thing that's killing us is the Pay-What-It's-Worth Subscription Plan. He says an idea is no good if it doesn't work which is what he got from Saul Alinsky. So from now on, Pasha says, it's still Pay-What-It's-Worth but it better be worth at least a buck or no more free rides. That's where I come in. Pasha says I'm the brawns of the outfit. I got to chew up the delinquent cards. The Boss just shrugged when he heard the news and threw his Frisbee out the window.

Now I handle the bookkeeping and Pasha sleeps on a copy of *Do You Sincerely Want to Be Rich?* He says that in a classless society it's called a division of labor.

The Next to Last Bridge

Death and Transfiguration. I don't kid you, Death is Transfigura-
tion. And it's distasteful. But the way to de-bug what bugs you is not
to let it bug you. It is a question of perspective. Like the Hollywood
back-lot sets, you must get behind it to see what is missing. But you
know that. That's why you read, which is something in these days
of the Great Thief Television.

A woman and I started talking on the train one day. About writing.
She was from England and quite well read—not that they all are, by
any means, but as S. J. Perelman said, they are more civilized—and
she said that she was amazed to find that so many people here are
writing books. We are not a very literary people, you know. With
better than two hundred million people, it only takes thirty-five
thousand or so to make a Best Seller and double that to make one of
the top three. On television that's practically a negative Nielsen. I said
that I thought it was because we have made celebrities of our writers,
glorified them so. The Great Thief has made it even easier for us than
Hollywood. Now we can know all of their opinions without reading
their books or watching their movies. F. Scott in Paris, Papa at the
bullfights, Harold Robbins on his yacht in Monto Carlo. The dream of
every A in English Comp. But the difference between people who
write books and people who write books is people who write books.

My friend Harry writes books. Harry Pesin. I like to read his
writing. Short sentences. Funny fiction. He plays with words. With
purpose. Anyway, Harry calls me one day about the new novel he is
writing called Welcome, Stranger & Partners *by Harry Pesin. I hope*
you get to read it. It's about God and the president of an ad agency
changing places for twenty-four hours. Towards the end, God
(in Michael's body) learns that he has cancer and Michael (in God's
cosmos) thinks about what he can do to help and Harry (on his

phone) asks me what would I do if I had the chance to redesign the human body? That's the way Harry does research. I said, call me back in two hours.

I thought about it. What would I do? I could have men menstruate. That way men would be reminded monthly of the fallibility of their bodies. It might not end wars, but at least it would make them better patients when they get sick. I could give men the ability to bear children and women the ability to impregnate men, without eliminating the vice versa of course. Then men would know about the fear and politics of rape. I thought about making everybody the same color, but I remembered Ireland, so they'd have to be the same religion too. But the blue eyes would despise the brown eyes, the freckles would hate the warts and things like that, so naturally everybody had better be exactly alike.

When Harry called I said forget it, I wouldn't change a thing. Our imperfections make us human. To rid us of them would be to create our own successors. We'll do that soon enough ourselves, with no help from God.

Still, that's no reason to pack it in. That the Future may be no better than the Past is no reason to suffer in the Present. Something can be done to improve the quality of living. We can agree on that at least, can't we? that we should each like to improve the quality of our own life? and if, because we share so many of the same problems, we should happen to solve somebody else's problems in the process, why not? Why not indeed, which leads me to Doctor Jim.

Oh listen, I wish you could meet this man, this Dynamite Man, who makes you pleased to remember that there is another side to the coin. Doctor Jim and his Cosmic Consciousness. Doctor Jim doing good karma in Appalachia while so many others spend a lifetime searching for the wrong thing. Baba Ram Dass after the long and painful journey from Harvard through Acid to Maharaji in search of Identity in the end discovers that you need search no further than yourself to find it. It is not important to know why you are. What matters is who you are. Besides, as Harry says, why is a crooked letter.

This is The Next to Last Bridge. An old skiers' shibboleth has it that you should never make the last run of the day, or sure as hell that's the one you'll break something. I haven't yet, so no last bridge.

About "my." I have the feeling that if you know too much about a writer, it can be a distraction. Yet the reader should have some protection against anonymity, some identity on which to heap praise or scorn. "my" is the compromise.

Once Norman Mailer made a personal appearance which I attended. He read from Armies of the Night, *mostly, and I thought he read superbly. Towards the end of the evening, he opened for questions from the audience. They were particularly innocuous and he was visibly annoyed. Finally he announced that he would take one more question before his last reading, following which he would depart from the auditorium. Hands shot up, all eager to ask the One Definitive Question. Mailer was pleased. He smiled, and chose. "Mr. Mailer, could you tell us . . . what has been your single most exhilarating experience?" Long pause. Slow burn. Then, in dependable Mailer fashion . . . "Fuck you."*

Mine has been life on the treadmill. Not so bad, really. I have met a lot of nice people on the treadmill, had some good times too. Like I say, it is a question of perspective. Is the glass half empty or half full? Neither one. The glass is always full . . . until it is empty.

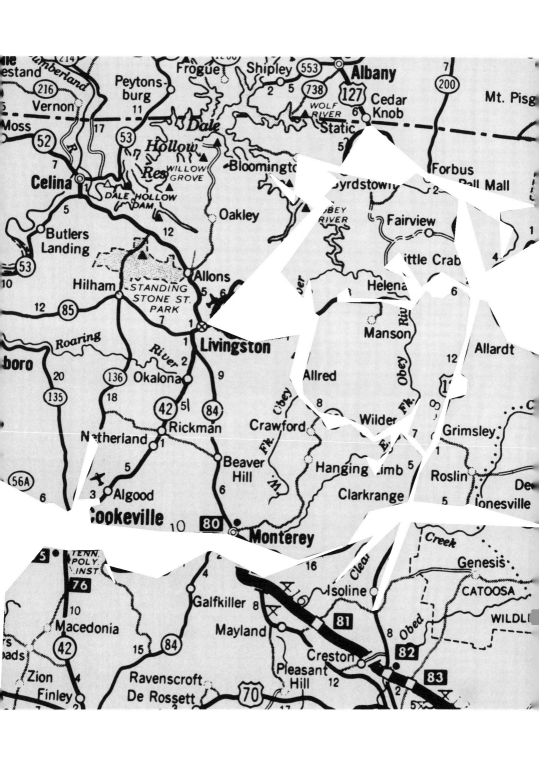

Doctor Jim

"I went to the living waters to drink and found the waters drinking of me."

—KAHLIL GIBRAN

Nashville. East on Highway 40. Cookeville, and North on 42 to Livingston. Then 52 to Alpine. Ever hear of Alpine? No? Well it's there all right, smack dab in the middle of the Upper Cumberlands near Hanging Limb and Deer Lodge, Little Crab and Gum Springs and Brown Town. Still doesn't ring a bell? Maybe you know the area by its other name. Appalachia.

Put a circle on your map around Alpine in east central Tennessee, because that's where we're going. To spend a few days with James Wesley Turpin, né Tom Dooley, né Albert Schweitzer. Doctor Jim and his Band-Aid and Aspirin Troupe. Hong Kong. Vietnam. Tijuana. South Texas. New Mexico. Appalachia. They haven't the sense to get in out of the rain. Hey, Doctor Jim, nobody gives a damn about his fellow man these days, haven't you heard? Not if there's no television camera around. This is the age of confrontation politics, man. You're out of style. (He doesn't hear. They never do.)

Appalachia. Poor kids quit school by thirteen, have babies by fifteen —five or six by twenty-three—and lose all their teeth by twenty-five. Appalachia. If you're lucky, a buck-sixty-five in one of the few garment factories or sixty-five cents a thousand catching chickens. If not, there's always Welfare. Maybe. Appalachia. The strip mines and lumber mills are mostly gone now, leaving behind scarred hills and black lungs. Appalachia. Where OEO, CID, and VISTA mean more than just budget items to be cut in Washington, and where the only medical and dental care for thousands of indigent mountain people comes out of a mobile van. From Jim Turpin and his Project Concern.

THE FIRST DAY

Highway 40 connects Knoxville, Nashville, and Memphis. It is a big divided concrete super highway. The speed limit is seventy-five. See the USA in your Chevrolet. Not from Highway 40, you don't. Cookeville is a pretty fair-size town. Tennessee Tech, a hospital, almost stylish shops, neatly dressed people. 42N to Livingston is a two-lane blacktop that watches Tennessee start to roll into hills. Some cattle. Some hay fields. Tidy brick houses along the road. Where's Appalachia?

The Rotary, Lions, and Kiwanis Club signs at the Overton Motel let you know that you're in Livingston. Little 52 winds off into the hills to Alpine, which you can spot because of the freshly painted one-room shack with the sign that reads US Post Office Alpine, Tennessee. Here's the turn in to Project Concern, Appalachia. Up the dirt and stone road to four mobile homes anchored to a gentle slope of grass.

Inside the one marked Headquarters are Judy Vetter and Dale Morris. Judy is "sort of in p.r." for Project Concern in Virginia, and Dale is Director of U.S. Field Projects for P.C. Judy is tired but still

excited from last night. She and three others were up most of the night with Doctor Jim and his patient at the hospital over in Livingston. "It was natural childbirth and it was the first baby I ever saw delivered and it was so exciting! Doctor Jim explained everything as he went along. He's really terrific!"

The wall map has pins stuck in the towns where Project Concern holds clinics. Chanute. Byrdstown. Pine Haven. Sharp Place. Oak Grove. Alpine. Armathwaite. Crawford. Hanging Limb. Davidson. Grimsley. Stringtown. Mayland. Crab Orchard. Monterey. Pleasant Valley. They stretch over seven counties and service about thirty thousand mountain people. They've been at it here since 1968, treating about 450 medical patients and 600 dental patients per month. Right now, Doctor Jim with about two hours' sleep is holding clinic at Hanging Limb. Dale gives me a lift in his car by way of Cub Mountain, a narrow steeply winding road that tops out past the ugly scar of a deserted strip mine.

Dale Morris, thirty-eight. Three boys and wife Sharon. Home is Tulsa, Oklahoma, when he gets there, which is about one or two days a week. The rest of the time he's in Tennessee or Bisti, New Mexico, or Mercedes, Texas, where a new clinic is being set up for migrant workers, or San Diego, which is Project Concern's home base. He travels a lot. Morris has been with P.C. four years, the first two as a summer volunteer on his vacations, the last two on Staff. One of which he spent with his family at Bisti setting up the Navajo clinic. He is an aerospace engineer and worked on Apollo at North American until he was laid off in 1970. It was a big decision for him to change careers.

"Sure I'm disappointed. I would be less than honest if I didn't say that I enjoyed my work there. I wouldn't have stayed with it, gone to night school 'n' gotten two engineering degrees 'n' spent so much time in it if I didn't enjoy it. I liked those high salaries, too. So did my boys. I didn't stop doing that work because of moral reasons or anything like that. I got laid off, that's all. And it was a really bad job market. This came open and I took it. I really enjoy it, especially the youth projects we're doing—the Adventures in Concern. After our first experience with Project Concern, Sharon became a nurse so she could be of more value. We're really looking forward to working together again.

"One thing I like about Project Concern is it has a family-type spirit. Jim and I are close. We disagree, but we're close. The whole organization doesn't agree on everything, but when we get together as a group . . . it's a big family. Jim involves people spontaneously, ya know. He's a spontaneous person. I'm a—uh—methodical person. It's my industry background, I guess. People like me follow around behind Jim and pick up all the loose ends he leaves behind."

Hanging Limb Clinic

The white Medical Van is parked with its umbilical cord plugged into the Hanging Limb Recreation Center it says on the Pepsi sign out front. Doctor Jim is inside the building doing an EKG on an eighty-seven-year-old woman who can barely walk. Three young boys hang around outside the door. "They wouldn't be here if he wasn't here," says Marie Strain. "They really love Doctor Jim." Marie is a volunteer Regional Director from Memphis. She's responsible for P.C.'s activities in Kentucky and Tennessee, especially the Walk for Mankind, the principal fund-raising device, since P.C. is a private nonprofit corporation. Marie is dressed in white, shiny white boots, blond hair. A Memphis Nightingale. With a drawl.

The van is air-conditioned and well lit. Drawers full of medicines and pills in peanut-butter jars. Much of Project Concern's stock is collected by volunteers from doctors who donate their samples. A small centrifuge. A microscope. A file cabinet of case histories and medical records. And a box of balloons for the kids. A sliding screen closes off the back of the van into an examining room. An examination table, a wash basin, a stool, and Doctor Jim's clipboard. Adequate for a good country doctor.

While I wait for Doctor Jim, I watch three men building a small cinderblock shed which will be a canteen. And I talk with Lemo Guffy, who has just been to see Doctor Jim. Mr. Guffy wears a broad-brimmed sweat-stained hat. His eyes squint, his voice is low, and there's a hint of tobacco juice just at the corner of his mouth. He is neatly dressed and freshly shaved. He walks with a limp.

What's the matter with you, Mr. Guffy?

"Not sure. Jus' had me a heartogram. Heart's not s'good. . . . May need a oporation on mah laig. S'all knotted up here [*pulls pants leg up*]. Waaall, ah worked all mah life. Worked sa cheap, got nothin' ta

show fur it. Ah'm broke down now . . . Fur's education's concerned, ah hain't got any. Not a bit. Cain't hardly sign mah name. Cain't work no more, jus' 'round t'house. Cain't even git mah breath up t'hill."

How old are you, Mr. Guffy?

"Fifty-four."

You could have fooled me. I thought he was easily sixty-five. The last patient has been seen at the clinic and Doctor Jim has made one house call nearby. We drive in the van to the Child Care Center at nearby Crawford. Funded by OEO and Head Start, the Crawford Child Care Center is one of eleven Centers in the Upper Cumberlands. Two teachers, four teacher's aides, one cook, one janitor, one driver, and Helen Allred, the Director. And thirty-five kids, who are at the moment napping. Except for the few still awake who flash big smiles at Doctor Jim who seems very proud. "These kids are bein' rescued, is what's happenin' and it just turns me on, I'll tell ya." That's the way he talks, honest.

James Wesley Turpin. This might be a good time to tell you about *Bacsi Hakkah* ("Doctor who remembers us") as he is known in Vietnam, or *Kai-Yeh* ("Godfather") the kids call him in Hong Kong. Ashland, Kentucky. December 18, 1927. Berea, Cornell, Bucknell. Ordained a Methodist Minister, Candler School of Theology. M.D., Emory University, 1955. A short struggling practice in Chickamauga, Georgia, followed by a considerably more lucrative private practice in Coronado, California, for five years. Married to Mollie who after four kids went back to school for pre-med and medicine, and finished her internship in July 1971. Two Doctor Turpins!

The inspiration for Project Concern came from Turpin's volunteer work with the late Señora Maria Meza in her Tijuana school and clinic known as Casa de Todos. In 1962 he up and quit his private practice, moved his family to Hong Kong on the basis of a newspaper article he happened to read, and started Project Concern's first clinic in a disease infested area known as the Walled City of Kowloon. Followed by a floating clinic among the sampan dwellers or "boat people" of Kowloon Bay, most of whom consider it bad luck to come ashore. Like Dale Morris says, Jim Turpin is a spontaneous fellow.

Since then it's been uphill all the way, but that's downhill for Jim

Turpin, and Project Concern continues to grow largely on his drive and vision. The budget for this fiscal year is two and a half million dollars, every cent of which comes from private sources. With it, P.C. staffs three clinics in Hong Kong, two hospitals in Vietnam (Da Mpao and Lien Hiep) as well as a training school for Hospital Medical Assistants and Village Medical Assistants, a clinic in Bisti, New Mexico, for four thousand members of the Navajo Nation, the medical and dental clinics in Appalachia, and the school and clinic in Tijuana now known as Fundacion Project Concern de Mexico.

Plans include a soon to open clinic in Mercedes, Texas, for Chicano migrant workers in the lower Rio Grande Valley, an eighty-bed hospital in Karen, Ethiopia, clinics and teaching programs in Trinidad and Bali, and a new fifty-four-bed pediatric and maternity hospital in Tijuana.

The first Walk for Mankind was in Santa Rosa, California, in 1969. Turpin pirated the idea from Canadian Jaycees in Edmonton, who had pirated it from the Oxford Famine Relief Society's Walkathon in England. This year P.C. will raise over two million dollars from the walks alone. Competition has set in, and P.C. has added Work for Mankind and Adventures in Concern to make the walks even more relevant. Ten per cent of the funds collected from the walks are turned back to each community for local humanitarian projects or for two week "adventures" working on field projects.

"We're not discouraged. We've been in the walk game as long as anybody. I believe that when the young people recognize a relationship and connection between walking and their own opportunity to become still more excitingly and rewardingly involved through Work for Mankind and Adventures in Concern, they're going to come back at the end of their two week period to their own communities determined more than ever that there be a still larger walk the next year, and I don't see any end to that."

Project Concern walks. Turpin runs.

Brown Town and Gum Springs

We part at Crawford. Dale and I arrange with Jim to meet him at Gum Springs later in the afternoon. We head for Brown Town with a short stop at Clarkrange, where Dale inspects the work being done to prepare for the move of headquarters from Alpine to here. Clarkrange is more centrally located. Cement pods are being poured for the mobile home in a nicely wooded but deserted area. We stop in Monterey at the Corner Grill for some lunch. Jim and the girls "brown bagged it," but made no provision for Dale and me. The waitress behind the counter: "You folks from Project Concern? Yeah, ah'm concerned too. We got a town? It's not a ghost town. Well, we only had one doctor. He was pretty old and he had trouble with his inner ear? Now he's r'tired 'n' they closed down our hospital. We ain't got no dentist at all? No ambulance service, nuther. Ya could bleed ta death."

We continue on to Brown Town, where twenty boys and girls from Peoria are working with some of the townpeople on a Community Center started two years ago by Teen Corps. The work was deserted when money ran out and Teen Corps disbanded. A picnic has been planned at the Gum Springs project, where the other half of the Peoria group is working on a nearly completed Community Center, also begun about two years ago. The Brown Town group is excited because Doctor Jim has promised to play in the softball game and because the Gum Springs group has running water and has rigged up a shower.

The Peoria group raised $53,000 in a Walk for Mankind. Their ten per cent—$5300—paid for transportation, materials, food, and incidentals. Some of their adult sponsors have joined them with their children. Most of the kids are high school juniors and seniors. Each site has a Site Coordinator who is a paid summer staff member with P.C. Part of the "adventure" is living in a tent and getting blisters in

Tennessee. But a bigger part is the thrill of doing something for somebody else and not getting paid for it.

At Gum Springs the girls are just as pretty, the boys are just as good-looking, and everybody looks just as tired as the Brown Town bunch. Days start early for adventurers. But when Doctor Jim arrives, they all come to life. Magic. You can see it in their eyes. For the rest of the afternoon they cluster around him, following him as he inspects the work, beaming at his nods of approval. He has a special word and a smile for everyone. One boy asks him: "You are an inspiration to all of us down here, but you're on the very top. Who inspires you?" "You do. You and you and you. When I see the work that you do, the spirit that you have, it gives me strength. I need you as much as you need me. That's our message to these people who live here, too. We need you as much as you need us."

Another boy: "Some of the townpeople have been coming around and that's great, but a lot of people just don't seem to care. They don't seem to care about anything at all."

Turpin: "You have to expect that. These are a defeated people. They're worn down. We have to build them up. When you leave, they stay. But somethin's been started here. They have this Community Center which they helped build. That gives them pride, self-esteem. You helped do that, all of you."

After a dinner of cold ham, hamburgers, cabbage salad, pie, and soda ("bellywash," Doctor Jim calls it), the softball game begins in a hayfield nearby. Doctor Jim pitches for both sides. A few of the local girls join in and one young and heavily overweight boy who seems to be the mascot of the Gum Springs Peorians. I talk on the side to a good-looking sandy haired seventeen year old senior from Peoria.

John Eastman. "I'm a Christian. I came down here because I want to help, to give my life meaning and purpose. But when I came down here it was an ego thing at first. Now I realize what I'm here for. I'd like to go on to pre-med—my dad's a doctor—or maybe engineering. Get a degree and maybe work four or five years with an outfit like Project Concern. But I'd get a degree first so I'd be more useful. I wouldn't have to just come to them with my two hands.

"I keep thinkin' and askin' why does there have to be war? I'm against all war and killing. If I were drafted, I'd think it was because God wanted me to be, but I don't know what I'd do. I wouldn't go to

Canada though. That's a cop out. If I were against it, I'd stay and tell people why.

"I don't mess with drugs. There's more to life. I used to live from day to day, but now I think more about the future. Some people say the world's all messed up, but I think there's hope. Some people call me a Jesus Freak, but I'm not. I believe in Him, though. I guess Doctor Turpin turned me on at my high school assembly. I was a freshman. You know what high school assemblies are like. But when he came, everybody got turned on. He's terrific!"

The game ends at dark and we drive back to Alpine. Jim and the others are bushed. They head for bed. I head for the Overton Motel. We leave for morning clinic at 7:30 A.M.

THE SECOND DAY

A hearty breakfast at the Overton Motel to tide me over until P.C.'s usually late lunch, and the seven mile drive to Alpine in the gray morning light. Looks like rain in the hills. The van leaves right on time, Doctor Jim driving and Pat Gariety, a licensed practical nurse, next to me in the passenger seat. Pat is from Fitchburg, Massachusetts, where she has a son and daughter, both married. Her other son was killed in Vietnam. "It seemed so pointless to have people spend money on flowers. So I looked around for something in Vietnam that they could contribute to. That's when I heard of Project Concern."

As we drive, Jim talks about the proposed clinic in Bali which is being done almost entirely by National Project Concern of Australia. There will soon be a national organization in New Zealand. Canada and Mexico already have their own organizations. He talks of the medical tutorial program for Trinidad which will include a modest hospital and classrooms in which to conduct the two year program which would turn out medical tutors who would then go to Central and South America to recruit and train young people in a six month course as Village Medical Assistants similar to the Vietnam program. "We're marking time here until we can build up enough local rapport, until we can have enough of a basic concept of what truly is needed here, what people want so that we'll know what area of medical education to move into in Appalachia. Only through medical education and preventive medicine will we ever make significant inroads."

A short stop at Fentress County Hospital, where Jim visits his patient of the night before and circumcises her little boy. He also pays a call on an elderly black-lung patient. I chat with Jim Clark, the hospital's Administrator. Seventy beds with ten more coming for an AA program. ("They come from the big cities where they get treated like bums.") A thirty-eight-bed convalescent home in back. Two doctors, one full time R.N., two part time R.N.s, and "a good supply of licensed practical nurses which are the backbone of this place." Over half the patients are on Medicare or Medicaid, the rest can't pay much if anything. The hospital had a profit of $141,000 last year. There is no ambulance. The morticians use their hearses as ambulances but a new law has been passed requiring a medical assistant in all ambulances by August 1, so the morticians will be out of the ambulance business. It pays to know when you're going to get sick if you live in Fentress County.

Pine Haven Clinic

We arrive at a little white building on the side of the road. Marie Strain is waiting there with Bertha Sanchex, P.C.'s registered nurse. Bertha is originally from the Philippines, calls California home, but travels the globe for Project Concern. "I usually open new clinics. I'm what you call highly mobile." Marie and Bertha have prepared the list of patients and done case histories on new patients. It's a busy

morning. Twenty-seven patients. The umbilical cord is plugged in and the procession begins, from the little white building into the Medical Van one at a time. The average is ten to fifteen minutes per visit.

#1. A mother and two week old baby. They hand me the baby to hold while the mother is examined. It smells sour.

#2. A teen-ager with an eye infection.

#3. A woman with a sore leg swollen at the knee and ankle. Arthritis.

#4. A woman. "Ah'm poorly. Ah'm nervous, cain't sleep, heart beats s'high. But ah wanna tell ya, ah hain't got no money. Kin ya doctor me fur no money?"

Doctor Jim: "Well, you come to the right place. We have good doctors and we'll take good care of you and we only charge one dollar. That takes care of everything, doctors and medicine. How's that?"

Woman: "Waaall, ah'll try ta git a dollar offen mah son."

Doctor Jim: "Well, we've also got a plan where it won't even cost a dollar. If you don't have a dollar, it won't cost you a thing. Is that fair enough?"

Woman: "Far 'nuff."

#5. A woman. Overweight. Has come to have the doctor complete a form attesting to her eligibility for Welfare. He does. She has diabetes and arthritis.

Bertha, Marie, and Pat are very busy. Marie continues to get information from new patients. Pat gets the old case histories from the files and prepares them for the doctor. Bertha fills the doctor's prescriptions after patients have been examined. Every patient gets two or three bottles of pills. They wouldn't feel treated without the pills. Bertha also does an occasional urinalysis or blood count.

#6. A woman. Early middle age. Overweight. Doctor Jim steps out for a minute and before going back into the examining room explains: "This is a minor victory. She lost four pounds in two weeks. She looks like a Sherman tank but she's real proud. This is my fat clinic. Seems like so many of the women are overweight, hypertense, high blood pressure. I decided to make some inroads. I get 'em off bread, potatoes, and pig fat. Does 'em a world of good."

#7. A man. Possible stomach ulcer.

Doctor Jim keeps using terms with patients like "Does your head swim" or "Are your bowels free." A father brings his small boy to the door of the van. He's not on the list but Bertha asks the doctor to step out and take a look at two huge and ugly warts on his little hand. They schedule him for minor surgery next week.

#8. A woman. Mouth infection. Hot salt water three times a day and penicillin tablets.

#9. A woman. "Some o' the doctors say ah got a weak heart, but ah don' know." She needs an extraction but the P.C. dentist wants her checked out by the medics first. Diabetic. Fainting spells. "Yeah, ah passed out yesterdee." High blood pressure. They'll put the extraction off until they get the blood pressure down.

#10. An older man with a tumor on his leg that will have to come off. "Ah don' want no surgery, but ah will ifn you say so. Ah'll go ta Nashville, ifn you want." No, he'll go to Fentress Hospital next week. Meanwhile his blood pressure is up. (And he's got booze on his breath.)

#11. A woman. Overweight. High blood pressure. She's on Welfare. Medicaid will pay the dollar.

#12. A woman. Doctor Jim kids with her. "How old are you, old lady?" "Waaall, ah was born in eighteen and ninety-one." Hard of hearing. Leg hurts from arthritis. High blood pressure.

#13. A woman. Doctor Jim: "What kin ah do fur ya?"

Woman: "Ah jus' been sick fur a long tahm." Joints hurt. Fingers go to sleep. Burning stomach. Can't sleep.

#14. An old man. Stomach ulcer. Cough. Cut his finger with an ax. Medicine for the cough, tablets for the ulcer, dressing for the finger.

#15. A young woman. Pregnant. Doctor Jim: "C'mon in, fats. I'll be away for a while in Africa, opening a new hospital. We'll have another doctor here next week. Doctor Stanley. A very fine young man. Then my wife Mollie will be here for ten days. She's a very qualified doctor. Looks like one of them will deliver your baby. Unless you're pokey and wait for me. Then ah'll do it."

#16. A mother and two small girls, one with a bad earache.

Doctor Jim: "It looks like she's gettin' better. We have two choices. We can let her get well by herself or give her medicine. There's an advantage to lettin' her throw it off herself. See, the body builds up antibodies to fight the infection. Next time she gets the germs, the antibodies will help her fight it off better. Let's do that." Both girls get medicine for worms.

#17. A woman. Headaches. High blood pressure.

#18. A young woman and child. Post-operative maternity patient. Delivered a dead and decaying eight month fetus. Complications included infected kidneys. She almost didn't make it. Now she's doing well. Her two year old daughter has diarrhea and won't eat. She cries when examined and Doctor Jim sings softly to her . . . Linda Loo, Linda Loo. I blow up a balloon for her.

#19. A young woman with a little girl. The little girl has impetigo. I blow up another balloon.

#20. Father and son. About three. Sutured knee. Dressing changed. I'm getting rather good at balloons.

#21. A woman. Overweight. High blood pressure. She gets pills and the Turpin diet.

#22. The sixteen year old son of #21. Peach fuzz on his face and dust in his lungs. He's a Chicken Catcher. They work in groups catching chickens, crating them, and loading them on trucks. They get sixty-five cents to catch a thousand chickens. Four in one hand, three in the other. "Shucks, ah kin ketch a thousand in mebbe a are." Nine of them caught forty thousand last night, well oiled with beer and White Lightning. The boy has a bad cough. Ampicillin shot.

#23. The father of #22. About sixty. "Ah got a sore on mah back. It burns 'n' sometimes hit bleeds." Ulcer. Schedule surgery for next week. His other son says: "Hafta hogtie ol' Daddy, git him out hyar next week. Almost dragged him ta the car, git him out hyar t'day."

Bertha: "You bring him back here in the car next week, okay?"

Son: "Dunno, he's liable ta haul off som'eres fore ah git up."

Bertha gives the Chicken Catcher his shot after asking if he's allergic to penicillin. He says nope. A few minutes later he slumps over on my shoulder in the front of the van. Bertha spots it and calls Doctor Jim. A hectic few minutes for Jim and Bertha, but the boy responds quickly. A little weaker but a lot wiser about his allergy to penicillin. It could have been serious. It wasn't.

The last four patients take about ten minutes each. I step out of the van to talk to Jim Rains. He helps P.C. by driving patients to and from the clinic, answering phone calls, etc. He's been dying to tell the stranger about his brother-in-law, Sergeant Alvin York, World War I hero and just about the most famous resident of the area.

"Ever seen the picture *Sergeant York*? 'Member the little girl in pig-

tails? Mah wife. Ah got Sergeant's picture right in hyar. Wanna see?"
He takes me to a little back room with a table on which is a framed
picture of Sergeant York in a dark suit (he looks more like Senator
Scott than Gary Cooper) and a vase of flowers. "Gary Cooper played
his part, 'member? Mah wife was his baby sister. June Lockhart
played her part. Yup. Shucks yeah. Mah wife was born 1910. She's
sixty-two now. Ah knowed him 'fore he went t'army. He was workin'
on t'highway, best ah 'member. When he come back, they widened it
out, called it York Highway. Lotta public'ty.

"Thar's a spring down thar, sep'rated the York fam'ly from the
Brooks. Went by the Brooks Spring 'till after that, 'till after he come
back. Wasn't long 'till 'twas the *York* Spring. Hah, hah, hah! Boy,
that's a long tahm 'go. Wasn't long 'till 'twas the *York* Spring. Hah,
hah!"

I go back out to the van. Chicken Catcher's brother tells me about
his brush with the law. "Ah got busted t'other day. Caught me with
thirteen cases o' beer and some White Lightnin' in a tanker ah was
drivin'. Ah know jus' 'bout what it's goin' ta be. 'Bout one ta fahv.
An' they won't give me probation nuther 'cause ah been in too much
trouble a'ready. Mah other brother was busted in Jamestown 'n' onct
in Ohio three years ago with sixteen hunred dollars wuth o' counter-
feit money. He got a trial comin' up soon fur poachin' outta season. I
was busted afore fur 'sault 'n' battry, 'citin' ta riot, 'sturbin' the peace,

carryin' a switchblade, concealed weapon. Jus' 'bout everythin'." He smiles. It's a quiet life here in the mountains. We leave for afternoon clinic in Deer Lodge. An hour and a half late.

On the Way to Deer Lodge

On the way to Deer Lodge with hamburgers and bellywash. Doctor Jim eats cottage cheese while he drives, the container perched precariously on the dashboard. "What we're not bringin' to the people of these remote areas such as here in the Upper Cumberlands is the kind of sophisticated specialized care, including the diagnosis and treatment of these conditions, that people in the urban areas have access to. This bothers me because ah think just because these people are poor, there's no reason why they should be cut off, isolated from that kind of service. We've got a good Band-Aid and aspirin outfit. We do a lot of hand holdin'.

"Ah'm not knockin' the validity of aspirin and Band-Aids and hand holdin'. This is important also, psychologically mostly, and in terms of controllin' hypertension, diabetes, this sort of thing. But ah cannot enjoy it when ah have a problem or two like ah did this mornin'—and do every day, every clinic—until ah feel they have access to the kind of referral services that ah would be doin' in a very grand private practice.

"For example, I had one patient this morning with hypertension in the range of two-forty over a hundred and twenty. She's not responding to the kind of usual therapy that the general practitioner would use. So she needs an internist, she needs a specialist in the field of high blood pressure. I've got that man with a chronic ulcer on his back. I don't know what kind of ulcer it is. He's had it about twenty-two years and it's getting slowly larger. It's beginning to hemorrhage. Well I need somebody for his sake and for my sake who can tell him with some confidence what it is and what we need to do about it. Now if we had a dermatology clinic, holding once a month, then he'd be there and we'd know about it.

"At Deer Lodge this afternoon, we'll have the same sort of thing. There'll be one or two out of twenty or twenty-five that I'd just give my eye teeth to know what to do with. . . . Psychological problems? Well, I'm seeing not an abnormal amount of psychiatric problems, certainly not an abnormal amount of severe problems. But I see a

[268]

higher percentage of emotional problems than you'd have in a general patient population.

"I think these people are affected by the stresses under which they live and they respond normally with stress symptoms. A lot of depression, a lot of what we call essential hypertension, a lot of hemorrhoids, a lot of ulcers, a large amount of peptic ulcer and hyperacidity. Just like a city practice, but those good people in those good city practices look upon a remote rural area like this and say, my how I envy the simple life. They don't recognize that the substandard housing and the substandard diets and the substandard education for the children, the substandard medical care, the substandard hospitals . . . all begin to have a somewhat disastrous effect on the psyche of these people.

"We tend to forget the teachings of the 25th Chapter of Matthew: Even as ye have done it unto the last of these, so ye have done it unto Me. I was naked and you clothed Me. I was hungry and you fed Me. Et cetera. I think there's an added dimension of pleasure and satisfaction from being involved in those places where those people whose painful conditions are such that God's heart obviously is torn and twisted by their suffering.

"The misleading part of that is that you begin to sense that *only* in those areas can you find satisfaction, because I insist that Christ is everywhere—I prefer to say God because although I am a Christian and believe that Christ was an extremely sensitive and enlightened individual, I find some satisfaction in the innate goodness and godliness of all people even though they've never heard perhaps of Christ, and have to believe that God in his infinite wisdom and love would understand that if some person livin' in India, who was a good person . . . a good Hindu . . . a good Mohammedan . . . a good Yoga or whatever—that he was entitled to as much of whatever reward is waitin' for us as anybody."

That's the way he talks, honest.

Deer Lodge Clinic

Another little town. Another little white building. This one has a sign out front that reads United Health Clinic. A number of beat-up old cars are lined up outside. Inside, the waiting rooms—there are two of them—and the examining rooms—two of them. One has been freshly painted and decorated. Doctor Jim makes the expected fuss over the surprise, to the obvious pleasure of the patients. Both waiting rooms are full. Some people have been waiting since midmorning. Again Bertha and Marie had gone ahead and the patient list is ready.

Outside, a man talks to a late-arriving woman patient: "Boy, they let the ugliest people in here."

"Don't they?"

"You'll be here till midnight, looks like. They's twenty-two in thar a'ready."

"They is?"

"Yup. Doctor jus' got hyar."

"He did?"

"Yup."

As Doctor Jim begins inside, I stand around outside. The sun has come out. So has the heat. One car parked out front has three small kids in the back seat. The smallest one cries most of the afternoon. Mom is a patient inside. A man sits on the porch whittling and sneaking glances at the stranger with the cameras. Mountain people are quiet, conservative, suspicious, superstitious, emotional, and easily triggered. There are frequent explosions of violence. Guns are a way of life. Turpin says that the Montagnards in Vietnam have much the same temperament.

I sit down on the porch, three or four feet from the whittler. He rolls a cigarette with tobacco from a can of Prince Albert. Neither one of us speaks. After about ten minutes, his mouth begins to purse up. Finally, without looking up from his whittling, he says in a quiet monotone: "Had ta git a new batt'ry t'is mornin'. T'other one jus' plum' wore out."

"That's all. I wait for more. Nothing. So I ask: "How much did it cost?"

A long pause. Then: "Twenty-two dollars with tax."

"That's a lot of money."

Pause. "Yup." He gets up and goes inside.

As the afternoon wears on and the patients thin out in the waiting rooms, this conversation between a man and three women:

Man: "Ah went to hear that trial this mornin', but they didn't have it."

Woman #1: "They didn't have it? Why not?"

Man: "No, well Carl's law-yer couldn't be thar."

my: "What kind of trial was that?"

Man: "One of our boys. Got him fur marijuana, growin' marijuana."

my: "What'll happen to him?"

Man: "Ahh, nobody'll do much 'cause thar hain't nuthin' they kin do. He didn't own the place and uh . . ."

Woman #2: "Reckon he was a-doin' hit?"

Man: "Ah don't know. It wuz thar at the place whar he li-yuvs."

Woman #1: "Waall, ah said ah didn't know what they'd need a witness fur, because it wuz right thar."

Woman #2: "Well, somebody's a-doin' it, hain't they?"

Man: "Yessm, but ah . . ."

Woman #2: "Well ah think somethin' ought ta be done about that."

Man: "They ought to, but ah don't know what they're gonna do. They won't do much though, it's prob'ly the fust time."

Woman #3: "Thar's 'nuff a thet stuff goin' 'round."

Woman #1: "Ah guess thar's mor'n we know about. It jus' worries me so."

my: "How do you feel about that stuff?"

Man: "Ah jus' don't feel it's any good, m'self."

my: "How about whisky?"

Man: "It ain't either."

my: "Would you feel better about a boy smoking marijuana or drinking whisky?"

Man: "They shouldn't do either one."

my: "But if they did one or the other?"

Man: "The way they claim . . ."

Woman #1: "Ah'd rather they take whisky anytime, sure ah would."

Man: ". . . any of it'd hurt ya, I b'lieve whisky 'r marijuana, either one. I b'lieve marijuana'll lead ta somethin' higher."

Woman #1: "Ah know one thing, scares me ta death ta think about it bein' s'close ta home.'"

And:

Man: "Ah guess they tried two or three cases. They tried Billie 'n' . . ."

Woman #1: "What's Billie done?"

Man: "Beat his woman up last night, she claims. Midnight. She called the sheriff. He came an' got 'im."

Woman #2: "Ah thought they got along good."

Man: "They don't git along good 't'all. People live 'round thar say they never did git along, 'cuz she wouldn't let 'im. Fined him ten dollars. Tried ta put him under peace bond, judge says no grounds fur peace bond. Said ah'll charge ten . . . said ah'm gonna fine ya ten dollars 'n' costs."

Woman #2: "They ain't no law down hyar. We ain't got no law."

Woman #3: "Waall, they take 'em in thar and they hain't tried an' they let 'em loose. What're ya gonna do about thet?"

Man: "Waall, he didn't have no lawyer. He pleaded his own case 'n' he made both of 'em tell they came in thar, both of 'em jumped on 'im. She had first licks. Hit 'im on the jaw. Then she went 'n' got her sister and they come back 'n' she come in with a poker stick. Yeah, he said, you had the poker stick in one hand and mah har in t'other, didn't ya?"

Woman #1: "Thet'll wind up in divorce, wait 'n' see."

my: "Word gets around here pretty fast, huh?"

Man (laughs): "Yup. We don't need no newspapers. We got a grapevine here. Faster'n a phone."

my: "Yeah, I just saw it working."

A man comes out of the examining room. The Editor of the Grapevine asks: "You all through?"

"Looks like."

"They say you're gonna die?"

"Ah told 'em ta make it 'nother day."

That evening one of the more affluent families of Byrdstown hosts a picnic dinner for the Project Concern staff. A very charming reconstructed log cabin with a thatched roof imported from Canada. Doctor Jim is relaxed and chats easily, first with one group then another. His energy is boundless, his charm devastating. I chat with Fran Baker, a CID (Community Information Depots) worker in charge of Pickett County for the LBJ&C Corporation. LBJ&C is an OEO funded organization doing job training, youth programs, headstart, summer recreation, legal services, etc., with a budget of over three and a half million dollars. The initials stand for the original four counties for which they were responsible. They've added three more. Fran is from Vermont, but married a local girl and moved here fifteen years ago. "I'm still an outsider here," he says.

According to Baker, the average income in Pickett County is up to $4200. My comment that from the looks of some of Pickett County's poor the average is deceptive, gets the subject changed. How is it that there are no blacks in the area, I ask. I haven't seen a black since I left Nashville. The answer, he says, is that historically Negroes never settled in the mountains but there's no reason they couldn't if they wanted to, there probably wouldn't be much fuss. And the subject gets changed again. People here only talk about what they want to talk about. Even the outsiders.

Doctor Jim calls a brief medical staff meeting which is held inside and chaired by J. Richard Wright, a member of Tennessee Tech's faculty and Project Concern's Regional Director. The principal subject to be discussed is housing for the coming weeks. Wright calls it "musical trailers." It is a half hour of absolute confusion.

Turpin leaves next week for Ethiopia. The Stanleys come in for one week. They leave and Mollie Turpin comes in for ten days. Paul Gehan leaves on the 30th for San Diego. Two dental assistants leave for two weeks for special training. A new dentist and his wife have just arrived. Another dentist will be coming in, to be joined later by his family for part of the summer. Regional volunteers, a husband and wife, will be coming in July for two weeks. One dentist coming in for two weeks will have his own rig. Another couple will follow in their rig. A volunteer is coming from Monterey Peninsula for a week but wants to be here when Jim is. All of these, plus the staff already in Alpine, to be juggled between the four trailers. The problem is solved by the decision to buy an auxiliary tent, though for the life of me I don't know how.

THE THIRD DAY

Another day, another early breakfast at the Overton Motel. There is the usual group of locals having breakfast or a second cup of coffee. The talk is about who got their hay in before the rain and about fox hounds and fishin'—are ya goin' with us, Ed?—and is Wallace out of the runnin' now 'r what? They flip quarters to see who pays. The same one loses as yesterday. He's on a streak.

This morning a film crew is coming up from Nashville to film the clinics. None are scheduled this weekend, but Project Concern is very cooperative. They can use all the help they can get. Paul Gehan has lined up some patients and will conduct a dental clinic at the Pleasant Valley School. The Dental Van stops at the Overton Motel at 8:30 and Paul drops off one of the dental assistants to act as my guide in case I lose the van. Paul Gehan is a dentist from Billings, Montana, and he heads P.C.'s Dental Program.

My guide is Suzanne Kirsch from Cowlesville, New York, near Attica. She worked for a dentist in Buffalo who "sometimes helped poor patients, but he said we still have to eat don't we?" So she and her friend Rita, the other dental assistant, joined Project Concern. She likes the work here very much but doesn't think you can really know people or a place until after several months, and they haven't been here that long. They will be. They're signed up for a year.

The van pulls in ahead of us and plugs into the Pleasant Valley School. First to eighth grade, forty students, three teachers. School has been out for over a month. There are two cars full of kids waiting, but no film crew. We wait. Standing outside the van, I chat with Dick Orlowski, Project Concern's new Appalachia dentist. He has just graduated from the University of Connecticut School of Dental Medicine.

Dick Orlowski, twenty-five. Married for four years. Tall. Thin. Mustache. Arrived in Memphis last week to take the Tennessee Dental Boards and learned this morning that he passed. "I wrote to the Peace Corps and some of the others, but these bureaucratic outfits, I just kept filling out the same applications over and over. Then this opening came along and I took it.

"This is the thing, we wanted to do something like this. I figured if I don't do something like this now, something I've been wanting to do, before I start getting caught up in going on to a specialty or practicing, I'd never do it. So many older guys at school said jeez, I always wanted to do something like that but I never did it. So if I don't do it now, I never will. I passed up a fellowship in oral surgery to come here. It wasn't an easy decision.

"Parents are funny. The measure of success is money. They were quite surprised that I wasn't gonna go on to school or set up a prac-

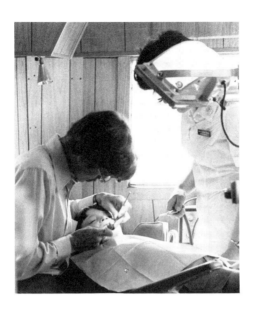

tice. They didn't really understand at first. My folks are second generation in this country. I'm the only one in the family—the Orlowskis
are a very large family—out of all those, I was the only one to go to
college and the only one to go on after that. So it was a little bit of a
shock, our coming here."

Paul Gehan, sixty-two. Married. Wife Jeanne is a dental hygienist.
They work together sometimes. But not lately, and Paul says this is
no way to live, without the Boss. She is at home in San Diego working
in Project Concern. Paul's daughter was in Vietnam with the Red
Cross when she heard P.C. was looking for someone to head up their
Dental Program. So four years ago he quit his practice after thirty-
two years and went to work for Project Concern. Quiet. Easy. Efficient. A wry sense of humor and a genuine concern for people. And
their teeth.

"I hope that in three generations, in this little pocket, I'll have a
bunch of people with good teeth when they're adults, when they're
grandparents. And their kids, and *their* kids, will have good teeth. But
they sure don't have them now.

"We give a fluoride treatment whenever we clean their teeth. Livingston has fluoride in the water. You can tell the minute you get to see 'em. Practically no decay. Ya live outside of town, ya got well water. No fluoride.

"It's partly diet, partly bad dental hygiene. Most of these kids drink six or seven bottles of soda a day. Too much refined sugar. You can't bathe your teeth in sugar syrup all the time and expect not to get lots of decay.

"It starts out mostly as a surgery clinic, mostly extractions 'cause the people haven't had any dentistry. The first thing to do is to relieve pain which you do by extractions, and then you gradually get enough extractions out of the way, and you get enough time, and you can start lookin' out for a person. When we came here I think we were doin' four extractions to one filling. Now the trend is reversed. With the pain relieved, we start tryin' to talk 'em into restorative work and this is difficult. You know. What was good 'nuff fur Ma 'n' Grandma is good 'nuff fur me 'n' ah don't want no fillin's in mah here teeth now, see?—Well, you're gonna get more toothache and you're gonna lose your teeth by the time you're twenty-five.—Ah don' care. Ma lost her'n 'n' Grandma lost her'n 'n' ah'm gonna lose mahn.—You know, it's such a fatalistic attitude.

"You get kids fifteen and sixteen—young girls—beautiful. And when they smile they look like they caught a load of buckshot. Big black holes too. Lot of 'em chew tobacco."

The film crew shows up finally. A cameraman and a producer/director. By now all of the patients have been treated except one, a little boy who's been sitting patiently in the chair for the better part of an hour. Rita Golaski, the other dental assistant, and Suzanne go into the school with a giant toothbrush to give a dental hygiene talk for half a dozen kids and the camera. We wait a little longer. The talk gets around to some local color.

Juanita Jones, a dental hygienist from Alpine ("Nobody believes me") tells the story of a local family of nine kids, eleven actually but the Welfare people put the last two in foster homes. The nine kids and the mother and father all live on a pig farm where the father works. The owner of the farm in great charity lets the family live in the hog house for free. With the hogs.

Paul tells the story of another family of ten kids, one a year. P.C.

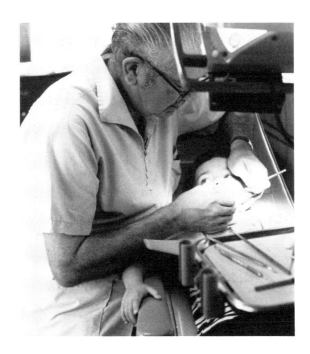

finally talks the mother into birth control pills and for almost two years there's no kids. The husband is climbing the walls. All his friends have started to kid him about "losing it." Then he finds the pills. He beats her up, throws away the pills, and makes her pregnant again. She delivers twins. He can hold his head up again. It's still one a year.

The Tooth Fairies are through with their talk. The camera crew is back inside the van getting a shot of Juanita blowing up a balloon for a little girl. The producer/director explains to the little girl in his best directorial fashion that "we'd like a real big smile for the camera now, honey, okay? We'll do that now, won't we honey?" The camera rolls. The little girl glowers. That's show biz. It's the little boy's turn. Doctor Gehan replenishes the Novocain which by now has worn off, and starts working.

P/D: "When we're shooting, you think you could talk to him in such a way as to get a response? We have sound on film, now."

P.G.: " 'Bout all you'll get is a grunt, but I'll do what I can."

Paul doesn't need much coaxing. He has a way with kids. The touch. A steady stream of friendly chatter. He really likes them. "Four years, I've yet to see a homely kid. Look at this kid. He's beautiful."

Doctor Jim (Conclusion)

We sit in his mobile home after lunch. He's been working on a speech he has to deliver next week in Atlantic City before fourteen thousand Kiwanis. Turpin is big with Kiwanis. And Jaycees. And Spars. And the UAW. Et cetera. He gives them a piece of the action, Turpin style. This is the largest group he has ever addressed and he is nervous. The President or the Vice-President will be there. It's an important speech and he's sweating it. But it'll go well. He is his own message and he turns on the Light.

"I feel like we're being attacked, humanity is being attacked by these privations. Hunger. Sickness. Poverty. Illiteracy. Overpopulation. Pollution. Human pollution. Intestinal parasites is human pollution. Tuberculosis is human pollution. Iron deficiency anemia is human pollution.

"When the idea of Project Concern first occurred to me I thought that if we ever started anything so humanitarianly oriented, that obviously everyone would want to cooperate and support it and that there would not be any conflicts, there'd be no real problems. But that's naïve to the point of bein' ridiculous because we do have problems. We have some conflicts in terms of personalities. We have certainly differences of opinion within members of the Board of Directors. Some are very liberal, some are extremely conservative, some are what you'd call middle-of-the-roaders. I think our Board reflects various positions, which is a healthy thing, but still we get into some pretty heated arguments.

"I guess the biggest problem of all is trying to decide what our priorities are. We've made a decision recently that the greatest priority has to be with existing programs, so we're not going to commit ourselves to any projects that would in anywise compromise the programs that are already under way.

"We have the problem of recruiting staff. That, probably, in terms of specific problems, is our biggest one. Four months ago I'd of had to say that we couldn't pay a professional man going into the field more

than ten, eleven, maybe twelve thousand at most, but now the Project has raised the salary range considerably, in fact we've doubled it. We can offer now a top salary—although no one gets a top salary, not even me . . . my salary's eighteen thousand a year, which is about a third of what I was getting in private practice ten years ago—we can offer a really good man as much as twenty-two, twenty-three, even twenty-four thousand dollars, a place to live, and a food allowance as well. We're lookin' for 'lifers,' and to get them we had to come up with a more adequate salary. We had an administratіve problem, but that was solved with Bob Cronk, our Executive Vice President who joined us from the US Jaycees."

Vietnam. "We treat VC regularly. No doctor in Vietnam who would be critical of that knows who he is treating, because they all treat VC daily. There's no real way to tell them apart. We have had no political problems, which is a tribute to the Ministers of Health under whom we have worked. . . . The policy of Americans and South Vietnamese is to destroy Viet Cong hospitals when they come on them in the field—they're deserted—but despite this policy and despite the fact that the VC know that most of our staff is American, they have not chosen to harm our people or our hospitals. The couple of times we have had people hurt, in fact we've had two people killed, they have been as a result of accidents."

Appeal to Middle Class. "I think this is our strength. There are times I think that the easiest thing to succumb to is the temptation of radicalism. I've wanted to go out and sit in front of the strip mining machines—by my usual behavior that would be radical—because I think it's one of the most damnable things that ever happened to our country that we would put power sources in such a high priority that we would pay this kind of price for it. This to me is unthinkable. But we have avoided, thus far, being identified with that which is extreme, even when perhaps publicity would have come our way more quickly and more extensively if we had been 'off-center.' But we've paid a price for a basic, honest kind of efficient program, gaining support largely from middle income people, not very poor or not extremely well-to-do . . . not illiterate and not sophisticated and educated."

Revolution, Turpin-Style. "I think eventually that's gonna pay off for us, because I think if the revolution comes about in the United States that I feel has to come about—which would come about because of the changes that would be made, because of one man's re-lating to another, of the government and the services it provides, the whole structure would tend to meet the needs of all the people much more directly, much more efficiently—it's gonna come about through the middle income people.

"Now, people tell me that's impossible, that these are the un-movers, that these are the people who are complacent, that if you want to have a revolution you go to the five per cent on either end of the spectrum. You get the John Birchers all excited and marching on Washington. Or you go to the SDS or the Weathermen. But you're not going to have a revolution across the broad spectrum. Well I've got fourteen thousand people to talk to in New Jersey and I'm going to try to persuade them to become revolutionaries.

"And I think I might have modest success, because I'm a middle kind of a person. I'm not a radical. And I think you have to speak to your own, and if I have any ability it's to speak to people whose back-grounds are not dissimilar from my own. And I'm gonna persuade them that the trouble we have with government welfare is that we haven't enough *private* welfare, and that if there's gonna be a kind of government of the people, by the people, for the people . . . if that was something other than a bunch of early patriots hopped up on weed or somethin' . . . then it means that we, in contrast to the Institu-tional Church, are going to have to become the government. *We're* gonna have to make the decisions. *We're* gonna have to insist on have those prerogatives. *We're* gonna have to be involved in im-proving the quality of life. *We're* gonna have to do enough for our fellow man that perhaps the government then becomes a more modest, moderate kind of function. We've become a socialized state. The only thing that's going to turn it around—that's why I called it a revolu-tion—is for people to become personally involved."

Why does P.C. have a religious connotation? "I'm not sure it does. If zeal is considered a religious connotation, then perhaps we are. We interpret our enthusiasm—which I trust is genuine—to be on the basis of finding our own selves in this kind of work. We find our own need fulfilled à la Kahlil Gibran: I went to the living waters to drink and found the waters drinking of me. The people here feel we have come here to help them. They don't know—although they're finding out, slowly but surely—that we have come here to help ourselves."

Religion. "It's very hard for me to define what religion is. The word that comes to mind is relevancy. To me religion is what makes me feel a part of what really is. I like to think that Project Concern is in part a practical expression of some early Christian concepts that I was taught. Possibly, without knowing it, one of the things I'm really after is rather than leaving the organized church, the Institutional Church, I have kept at least a hand or a foot or a part of a heart in it, refusing to give it up as an entity.

"If I can get these young people to believin' that this is quote church work end of quote . . . if they can grow up feelin' that the Church is here, and that this is it as well as their sanctuaries, their temples, their synagogues, whatever . . . then I think we've taken a giant step forward. Because we certainly took a giant step backward when the Church surrendered by selling its institutional soul for mediocrity. Wouldn't it be wonderful if in addition to the prayers and the scriptural readings and the offerings and the hymns and the responsive readings and all, if we also included in terms of quote religious service—what an interesting word—end of quote, a reporting on the progress that's bein' made in terms of rescuing families. It would bring people *into* the church because our younger people are going to go where the action is."

Doctor Jim's Philosophy of Life. "I've come to decide if there's a synonym for the word Love, it's the word Identification. I can identify with you.—'Love you? I am you.'—If I can identify with these people, I can identify with the Montagnards, I can identify with the sampan dwellers, I can identify with the people in the canyon slums and the migrant camps . . . then it is possible for a human being in a lifetime to sense something of the eternity of the soul. And by becoming identified with it, at one with it, then to experience a kind of cosmic consciousness that is perhaps the most singularly exhilarating experience available. If I can find that sense of identification by improving the quality of their lives and having them accept me as I accept them, then something very special is happening."

And that's the way he talks, honest.

We are really rich, you know? Ninety-five per cent own television sets. About a hundred million own cars. Our average life expectancy is better than seventy. We have the highest standard of living in the world. And we're generous too. Didn't we have the Marshall Plan? And Welfare, don't forget that. When people were starving in Biafra, didn't somebody start a relief fund with a picture of that skinny kid with the big belly? Didn't we send some wheat to Afghanistan and some medicine to Burundi recently? Or was it medicine to Afghanistan and wheat to Burundi? And what was that can they passed in the movies last week, MS or MD or VD or something like that.

Poor people? Hell, there's gotta be *some* poor, otherwise how would ya know who's rich? But they don't hafta stay poor, right? They can do somethin' about it, pick themselves up by their bootstraps like we did, right? Nobody says they hafta stay in Appalachia or Watts or wherever. They can leave anytime they wanna. It's a free country, ain't it?

Poor people. We never seem quite to know whether to pity them or hate them. To feel embarrassed by them or guilty for them. So we keep them tucked away and out of sight where they won't cause us too much trouble, except now and then when they raise their fists or camp in Washington which we tick off as either subversive or cheaply melodramatic. Then we form committees and talk until they go back where they came from. Only now and then along comes somebody who does more than talk, and we tick that off as a missionary trip. Jim Turpin? Oh well, he's a missionary type. Cosmic consciousness . . . Early Christian concepts . . . We need you as much as you need us.

Except he means it. He really does. If you're sick, Project Concern will try to make you well. For a buck. If you have it. If not, they'll do it anyway. That's no slick con job. There's nothing to buy. You don't have to read the Book or pray to Jesus on Sunday or get a job on Monday or honor your father or give up booze. Sure Jim Turpin is on an ego trip, it's the greatest ego trip there is. We should all try it.

If you can, work for him. If you can't work, walk. If you can't do that, send him money. He's paying our dues. James Wesley Turpin. Project Concern Inc. 440 West B Street. San Diego, California 92101.

[July 1972]

The Perils of Parity: Part VII

Memo to: Saul Alinsky
From: Shofar the Dog
Subject: Hegelian Dialectic

Sometimes I get the feeling Pasha the Cat may not be as smart as he looks. The other day the Boss leaves me this big pile of delinquent cards and I asked Pasha what happened to his famous Alinskyism: An idea is no good if it doesn't work. See, Pasha had asked the Boss what about fringe benefits and the Boss threw one of your books at him. "Get your own fringe benefits," he said. "I'm broke!" So Pasha got this idea we should change the Pay-What-It's-Worth Subscription to Pay-What-It's-Worth-But-Pay-A-Buck-Minimum-Or-Else. Or else I get to chew up your card.

So I ask Pasha how come the big pile of cards, isn't our new plan working? I mean he's got me plenty worked up with all his talk about nobody caring about old cats and dogs. But he keeps talking about future security and I'm getting worried about present bones. My supply of bones is going down about as fast as the pile of delinquent cards goes up.

Well Pasha gives me one of his slow what-can-you-expect-from-a-dog looks and says what we got to work on is a Hegelian dialectic. He says the Boss's idea of Pay-What-It's-Worth is inspired . . . but it's not working. And his idea of a Minimum is also sound . . . but it's not working. So Pasha says that to reconcile these two contradicting ideas, we need a higher truth. Then he goes to sleep mumbling something about to each according to his needs.

So here I am. The Boss is contemplating the basic Nature of Man and throwing the Frisbee like it's the I Ching. Pasha is stretched out like Nureyev on three feet of Hegel's books, catching some zzzz's. Being the only Proletarian on the staff, I got to decide what to do with these cards. Destroy them, and a lot of procrastinators and free-loaders lose their integrity. Keep mailing to them and the Boss goes broke, I go to the City Pound, and Pasha ends up worse than Mehitabel.

I figure the only pragmatic thing to do is go to *the* Pragmatist. Maybe I'm not as dumb as Pasha the Cat says I am. What do you think we should do?

The Perils of Parity: Part VIII

Memo to: Dear Readers
From: Shofar the Dog
Subject: My First Official Act

Did I tell you the Boss made me Business Manager? Me, who never had to manage more than where I buried the last bone and I never seem to manage that very well. And right in the middle of tick season, as if I don't have enough problems.

Where he got the idea was my memo to Saul Alinsky. See, the Boss' plan for a Pay-What-It's-Worth Subscription is good but it doesn't work, and Pasha the Cat's plan for a One Buck Minimum is good but it doesn't work, so I figured a pragmatist like Alinsky could come up with a Higher Truth. His answer came after we had already gone to press on the last issue:

Telegram to SHOFAR THE DOG:
HAVE READ YOUR OBSERVATION AND COPY OF
TREADMILL YOU HAVE A SUBSCRIBER BILL US
OKAY TO PRINT
                                        SAUL D ALINSKY

I wrote and asked if he meant we should bill everybody and how was that a Higher Truth, but I regret to say that Saul Alinsky died before he could answer my letter. A good man gone, and us back where we started.

So I called a Staff Meeting for new ideas. I figure if half the readers still don't pay, but keep sending change-of-address cards and lists of friends, our subscription plan may be ahead of its time. Well the Boss sticks his head in and says don't let a good idea die just because it doesn't work because this could be the one that gets them to pay and how will we ever know if we cut them off? Pasha the Cat hands me a list he has researched of what you can buy for a buck like ten ounces of Haley's MO, eight nickel candy bars which cost twelve cents each, a bridge ride or tunnel ride into New York which is free going out, four cans of cat food, or eight Birth Control Pills which won't quite make you half-safe. What you can't buy for a buck, Pasha says, is three days with Jim Turpin in Alpine, Tennessee.

So after the Staff Meeting I made a big decision. I decided that my first official act as Business Manager is to do nothing. Pasha says that's how the Government reacts decisively to failure. That and appointing a Study Commission. Pasha says we should ask some of our delinquent readers to investigate why delinquent readers are delinquent. He says that's the way it's done in Washington.

So that's my first official act, Dear Readers. To do nothing. The Boss is busy finishing his book for The Viking Press, I am managing the business, and Pasha is sleeping on *The History of the Occult*. He says he's preparing for his next life. When I ask him which life he's on now, he just smiles and says who keeps count? Sometimes I wonder if he's as smart as he looks.

Fun City

Penn-syl-van-ya
Penn-syl-van-ya
Pennsyl-vanya Pennsyl-vanya
New jersey newjersey newjersey newjersey
Newyork newyork newyork newyork
Nuuuuuu Yawwwwwwk!

Out on the street, everyone hurries
Smog in the air, no one worries
Trucks and cabs and busses and carts
And out-of-town drivers, the goddamn farts!

And night's level roar becomes day's shrill scream.

Nice people leave nice houses to become animals.
Pushing and shoving and bumping and cursing.
In crowded subways you can smell armpits and crotches
In spite of perfume and deodorant and lemon scented vaginal spray.

They read the Daily News.
Murder. Rape. Mugging. Drugs. War.
Prices up. Market's down. Hurry up. Hurry up. Hurry up.

Horns blare and drivers swear and jack hammers tear
And sirens wail and busses roar and motorcycles cough
And generators go topoketatopoketa.
Buildings go up with a clangggg and down with a bangggg.
Subways rumble and screech
And irritated people yell to each other above the noise. . . .

So I said and to hell with her and screw you and fuck him
And we bought on margin so he sold short with their bonds
And my new dress is your new hairdo is his new car
And he's wigged out and I was stoned and she's a gas.
And see ya. Hurry up. Hurry up. Hurry up.

The soothingest sound in this screamingest dung heap is
The soft sweet kerplop of lovely liberated braless tits
Bouncing up and down and up and down Fifth Avenue.
But who can hear them with all the noise?

The awful shrieking hammering shattering mindblowing noise!
The straining draining paining maiming noise.

New York
New York

New-york New-york
Newjersey newjersey newjersey newjersey
Pennsyl-vanya Pennsyl-vanya
Pennsylvanyaaaaaaaaaa.

The Perils of Parity: Part IX

Memo from:	Shofar the Dog
To:	Dear Readers
Subject:	Double Dealing

This time Pasha the Cat has gone too far. I never was much for fights—my motto is bark and let bark—but Pasha the Cat meows out of both sides of his face.

The other day the Boss calls a Staff meeting. What are we doing about nonpaying subscribers, he asks. When the Boss says we, he means me because I'm the Business Manager. Nothing, I tell him, because that was my first official act, to do nothing. Which was actually Pasha's idea because he always says we should learn from the pros. When people demand that Washington do something, the politicians always do nothing so I figured if we want readers to do something, we should do nothing. So the Boss wants to know how my idea is working and I have to admit it isn't.

Then Pasha yawns and says it's the same old story he's been hearing for centuries, nobody cares. Pasha claims he's a transmigrator but between you and me, any cat with two different color eyes is a little flaky anyway. Then the Boss frowns and says the fact that the future may be no better than the past is no reason to suffer in the present, we need money. Right away Pasha agrees and that's when he does it. My friend and fellow worker stabs me in the back. The trouble is, Pasha tells the Boss, you're Aries and Arietians need help with finances. Now Shofar is a Leo, he says, and while Leos may be okay at public relations, everybody knows they're terrible gamblers and easy targets for free-loaders. Then he says since he's Sagittarius he should be Business Manager because Sagittarians can be ruthless when they have to be—which means he wants to cancel out the delinquent subscribers—and besides, he says, his chart indicates that everything is perfect for a Sagittarian financial success in the publishing business. Which is the longest speech I ever saw Pasha make.

With that he curls up and goes back to sleep on Sybil Leek's *Astrological Guide to Financial Success*. Sybil Leek is a witch, I yell. Pasha the Cat opens his eyes just a slit and purrs: I know, I know. And the Boss walks away scratching his head and mumbling maybe there's no room in the world any more for glorious impracticality. Now he's busy proofreading the galleys of his book, so I figure I got one more chance.

I hate to put it on this level but the way I see it, my job and my reputation as an Airedale are at stake and no double-dealing Persian is gonna beat me out of either one. What Pasha may not know about Leos is that we fight best when the chips are down and our backs are to the wall. So I'm asking all the dog lovers out there to kick in at least a dollar. You cat lovers will have to make a decision. Do you back a ruthless Sagittarian who'd double-cross his best friend, or put your trust—and your money on a hard-working, fun-loving Leo? As for you Sagittarians who may be confused by the issues, don't let anyone insult your intelligence by suggesting that you are a bloc vote.

The Boss always says that he wishes intelligent voters would vote intelligently. Here's your chance.

The Entire History of Man

Why should I tell you everything, when
   everything has been told and you
                  have done nothing?
No, I will tell you only
   one thing.

But what shall it be?

Youth is not innocent.
   Old Age is unwise.
Love corrupts.
   Power weakens.
Victims rob.
   Populists dictate.
Progress retards.
   Virgins abort.
There is more than one Infinity.
   And only ashes will rise up out of ashes.

But these do not diminish your insignificance.

I will tell you something.
Smile days. Sleep nights.
There is no Reason Why.